T0299292

Leading Business Teams

In a rapidly changing world, businesses must create a high-performing, metrics-driven workplace environment characterized by respect, inclusion, teamwork, innovation, and overall harmony—and it must be manageable and sustainable.

This book shows that returning to managerial basics will provide the way forward, as exemplified by legendary UCLA basketball coach John Wooden, the model for a new people management pathway: the SCORE paradigm.

Generally considered the greatest coach in history, John Wooden's recipe for team success was unique, culture-based, and ahead of its time. Building upon Wooden's 21 coaching principles and his own 35 years of experience as a human resources leader, Bill Kane has created the SCORE framework to guide people managers in creating and nurturing effective teams and steering their organizations through times of change:

- Staffing: Attracting and selecting talent
- Cultivating culture: Defining how people should interact
- Organizing and planning: The need for direction and focus
- Reinforcing desirable behavior: Managing performance
- Engaging your team: A leader's role and responsibility

Enlivened with stories from the careers of Coach Wooden, Andy Hill (a three-time national champion under Coach), and the author, the book clearly explains why each coaching principle works in practice and provides examples of success, as well as pitfalls to avoid. Readers will learn how to get the right people on their team, create meaningful participative and inclusive management practices, build a winning organizational culture, and achieve heightened results.

New and experienced people managers and leaders in corporate settings, as well as business and organizational psychology students, will appreciate this timeless reference tool, a roadmap to help people managers—as their own "work-in-progress"—develop strategies for success based upon a proven and simple model.

William S. Kane is a faculty member at the Rutgers University School of Management and Labor Relations. Prior to joining Rutgers, he was a highly accomplished leader in the Human Resources field in the *Fortune 500*. Author of *Thriving in Change* and a lifelong learner with four advanced degrees, Bill's specific expertise is in helping companies plan and execute sustainable people strategies associated with profitable business transformations.

Andrew Hill is a successful author and motivational speaker. His book, *Be Quick – But Don't Hurry: Finding Success in the Teachings of a Lifetime*, is now in its 15th printing. From January 1991 to April 1996, Andrew Hill served as president of CBS Productions. During Mr. Hill's presidency, CBS Productions became the network's leading supplier of primetime programs and returned more than $1.5 billion in foreign and domestic syndication income. During his tenure at CBS Productions, Hill was responsible for some of the decade's most successful primetime programming including *Touched by an Angel; Dr. Quinn, Medicine Woman; Walker, Texas Ranger;* and *Caroline in the City.*

Leading Business Teams

The Definitive Guide to Optimizing Organizational Performance

William S. Kane with Andrew Hill

Routledge
Taylor & Francis Group

NEW YORK AND LONDON

Designed cover image: © Getty

First published 2024
by Routledge
605 Third Avenue, New York, NY 10158

and by Routledge
4 Park Square, Milton Park, Abingdon, Oxon, OX14 4RN

Routledge is an imprint of the Taylor & Francis Group, an informa business

© 2024 William S. Kane and Andrew Hill

The right of William S. Kane and Andrew Hill to be identified as authors of this work has been asserted in accordance with sections 77 and 78 of the Copyright, Designs and Patents Act 1988.

All rights reserved. No part of this book may be reprinted or reproduced or utilised in any form or by any electronic, mechanical, or other means, now known or hereafter invented, including photocopying and recording, or in any information storage or retrieval system, without permission in writing from the publishers.

Trademark notice: Product or corporate names may be trademarks or registered trademarks, and are used only for identification and explanation without intent to infringe.

Library of Congress Cataloguing-in-Publication Data
Names: Kane, William S., author. | Hill, Andrew, 1964- author.
Title: Leading business teams : the definitive guide to optimizing organizational performance / William S. Kane and Andrew Hill.
Description: New York, NY : Routledge, 2024. | Includes bibliographical references and index.
Identifiers: LCCN 2023033763 (print) | LCCN 2023033764 (ebook) | ISBN 9781032599410 (hardback) | ISBN 9781032599410 (paperback) | ISBN 9781003456902 (ebook)
Subjects: LCSH: Teams in the workplace--Management. | Employees--Coaching of. | Personnel management. | Organizational effectiveness.
Classification: LCC HD66 .K367 2024 (print) | LCC HD66 (ebook) | DDC 658.4/036/eng/ 20230804--dcundefined
LC record available at https://lccn.loc.gov/2023033763
LC ebook record available at https://lccn.loc.gov/2023033764

ISBN: 978-1-032-59943-4 (hbk)
ISBN: 978-1-032-59941-0 (pbk)
ISBN: 978-1-003-45690-2 (ebk)

DOI: 10.4324/9781003456902

Typeset in Times New Roman
by MPS Limited, Dehradun

To Coleen, Billy, David, and Michael with all my love.

To Mom and Dad.

To Coach and Andy with all my gratitude.

Sorry it took twenty years, but pleased that it has arrived!

Contents

Testimonials

I thought of getting a slew of testimonial quotes for this book from prominent business leaders, human resources heads, sports figures, and academics; however, an early reader of this book's manuscript, who is director at a New Jersey state agency, unsolicited, gave a quote that best summarizes this book's essence:

"I wish I had this book last week."

Introduction and context

Sports and business equivalence

Vince Lombardi, Phil Jackson Bill Belichick, Pat Summitt, Dan Gable, Dean Smith, Bear Bryant, Coach K., Scotty Bowman, ... these legendary sports coaches mastered the ability to derive peak performance from their teams and individual athletes at the times it mattered most and to levels previously unknown. Among other leadership factors, they provided an organizational vision and strategy, implemented structure and systems, recruited and developed the "right" talent, aligned individual capabilities with responsibilities, built the "right" culture, and gave tactical guidance through x's and o's.

The systemic parallels of these successful sports coaching models to business are well known and uncanny, especially by those who have lived in and been taught by the experience. Specifically, competitive sports paradigms "work" for business as:

- Learning is fundamental to development and high performance.
- Learning is related to action.
- Changing behavior involves a fundamental shift in how people are rewarded.
- Behavior is changed when people transform the way in which they think.
- It is the relationship between performance disciplines that truly matters.
- Cause and effect linear thinking limits the potential for their organization.

Have any doubts? Research conducted by Ernst & Young found "94 percent of women who hold C-suite level positions are former athletes. What's more, 52 percent played sports at the collegiate level (compared to 39 percent of women at other managerial levels)."

They concluded, "There's an irrefutable correlation between athleticism (sports) and business success."

Why basketball is the perfect business model

Basketball, like business, is highly competitive, team-oriented, and pressure-filled. It requires players to be conscious of strategy and their own innate talent, much like the employees in any professional organization.

In a *Wall Street Journal* article featuring the Fuqua School of Business/Coach K Center of Leadership and Ethics, Thaddeus Herrick suggested that applying team building and

DOI: 10.4324/9781003456902-1

leadership principles to business from basketball, more so than any other sports,[1] is the perfect organizational model. He points out these similarities:

- The aggressive pace of basketball is akin to business: "fast, fluid, and requiring flexibility."
- The players must make decisions on the court as opposed to waiting for sideline instruction.
- The scale of the game (i.e., typically a dozen players per team) is comparable to the typical supervisory ratio of direct reports.
- The leadership skills required on the sideline in basketball, unlike other sports, parallel business, as an injury to a key player may cause the entire game plan to change, as opposed to just sending in a substitute.
- The general coaching style of basketball places a premium on cooperation and collaboration between player and coach, a philosophy and approach more and more relevant in today's business world.

In addition, like business, basketball has deadlines and a clock, which require real-time management, creative thinking, and crisp communication.

The role model

As Ken Blanchard, management expert, and author, stated, "What's fascinating about basketball and studying John Wooden is that basketball is a wonderful metaphor for life, for organizations, for businesses. His basic philosophy is that none of us is as good as all of us."

John Wooden, as a motivator, teacher, and coach, is one of the most important and lasting icons of his era—in and beyond the world of sports. His teams won a remarkable 80% of the time that they took the floor over his 40-year coaching career, including 16 conference championships, an 88-game winning streak, and 10 NCAA men's basketball championships at UCLA, 4 of which featured undefeated teams. These records, set in the 1960s and 1970s, have not yet been challenged, and many believe that they will stand the test of time. They are a testament to why Wooden is generally considered the greatest coach of all time.

How did he manage to attain such numbers? There was no magic to the Coach's success, but his recipe was unique. He simply reached and stayed at the pinnacle of his profession by creating a high-performing team culture based upon the timeless values and lessons learned from his boyhood days on a farm in Indiana.

His indelible mark: The pyramid of success

Coach Wooden's "Pyramid of Success" identifies and defines the 15 personal qualities necessary for success.

Coach first began to contemplate the definition of "success" during his sophomore year of high school in response to a homework challenge from his math teacher, Mr. Scheidler. After completion of that assignment, John was constantly editing and refining his thoughts on the topic, particularly as he commenced his own teaching career after graduating from Purdue University. He was both intrigued by and conflicted about determining the

---

1 I think "sport" is the correct term.

appropriate grade to assign to average students who were trying hard versus good students who were only partially applying their natural aptitude.

This philosophical predicament ultimately led him to search for a better way to motivate and inspire *all* who came under his tutelage toward maximum effort and productivity. To do so, he turned to a logical source—the lessons and values gleaned from his own upbringing. As such, the Pyramid is a compilation of his ethical, spiritual, and pragmatic reflections. They are organized in a manner that would become an introspective resource for his students to carry well beyond their college years.

These attributes would also serve as the philosophical basis for the principles highlighted in this reading.

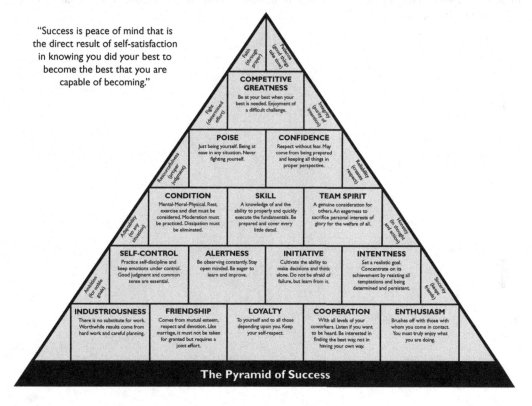

Figure 0a.1 The Pyramid of Success.

Endnotes: Introduction and context

Sports and business coaching equivalence

Long, S. (2002). *Competitive intelligence: An organizational development initiative.* Colorado Springs, Colorado: The Motere Institute, p. 20.

Hinds, R. (2018, February 8). The 1 trait 94 percent of C-suite women share (and how to get it). *Inc.com.* Retrieved on March 15, 2021, from: https://www.inc.com/rebecca-hinds/the-1-trait-94-percent-of-c-suite-women-share-and-how-to-get-it.html

Why basketball is the perfect business parallel

Herrick, T. (2005, March 14). Leadership as layup? *Wall Street Journal*, p. R-10.

The role model

Impelman, C. (2016, November 2). John Wooden's legacy is a how-to guide for a successful life. https://www.thewoodeneffect.com/success-december-cover-story-featuring-john-wooden/ (Blanchard quote)

His indelible mark: The pyramid of success

Bisheff, S. (2004). *John Wooden: An American treasure*. Nashville, Tennessee: Cumberland House Publishing, Inc., p. 26.

Background

An introduction

In 2001, Andy Hill, along with Coach John Wooden, authored the best-selling book, *Be Quick But Don't Hurry*. Part autobiography and part lessons learned for both professional and personal success, the book recounts Andy's relationship with Coach as a highly sought-after recruit, a member of three national championship teams, and the roller-coaster years beyond—through two plus decades of separation and their subsequent heartfelt reunion.

In the late 90s, Andy and I were colleagues at the Channel One Network. A few years later, around the time of *Be Quick But Don't Hurry's* publication, I was beginning my studies for a doctoral degree, with an eye toward finding an "ideal" leadership paradigm for the corporate world. To this end, Andy graciously suggested that I should spend some time with Coach.

Meeting Coach John Wooden would have been a "bucket list" wish for any college basketball fan (which I am), and I was certainly on an adrenaline high beforehand. However, I was also skeptical. How could any leadership model from the world of sports have significant relevance beyond that specialized realm? My admitted bias was that such paradigms were generically helpful but hardly lasting. Certainly, Coach John Wooden had been phenomenally successful; however, time and place were in the past tense. Universal application of any "sports coaching model" was likely a limited avenue.

I was wrong. So very, very wrong.

The challenges of managing people today

As you come across business articles and books from days gone by, they seemingly have the same recurring theme as to how much the world is changing and how that volatile period is unique and unprecedented. So too, today.

Our global world is rapidly changing with heightened uncertainty—socially, economically, and politically. We must think differently; we must act differently; we must lead people differently. There is little margin for error given the competitive landscape and the mobility of the best talent. Teaming and upskilling are critical. The differentiating influence and impact of leadership upon the organization's cultural and human elements are the focal points of stakeholder attention. Accordingly, managers MUST have a captivating vision, hire the "right" people and get them on the same page, clarify their roles and dependencies, agree on processes, hold them accountable for results, and do everything in a collaborative manner. They need to create a metric-driven workplace environment characterized by

DOI: 10.4324/9781003456902-2

respect, inclusion, teamwork, innovation, a solid work ethic, a competitive fever, a results orientation, and overall harmony. All of this MUST be done in a manner that keeps everyone engaged, satisfies multi-generations, provides individual challenge and meaning, and allows self-expression and participation.

Often, this expansive agenda of potentially overwhelming[1] supervisory responsibilities is met with minimal training, mentoring, or role modeling, straining the strongest of people managers. It is not an ecosystem for those who may be ill-prepared, inexperienced, or faint of heart. Yet, corporations precariously press ahead, knowing these voids in leadership exist.

We can do better. We must.

Returning to managerial basics will help address these concerns and provide the way forward. Enter Coach John Wooden as our exemplar, and model for our own enhanced people management pathway.

The SCORE paradigm

In their 2001 book, *Be Quick But Don't Hurry*, Andy identified 21 of Wooden's coaching principles. Standing on Andy's shoulders, I have taken these principles and built upon them—academically, pragmatically, and anecdotally. They are organized into five management practice areas: SCORE:

- **Staffing**: Attracting and selecting talent
- **Cultivating culture**: Defining how people should interact
- **Organizing and planning**: The need for direction and focus
- **Reinforcing desirable behavior**: Managing performance
- **Engaging your team**: A leader's role and responsibility

Why SCORE is unique

The roadmap toward optimal individual and team performance has been researched, clearly articulated, illustrated, and demonstrated with each of the 21 coaching principles. They are a unique blend of:

- Coach John Wooden's maxims and how he lived them—The succinctness of Coach's words and messages was startling. Here was a man that experienced the highest levels of personal and professional success, and he was able to synthesize his experiences into simple phrases and practices around hard work, self-discipline, loyalty, and selfless thinking. A brief summary of the Coach's philosophy and a sampling of his supporting practices are offered with each principle.
- Andy's relationship with and reflections on Coach John Wooden—Beyond Coach's immediate family, no one was closer to Wooden during the last decade of his life than Andy. Coach jokingly described them to be "thick as thieves." Many of Andy's insights are captured and shared; some will be new to even those most familiar with Coach.
- Traditional and contemporary research across multiple academic disciplines—Coach brought the best out in others using talent management techniques that were well ahead

---

1 Should stay as "people".

of his time. A true differentiator and not found elsewhere, each principle is innovatively analyzed and reviewed through the lens of academic scrutiny and research, highlighting why "it" works. Hundreds of sources are referenced, from Abraham Maslow to Susan David.

- Business case studies and best practices—As applicable, current corporate examples exemplifying correlating principles are cited and detailed.
- Prescriptive managerial guidance—Pragmatism rules. Each principle is a "how to" guide of application where I share lessons learned and pitfalls to avoid. (For example, the third principle is about creating and managing a successful DEI program, which is especially compelling in today's corporate environment.)
- My organizational observations and scar tissue—As a "student" of organizational behavior and as a senior human resources practitioner, I have seen first-hand the "good, bad, and ugly" of employee relations issues in the workplace. I weave applicable anecdotes into the principles to bring them to life.
- My relationship with Coach—I had the opportunity to extensively interview the Coach in his later years and our relationship blossomed into a warm friendship.

The end result is a definitive, step-by-step guide to help current or aspiring people managers create and build teams for heightened and sustained outcomes.

About this book

This book is for people managers who want to make a difference!

Before the pandemic, and even more so now, there is a dire thirst for leaders and team-builders.

> The need for leadership development has never been more urgent. Companies of all sorts realize that to survive in today's volatile, uncertain, complex, and ambiguous environment, they need leadership skills and organizational capabilities different from those that helped them succeed in the past. There is also a growing recognition that leadership development should not be restricted to the few who are in or close to the C-suite.
>
> *Harvard Business Review*, March–April 2019

Whether you are a recently appointed supervisor in a *Fortune* 500 company or a director in a smaller entity, you are or will be challenged on a daily basis to keep up with multiple stakeholder and marketplace demands, lest falling behind. This entails making constant course adjustments, juggling non-stop business priorities, and addressing an ever-increasing multitude of people's challenges. The latter task is particularly daunting.

Fear not. Help in the form of a time-tested leadership paradigm, whether as new knowledge or as a refresher, is found on these pages. And you will become an exemplary leader along the way!

This book is also for ...

People with career-minded interests, as well as in related roles and fields will find benefits.

- Coaches and leaders in a wide range of environments and industries
- Organizational development professionals and consultants
- Students (and their teachers) as future leaders
- Self-directed learners will improve their skills of self-discipline and self-awareness; becoming better and more capable professionals. This will potentially impact your career path and trajectory, as well as the vibrancy and productivity of your current workplace.
- For human resources practitioners, your role has gone from the back office to the front line, with talent management practices now at the forefront. This book contains the

DOI: 10.4324/9781003456902-3

informational framework and detail that will help you design and implement the organizational strategies and practices that will raise the bar in staffing, diversity, employee relations, performance management, and other related talent management areas.

- For corporate executives, if you are true to the mantra that "employees are your most valued resource," (and you should be!), this book provides you with an enhanced understanding of how your words and actions influence teamwork, culture, empowerment, and engagement within your organization. Most importantly, this book discusses the character of leadership.

This book's relevance

"Today, next year, a century from now, Wooden's teachings will still have value."

Craig Impelman
John Wooden's Legacy Is a How-To Guide for a Successful Life

A team's culture is a direct reflection of its leadership. It is the keystone of all high-performing teams, and it can be a competitive edge. Culture affects and permeates morale, engagement, and a sense of community. Leaders can do almost everything right, but if the culture is wrong, challenges will never be met.

Coach Wooden brought deliberate intention to shaping his team's winning culture. He was not about the "I" in leadership; he was about the "we" in culture. He knew what skills and behaviors were required to drive collective excellence. He set goals, defined responsibilities, held people accountable, built trust, and encouraged his team members to grow and develop. Every player knew their role and what was expected. No detail was too small; nothing was left to chance; no loose ends.

The 21 coaching principles are the fundamental underpinning of a successful and sustaining culture. They are not mutually exclusive nor timebound. They are all relevant today and will be going forward, as evidenced by some of the current and emerging trends in people management practices. Select examples of topics which are covered in detail include diversity and inclusion, values-based character, engagement and motivation, professional development, and coach as leader.

This book's style

The writing is mindful in its approach and detail. It has textbook profundity without a textbook feel. Each principle is presented with subject matter depth and pragmatic detail. It is written in a modular format to be a quick reference guide and a deep dive. Read it front to back or select a few chapters at a time. "Bullets" are used extensively as executive summaries.

As an easy-to-relate-to and easy-to-read compendium, the reader will recognize themselves and find something applicable on every page.

Potential reader outcomes

Readers of this book should experience the following:

- Confidence and action learning: Feel self-assured in applying what you have read.

- Focus: Have heightened self-awareness and confidence, and greater clarity when it comes to goal setting and attainment planning.
- Personal growth: With a fundamental underpinning of values, the reader may integrate this book's suggestions into what may be a transformative experience.
- Professional development: Become more analytical and conscious of your impact as the boss, especially when it comes to your leadership style and its influence upon those around you.
- Situational awareness and adaptation: Practicing these principles will help you adapt to the expanding needs of their organization and team to help them grow and develop.
- Appreciation of diversity: Come to know, appreciate, and value others.
- Current and future reference: This book is not a stagnant model of one-time or "quick hits." It is meant to be a timeless reference.

My point of view

I have been a Chief Human Resources Officer in the *Fortune 500* since I was 39. (Let's just say that was a while ago!) I have reported to over 30 different bosses, including a dozen chief executive officers. The places where I worked have largely been start-ups, turnarounds, or companies in some phase of distress or transformation. One of my more noteworthy undertakings was helping to take a company out of Chapter 11 bankruptcy. In another long-term role, ostensibly in a private equity model, I had oversight and responsibility for the HR activities of over 40 different domestic and international operating companies, touching numerous industries and thousands of employees.

Having worked in these diverse and dynamic environments, leadership—the impact of the boss—has always been a perplexing and curious topic for me. I have seen firsthand its influence in driving organizational change and managing people, often spelling the difference between corporate success and organizational inertia. To me, the mystery had always been why some leaders were able to make adaptable, quantifiable, and sustainable progress with and through people, while others treaded water in stagnation or dysfunction.

Fortunately, since meeting Coach Wooden, I have had these principles as guiding beacons.

This book as an "Icebreaker"

You might like this idea …

If you are having difficulty with or feel awkward in broaching what may be a touchy subject with your boss, your HR partner, a coworker, or a subordinate, marking the correlating page(s) in this book and sharing it with them might be a step in the right direction. In fact, it could be the start of an organizational movement … (with a nod to "Alice's Restaurant").

Where do we begin?

We begin our journey of leadership discovery by focusing upon the first and the most difficult step of building any team: staffing. This is the most critical principle because if you choose the wrong people for your team, the rest will really not matter.

I hope you will enjoy it.

Endnotes: About this book

This book is for people managers who want to make a difference!

Moldoveanu, M., & Narayandas, D. (2019, March–April). The future of leadership development. *Harvard Business Review.* https://hbr.org/2019/03/the-future-of-leadership-development

This book's relevance

Impelman, C. (2016, November 2). John Wooden's legacy is a how-to guide for a successful life. https://www.thewoodeneffect.com/success-december-cover-story-featuring-john-wooden/

Potential reader outcomes

Melville, K. (2016). *A passion for adult learning: How the Fielding model is transforming doctoral education.* Santa Barbara, California: Fielding University Press.

The coaching principles

The coaching philosophies

Staffing

Attracting and selecting talent

The most critical role and challenge for the leadership of any organization is to attract and carefully select the *best talent* for your team. Coach Wooden understood this responsibility through his own belief that teamwork resulted from the seamless integration of individual mastery.

The following coaching principles exemplify his philosophy:

1 The team with the best players almost always wins.
2 Surround yourself with strong, opinionated people.
3 Balance is everything.
4 Teamwork is not a preference; it's a necessity.

DOI: 10.4324/9781003456902-5

The team with the best players almost always wins

Coach knew, "No one can win without talent; not everyone can win with it." He understood the difference between having the *best twelve* individual players on his team versus the *twelve best* that could play as a cohesive unit. This approach was dramatically illustrated in the meticulous way he attracted and selected talent for his program.

Wooden recruited by keeping a "pulse" on the marketplace. He read newspapers. He utilized former players and alumni, managers, and players' parents and friends as sources to locate and screen potential recruits. Once identified, he obtained the student's transcripts to assess their academic capabilities and preparedness for college. Further, he investigated each prospect's background through scouting reports, checking with the player's high school coach, surveying opposing coaches, and meeting the prospect's parents. The goal of these inquiries was to validate a player's current and potential skill set and to explore the player's personal character, temperament, motivation, and ability to withstand pressure and adversity. Coach was also interested in the player's team orientation, as he understood the importance of integrating roles and individual competencies.

One physical attribute that Wooden insisted upon was "quickness" (although, certainly height did not hurt). He observed and assessed this attribute in a somewhat unique manner by scouting from the corner of the court (as opposed to mid-court), as he thought that he could get a better perspective of the player's vertical and horizontal movement from that vantage point.

During the recruiting process, honesty and candor were paramount. No promises were made to the prospects; Coach simply advised them that they would have the opportunity to gain a solid education and to play basketball, in that order. It would be up to each individual to manage these priorities and to determine their own level of performance, participation, and advancement.

Your coaching imperative: Get the "right" people on your team

When one considers the organizational implications of the Coach's rigor in recruiting, the message is clear: talent, *the right talent at the right place at the right time*, is critical for your "system" and organizational success.

Maintain a "pulse" on the marketplace

Just as Coach had his own recruiting "pipeline," identify talent by staying current with your professional readings, participating in professional organizations/conferences, developing a

DOI: 10.4324/9781003456902-6

network, nurturing key relationships with vendors and/or customers, and keeping abreast of changing demographics, compensation trends, and competitive situations. Specifically, you should:

- Welcome referrals from your professional associations and communities.
- Establish or leverage an existing incentivized employee referral program.
- Pay attention to any internal referrals (of outside talent), especially from your most productive contributors. Talent knows talent.
- Stay in touch with external recruiters. They can keep you apprised of local talent and its availability.
- Use job boards and social media to the extent appropriate and applicable.
- Keep in touch with the academic community. They are often keen on market and talent developments.

It also does not hurt to keep outside talent on your radar by grabbing an occasional lunch with said parties or with trusted advisors who can point you in the right direction. Networking* is an unbelievably valuable activity for these means.

*Note: I am using the term networking in a positive, proactive manner to reflect "bridge-building" interactions that will be mutually beneficial and longer-term in nature.

Raise your organization's profile

UCLA's reputation as one of the nation's top destinations for the best players grew over time; yours can too. To do so, your organization must become an "employer of choice."

There are many benefits for your organization to become known as a good place to work. Recruiting becomes easier given the increasing number of applicants knocking on your door. Over time, this will improve the quality of your workforce. Likewise, your employees will be more dedicated to your success, taking greater pride in their work. They will work harder, stay longer, and be more productive. Reduced team turnover impacts your bottom line.

To become an "employer of choice" takes a strategic commitment and an organizational-wide effort. To get started, you should conduct an audit of your current workplace and gauge its reputation in order to determine your organization's value proposition to current and future employees. What draws prospective employees to your firm and retains them? Is it challenging work, compensation, benefits, work/life balance, career development opportunities, potential impact, leadership, a noble cause, or some other intangible aspect?

If your company's employee value proposition needs refinement or overhaul, you must focus upon your brand and reputation, and have your teammates join you as talent acquisition ambassadors. Check social media sites and exit interview notes for clues and speak with your team members. Internally, it may be time to enhance your healthcare benefits program, adjust compensation scales, refresh your workspace, or introduce some employee-friendly policies. In the public domain, you may raise your company's "envy index" by selectively increasing your organization's visibility and exposure through social media platforms, job fair attendance, philanthropic causes, and interactive website and association memberships. Other approaches might include local school partnerships, key advertising placements, and other community involvement activities (blood drives, activity/event sponsorships, food drives, walk-a-thons, and similar activities).

Develop your personal brand

Why would anyone want to work for you?

Your personal brand is the image people have of you, inside and outside of your organization. It is important. It differentiates you; it helps distinguish you from the crowd.

Building your personal brand is done over time. Within the organization, you want to be known as someone that fosters meaningful and productive relationships. You want a rightful reputation as someone that "gets it done," "goes the extra mile," and "rolls-up their sleeves." You want to be recognized as a "people person," a team player, and a team-builder. You want to be seen as highly credible, trustworthy, and as someone having a steady moral compass. Might you even be fun?

A recent *Harvard Business Review* article outlined four steps to build your personal brand. First, understand through deep reflection who you are: your uniqueness, values, and your contributions. These three factors are foundational to your core being. Second, work on projects and initiatives that are aligned with your brand. This is how your brand becomes integrated with your daily work and routines. Third, become an active part of your workplace community with those of similar interests, especially any group with high profile or visibility. These people will lend support, share ideas and perspectives, and help refine your thinking. Last, share your learning through content development. Reaching colleagues with thoughtful communication may inspire others.

For personal brand building outside of your work environment, you might consider updating and optimizing your LinkedIn profile and presence (LinkedIn has several tips on how to do this and other related activities). Further, you could speak at conferences, guest lecture at a nearby college, volunteer your time and efforts for areas of interest, publish papers, have a presence on social media, be part of mentoring programs, be an active alumni, and connect with key players in your field.

Do your homework

Before determining "who" to go after, you must identify "what" you need. To this end, you should initially contemplate several related organizational factors:

- How will this role contribute toward your organizational goal?
- What voids or gaps will this role fill?
- What will success in this role look like—short- and long-term?
- What is the ideal background and experience for this role?
- What else needs to change in the organization to ensure this role's success?
- What are the related metrics around tracking your recruiting costs, timing, and success?
- Are there any political sensitivities or critical cross-functional dependencies?

Update (or create) the job description

Job descriptions state how the position fits into the team, along with its expectations—inputs, throughputs, and outputs. Typically, this includes a brief summary of the job's major responsibility areas, along with correlating task statements. The description will also highlight the knowledge, skills, and abilities needed (preferred or required), as well as the required experience or education.

Do not underestimate this step. This is your hiring roadmap. It outlines all the critical selection criteria required for success. All parties of interest should contribute toward it; interviewers should have a thorough knowledge of it, allowing you to examine and assess each applicant's background. This includes their general qualifications, past performance and related accomplishments, functional skills, and leadership capabilities. *(Note: Job descriptions are also the basis for grading structures that yield career paths, compensation ranges, bonus considerations, training program participation, etc. They should be annually updated.)*

Consider other staffing options

Whether you are a people manager in a *Fortune 500* environment or serve as the chief cook and bottle washer in a smaller environment, the ways in which we staff our teams are changing.

- Globalization is here. The gig economy is upon us. The pandemic has rocked the employment markets and local markets. Technology is marching ahead, and jobs are being redefined. Virtual teamwork is becoming the norm, and, as such, your hiring needs may need to consider such.
- Related to these seismic employment shifts, the trend of short-term work assignments is growing and gaining popularity in the United States. A recent study by Intuit predicted that in the near future, 40% of American workers would be independent contractors, farming out their services to the employment marketplace. Technology is the primary driver behind this accelerating shift, enhancing the ability to freelance, communicate, and work from any location.

  Hiring for the short-term makes sense in many cases for your "on-demand" or "as needed" staffing needs. Beyond contractors, there are part-time workers, retirees, consultants, and other professional service providers. *(Note: As a word of caution, the field of how you buy, build, or borrow talent is quickly evolving, and there are legal issues of concern. Get advice.)*
- Outsourcing of staffing is a possibility. This has been prevalent in specialized, professional services fields like information technology and accounting for years. It is currently expanding across other corporate functions, as well as R&D and manufacturing. Its advantages include some combination of cost savings, reduced overhead, presumed operational or systemic efficiencies, real-time expertise, potential innovation and technology advancements, and someone else has to do the hiring and firing. Disadvantages may include a lack of exclusivity, poor responsiveness, potential cost overruns, quality concerns, and your time commitments to oversight.

Use an external recruiter?

Depending upon your staffing needs (i.e., timing, budget, talent availability, confidentiality, and level), you may wish to use a recruiting firm to assist with candidate sourcing.

Briefly, there are two types of firms. First, *contingency* recruiting firms generally focus upon placements at or below director level. They charge your firm a fee upon placement of the individual. Their fee is in the 20% range, and you might engage one or more firms concurrently to assist you. Second, *retained* recruiting firms have an exclusive arrangement with your firm and are generally used for more senior or specialized positions. Their fee is in the 30% range of the position's annual salary, payable at various process milestones.

I have worked with both types of firms, more so the latter. My experiences have been generally positive; it is a relationship-based business. I will suggest that in order to optimize success on your side of the effort, open your organizational kimono. Share with your recruiter everything about your organization, your team, your management style, the role's responsibilities, the expectations for results, etc. The more you can share, the higher the probability that your search firm will help you get the right talent.

Thoroughly evaluate talent

When you are reviewing the resumes and applications, bear in mind that many of today's movers and shakers have not always had the traditional "one rung at a time" career progressions. The best talent has passion and chases challenges. Instead of steady upward mobility, you may see backgrounds that involve a series of lateral moves (or jumps) to multiple companies or different functions. The key is to discover what the candidate has learned from and applied at each step.

As an additional resource, there are several different types of screening and predictive software that can also assist with resume evaluation. This software will scan or filter for keywords, and even conduct preliminary (and beyond) interviews. Also, technology can assist with video interviews and predictive analytics; early-stage interviewing, chatbots; talent management solutions; and detection and analysis of behavioral and personality traits. All of this scrutiny will allow you to determine an initial list of candidates to initially (or continue to) interview.

When it comes time for a face-time interview, review each candidate's background and come prepared with appropriate questions.

Each candidate you interview will likely be punctual, dress the part, be well groomed, have some basic level social skills, and will be able to describe their responsibilities in current or past roles. All of those boxes must be checked, and they are all important. However, for recruiting purposes, it is critical to focus on how each candidate's background can help with your future performance *outcomes*. To this end, consider all or a combination of some of these time-tested practices.

To prepare:

- Identify who is involved in the interview process—most notably key stakeholders with whom the prospect will interact. This includes peers and subordinates.
- Know each other's role.
- Who is the decision-maker?
- Know your "must have's" (more on this to follow).
- As part of your planning, use a coordinated approach for questions. The candidate should not have to answer the ubiquitous "Tell me about yourself" multiple times.
- Compare notes with your colleagues throughout the interview process.

Conducting the interviews:

- Utilize behavioral interviewing. Do not just ask candidates "what" they have achieved; ask them "how" they accomplished their past results. Dig deep here and be persistent. In many cases, when attempting to "match" the person to the tasks, the detail and process is more important than the results. *(Note: This "detailed-asking" approach is highly recommended as candidate resumes, unfortunately, may contain lies, exaggerations, omissions, misrepresentations, and non-substantive keywords intended to "game" the system. Candidates may also be professionally coached in interviewing. Be sure that you have high confidence that any prospective hire knows their stuff.)*

- Explore why people have made career and life decisions. There is a great deal of insight to be gained around these thought processes. *(Note: The millennials in my classroom tell me that they are more interested in lateral career and experience exploration versus career ladder-climbing in the early stages of their career. This might explain some job-hopping and should be a topic to probe.)*
- Ask about mistakes made and lessons learned.
- If you have a team-oriented environment, probe how the candidate has collaborated with others to help them fulfill their obligations.
- If you are doing college recruiting, note that there are many good to outstanding students in the marketplace. Look for the ones who are most hungry. Students who worked their way through school or have had diverse life experiences may have additional appeal.

Sensitivities:

- Be conscious of your own reflective signals to the candidate. Unintentionally, you may be positively reinforcing his/her answers with head nods or other affirmative non-verbal cues. Called the "Greenspoon effect," it is something to keep on your radar.
- This is an important decision for you and your team. If it means inviting the lead candidate(s) back for a second or third round, you should do so; however, be as accommodating as possible.
- Be wary of "cookie cutter" candidates for your culture. While you want people who "fit" your current environment, you also may want to add someone who is unique and/or challenges the status quo.
- For key positions, psychological assessment, simulations, or competency testing is becoming more common. Caution is urged in interpreting and using the findings from these tests, as many were originally intended for self-discovery and not necessarily to be used as the final word for selection.

My personal favorite: It is noteworthy to gauge whether a job candidate is running to you or running away from somewhere else. If it is the latter, strong caution is well advised. People often leave toxic work environments and have trouble distancing themselves from that baggage.

In the end, you are ultimately concerned with comparing the candidate's knowledge, abilities, and aspirations with your team's mission and needs.

You may not find the "perfect" candidate but taking these evaluative steps should help minimize staffing mistakes.

Avoid the "quick fix" temptation

A former company of mine was once so desperate for a specific skill that they hired someone despite opinions to the contrary from one of the candidate's references. That is right ... your eyes do not deceive you. One of the candidate's references went so far as to say that he would NOT rehire this individual!

I raised my "tap the brake" voice on that one. I was over-ruled and we hit the gas. To no one's surprise—other than the hiring manager—this individual's flaws quickly resurfaced to the point of significant disruption and inefficiency. Six months later, I was discussing an exit strategy with the individual, and we were facing far more organizational trepidation than we could have imagined.

While the short-term needs of any business can be pressing, try not to act in a way that detracts from the long-term horizon.

Know the must have's

Coach looked for quickness and team orientation. Here are some factors for you to consider.

Hire team players

In August 2004, the U.S. Men's Olympic Basketball Team suffered an embarrassing first-round loss to Puerto Rico. The lop-sided loss was this country's third in the history of the games.

What was wrong with this version of the "Dream Team?" One television commentator put it succinctly when she stated, "They need to learn how to pass the ball."

The implications of selfish play also ring true in organizational life, where there is often a premium placed upon individuals with "been there, done that" reputations or employment records.

A word of caution: Hiring managers should avoid the temptation of recruiting an ego-driven star, for doing such without holistic consideration may have an undesirable consequence on the balance of the team. During the interview, pay particular attention to the candidate's use of nouns and pronouns. *When discussing past or current experience, I suggest listening for "we" and "us," which are preferred over "they" and "them." Likewise, too many "I's" is a yellow flag.*

Hire "A" players

While your organization has and needs its share of "B" players, as valuable corporate soldiers to make things happen, your "A" players are the foundational pieces upon which you should build. They are in critical roles and are hard to replace. Smart & Smart suggest that "A" players have, among other characteristics, high intelligence and the associated ability to be quick studies. They must be able to facilitate and create vision, initiate change, be highly adaptive, and possess a high energy level. They should put forth maximum effort and obtain maximum results. They will want to optimize their own contribution and motivate others around them to do the same.

So how do we recognize an "A" player?

There are a lot of definitions and paradigms. Pronexia, a Canadian search firm, publishes the best that I have seen. It highlights eight distinct characteristics to bear in mind as you shape your interview questions:

- Smart and always learning—always curious and eager to expand their horizons
- Intensely observant—always know what is going on in your business
- Work-life juggle—sacrifices and trade-offs to be made
- Shape their own job descriptions—finding their place and assuming ownership
- Mindful of boundaries—being professional, respectful, and appreciative at all times

- Reliable—willing to do what it takes to get the job done
- Trustworthy—upfront and honest; your most valued ally
- Alignment—exemplars and advocates for your mission, values, and culture

To determine if the interview candidate in front of you is an "A" player, the Young Entrepreneur Council lists some questions you can ask. You may want to think a bit "out of the box" to create your own. The questions can be creative, and they should be insightful. Samples include, with some variations:

- What skills and experiences make you the ideal candidate?
- What is the last thing you taught yourself to do?
- What is the biggest mistake you have made?
- Describe your values and give an example of how they have been tested.
- How have you stretched your job description?

Character counts

Bruce Weinstein is "The Ethics Guy." In his book, *The Good Ones*, he outlines ten crucial qualities of high-character employees. These include honesty, accountability, care, courage, and fairness. His research suggests that high-character employees work in a more agreeable manner, contribute more significantly to the company's bottom line, tend to be more loyal, advance the company's mission, and reflect positively upon the company.

Past behavior is generally a fair indicator of future behavior. Therefore, you should ask questions, hypothetical or reality-based, that will cause the candidate to reflect upon how they would react in situations where their values will be tested. The candidate's answers will shed light on their views and potential behaviors and will indicate if there is alignment between their personal values and yours.

Some potential scenarios to prompt this discussion, all of which where I have been a party, include:

- *The best performer on your team has a cocaine habit.*
- *A close colleague just told you that he has been cheating on his expense report but asked you to keep it confidential.*
- *You are aware that a colleague is skewing an inventory report in order for the bottom line (and his management of it) to appear in a more favorable light.*
- *A former employee and direct report who was a poor performer is asking you for a reference.*
- *A colleague claims to be "working from home," but you know that he is using this time for recreation.*

Probe why they would take the actions they suggest. This insight could be revealing and valuable for your decision-making.

Hire for intangibles

Some personal attributes are hard to describe and quantify, yet you want to be sure that candidates have them. In terms of attitude, look for colleagues with a "can do" approach and spirit, those who see the glass as half-full, and who appreciate their work as a form of gratifying self-expression. These people are passionate about what they do. They are explorers and lifelong learners with an insatiable appetite. They bring an intellectual curiosity about how things work and why, which drives them and motivates others. They bring enthusiasm and energy that is contagious; they are "movers and shakers." They push themselves and others in a collaborative manner. They are passionate and proud of what they do and, more importantly, what their team can do.

For behavioral attributes, beyond questions about "fit" and values, seek coworkers and teammates who have the courage to ask difficult questions or take on sacred cows. These individuals act with a sense of urgency and work inside and outside of their job descriptions. They roll up their sleeves. They place priority upon team needs over selfish interests, are cooperative and collegial, and demonstrate acceptable professional norms. They treat the organization's resources like their own and play well with others. They also make your life easier.

Hire for talent AND experience

Older workers ... tired, slow, set in their ways, expensive, not tech-savvy. Let us not be so quick to judge. It might surprise you to know that Coach Wooden was 53 years old when UCLA won its first championship!

Recognizing that there is value to a wealth of years of first-hand business knowledge, organizations today are finding value in retaining and recruiting employees with "been there, done that" perspectives. Thus, you should consider older workers to be part of your staffing solutions, as they have experience, broad and deep industry knowledge, more developed problem solving and critical thinking skills, tend to be very dedicated, and often produce a high-quality work product.

Something else to consider: Generally, the candidate with job-related experience, mastered skills, and a record of accomplishment will make a faster contribution than someone without. A case in point: *I joined a $500 million real-time technology company in the early nineties that had just entered Chapter 11 bankruptcy. True to the competitive times, the company, like other technology concerns, got itself into trouble by trying to be all things to all markets in that space. I joined the company as the turnaround was starting. We were, to the best of my knowledge, the first public company in the state to move forward with a plan to reestablish the firm without the guidance of court-appointed trustees.*

As part of our turnaround plan, we intentionally hired more experienced functional leaders, many, as it turned out, at or above a certain age. We needed "been there, done that," to help us get the company turned around on a dime. These were folks who knew the drill, ran through the proverbial brick wall, worked smartly and tirelessly, and were guided by lessons learned.

It was a turbulent ride. This was a good size company and we were bringing stationery supplies from our homes to avoid expenses. (Imagine that ... bringing paperclips and pens to work!) More dramatically, there was one Friday when we were not sure if we were going to make payroll. Fortunately, we did. And we made it every Friday after that. In fact, we were able to return the company to profitability in 18 months!

Hire for diversity

We will touch on this topic in detail in Principle 3; however, recruiting from a diverse, and therefore wider talent pool, allows you to attract and select the best talent. Include our veterans!

Approaching the finish line

Here are a few tips to help ensure a positive outcome.

Paint a true picture

Early in my career, as a prospective hire, I was told that I would participate in and influence the design of a much-needed global HR system and its associated processes. I accepted the job based largely on this challenge.

As well-intentioned as the interviewer may have been, the objective never materialized. When I periodically and gently reminded my boss about this critical objective, I was always told to be patient. More patient. More patient. Eventually, months became years, and my enthusiasm and patience ran out.

The last thing any hiring manager or HR practitioner wants or needs is for a new team member to be disappointed, disruptive, or disengaged, particularly if the root cause of any turbulence can be traced to incongruence between what was said during the interview and reality. This is a "lose-lose" scenario for all involved parties. Therefore, when recruiting, as an extension of establishing rapport, realistically state the pros and cons of the situation. If anything, you may wish to emphasize, with some gentle overemphasis, some of the position's most significant challenges. (This is called "negative selling.") If the candidate does not walk away—or better yet, expresses excitement—you could be looking at the person you need.

Make the candidate experience positive

Applicants and interview candidates are "touch points" with your brand and your people. Favorable impressions and experiences for them can turn into positive messaging in today's social media world and elsewhere. The opposite, unfortunately, also holds true.

As you would with any stakeholder interaction, treat all parties with respect, especially in making a positive first and lasting impression. Not only is this the right thing to do, but it may also pay dividends. A recent study by CareerBuilder found that 68% of job seekers said they would accept a lower salary if the employer created a great impression throughout the hiring process.

One related point: While the screening and selection process can take some time due to several factors, in fairness to the candidates and in the interests of filling your organizational void as soon as possible, you should do your best to nudge internal processes along. Related to this, keep the lead candidate(s) informed along the way. (This is called "keeping a candidate warm.") Proactive communications will go a long way here.

If one of your lead candidates did not get the role, personally contact them to advise of such. This goodwill, versus a standardized rejection notice, may carry forward.

Make the right offer

As the saying goes, "If you pay peanuts, you get monkeys."

I worked for a company whose philosophy was to low-ball new hires until they proved themselves. The problem was that we could never get around to making the proper (and deserved) increases with a 3% annual merit budget. As a result, good talent did not stay long. In another company, the executives displayed an arrogance that suggested employees should just be grateful to work there and to work with them; therefore, competitive compensation was seemingly an afterthought.

The marketplace for talented people in any economy is fiercely competitive. "A" players have choices. They are able to command better salaries and often dictate employment terms outside of your organization's norms. *It has been my experience that they do not want to play games with negotiating.* Neither should you.

Check references

In an engineering-driven company, we were going through an ISO certification audit (or the like) which prompted us to double-check the credentials of our professional staff. As it turned out, one of our most senior, longest-serving, and highly-respected engineers—who had been and was the lead on many of our critical projects —had not completed his undergraduate degree.

He had lied on his employment application several years ago.

What to do? As a policy matter, he falsified his credentials, which was worthy of termination. On the other hand, he had been a stellar performer over a prolonged period of time and was instrumental to our continued success.

After much debate, we handled it quietly by offering him the opportunity, with cost-sharing, to return to school and obtain his outstanding credits. A "win-win" for all, but not without a test of humility. Certainly, had the background check been properly conducted at his time of hire, this never would have happened.

Do not let it happen to you. Check references. As noted, do not be fooled by eye-candy resumes. Do not let your "hunch" or "gut feeling" tip the hiring decision scale. Do not lean too heavily on the candidate's hand-picked references. Estimates suggest that bad hires and terminations can cost anywhere north of five times an employee's base salary in hard costs and lost productivity! Try to obtain objective, reliable, and valid information, as recent as possible, about the candidate. This can be done by utilizing effective pre-employment screening procedures, including third party research assistance. Such information will help maximize the probability of selecting choice employment candidates and minimize what may have been "spin" on the prospect's resume.

If your company does pre-employment drug testing

Back in the day, this was pretty straightforward. The candidate peed in a cup. It was analyzed. If clean, a start date was selected. If not, the candidate was disqualified with no parting gifts. Today, in light of marijuana legalization trends, this is a gray area with little conformity. Your HR professional/outside counsel is your authoritative source on when and how drug testing may still be performed (or not) in your locality.

Putting your best foot forward

You have likely spent a considerable amount of time and effort to find a proper candidate; now it is time to close the deal. Do not screw around.

Pre-board

It is a great idea to begin the new hire's employee experience before "day one." Just be careful not to inundate him or her.

If doable and agreeable, share information about the company's history, mission, values, and structure with them. Make them feel welcome. Start building their confidence by reiterating that they made the right decision and that their landing will be soft and productive. It is never too early to start the new hire's learning curve and to build your brand.

Start your new hire on the right day

On my first day as director of human resources in a new job with a new company, I had an introductory team meeting scheduled for 9:00 a.m. I had rehearsed my comments the night before, and I was excited to meet everyone and to set an energizing tone for the road ahead.

But there was something wrong.

When my new colleagues trickled into the conference room, most of them were wearing black. In fact, the mood was sullen; words were few. Many appeared to have been crying. As it turned out, a popular coworker had died a few days ago. The funeral service, which most would be attending, was my first day.

Maybe I could or should have started a little later in the week.

Assist with acclimation

A friend of mine was a top graduate student from a premier university. He had a wide choice of positions offered, and he went to work for a leading financial services firm. After several years, unsolicited, he received a call about a significant promotional opportunity with a competitor.

After much personal debate and consternation, he took the interview. Ultimately, he joined the new firm.

On day one with the new company, his boss came to greet him. My friend was shown his desk, as well as the location of the men's room and the nearby vending machines. That was the end of human contact on that day. On day two, there was no human contact. The same for the morning of the third day. He was appalled.

At lunch time on the third day, my friend contacted his former employer, where he had been in good standing. He asked if they might take him back. Perhaps they could just consider his time away as a vacation. And that is what they did.

Be intentional. Have a socialization plan; don't wing it. Be or appoint an active "On-Boarding Buddy." Ask and/or assign others to help, especially if the environment is virtual.

(Note: I would also suggest that extra time and attention be given to the younger generation as they enter the workforce. I have heard many firsthand anecdotes in my classroom—undergraduate and graduate—about the difficulties anticipated and experienced by this isolated, COVID-worn, Zoomed-out, and potentially socially-anxious cohort group. At the risk of generalizing, many have not worked side-by-side with anyone before; they have not worked on teams; they do not know what to do at lunch time; their communications skills need professional honing; and they tend to be fairly reserved and cautious. For these new entrants to the workforce, working "on-site" may be a feared environment.)

Get into the needed detail

Your new team member reflects upon and is an extension of you. Therefore, it should be a primary concern of yours to make sure that he or she gets started on the right foot. This is particularly critical as the first three months are considered a time when the new hire is still somewhat vulnerable to the marketplace. In this regard, beyond the standard human resources orientation materials, be sure that you cover key responsibilities, norms, stakeholder introductions, key policy reviews, IT training, and departmental practices. It also would make great sense to assign team members to take the new hire to lunch at the onset to assist with socialization and set periodic check-ins thereafter.

The faster your new hire is comfortable, the faster they will begin to contribute, but do allow them time to breathe. One tool to consider early on in this regard is the General Electric ("GE") "New Leader Assimilation" model, which you can customize for your needs. It is intended to fast-track the "getting-to-know you" process between teams and their leaders. It is well worth a few clicks of research.

As a related concern, if the new hire is relocating and the move involves a significant cultural introduction and education, the organization should, in addition to the standard "on boarding" processes, assist in any way that is reasonable.

Set early expectations

In these early days, it is also imperative for you to lay out some short-term objectives for the new hire. These are typically in the form of 30-, 60-, or 90-day objectives and they should be the by-product of mutual agreement.

We highlight performance management methodologies in Principle 15, but I would be remiss not to share one "out-of-the box" approach.

I had just taken the top HR position in a several billion-dollar global firm with multiple sites, vast product and service offerings, and thousands of employees. I took the position with the understanding that the organization was about to embark upon a transformative path, and that I would help lead the way. In fact, I believed that I was hired to shake things up as soon as possible.

When I first sat down with my new boss, he said that he wanted me to do ... ostensibly nothing. In essence, he said that I should take three to four months to watch, listen, and learn about the company by meeting our people and visiting our sites. Be a sponge.

Wait! You are paying me a handsome salary to do what? I was troubled and restless. I certainly could make the rounds, but I thought that I should concurrently be changing policies, restructuring, assessing senior staff, shifting the company's culture, and streamlining organizational processes. Hey, I am a mover and a shaker!

As it turned out, I followed his advice (while attending to concurrent time sensitive matters) and it paid huge dividends. The knowledge and insights absorbed in that early period made me that much more valuable to the organization over time. I gained a true appreciation for the workings of the company and its heritage.

Three to four months may seem a long time and you may not have that baptismal luxury; however, the lesson is noteworthy.

If you get it right …

In a recent study noted in Adobe's *Future of Work: More Than a Machine*, three in four respondents said that they would work longer hours for a job they love versus shorter hours for one they don't.

Get and keep the *right talent in the right place at the right time* and you have established a strong foundational underpinning for optimizing your team's performance for today and the future.

If you get it wrong …

Hiring mistakes happen, even to the best recruiters and managers. *My best guess is that a successful hiring rate for more seasoned managers and talent acquisition professionals is in the 60–70% range.*

We have all seen the hiring of train wrecks caused by poor attitudinal issues, lack of work ethic, cultural misfits, or underperformance. Wine improves with age; these situations do not.

Despite everyone's best efforts and intentions, staffing decisions are still a combination of art and science. They are not fail-proof. Formal assessments and structured interviewing help, but you will make mistakes. These can be very expensive in the order of multiples of the position's base salary. When trouble is brewing, make the difficult separation decision as soon as possible and, as importantly, listen to the answers given in an exit interview that may yield critical insight for corrective measures. Post-mortems are well worthwhile.

How does this compare to conventional wisdom?

"I can coach anybody." "Anybody can sell this product."

You cannot. And they cannot.

While there are fluctuations in the economy between being a buyer's and seller's market, superior talent is a limited resource. It should not be taken for granted. It is your responsibility to seek out new talent, while nurturing and managing the productivity of the existing staff.

Endnotes for Principle 1: The team with the best players almost always wins

The team with the best players almost always wins

Wooden, J.R. (2002, August 22). Private conversation.

Pulse

Why hiring "A players" should be your number one objective. (Date unknown). Retrieved on May 14, 2018, from: https://www.icaew.com/en/technical/business-resources/hr-and-employment/recruitment/why-hiring-a-players-should-be-your-number-one-objective

Raise your organization's profile

Herman, R., & Gioia, J. (2000). Why become an employer of choice? Retrieved on May 11, 2018, from: https://employerofchoice.com/chapter1.pdf

Develop your personal brand

The Michael Page Team. (February 28, 2023). Building your personal brand: Tips and strategies for crafting the brand called 'you'. Retrieved on May 11, 2023, from: https://www.michaelpage.com.au/advice/career-advice/career-progression/building-your-personal-brand-tips-and-strategies

Orduna, N. (September 28, 2022). How to build your personal brand at work. *Harvard Business Review*. Retrieved on May 11, 2023, from: (https://hbr.org/2022/09/how-to-build-your-personal-brand-at-work

Rynne, A. (August 1, 2016). 5 Free ways to build your personal brand on LinkedIn. Retrieved on May 11, 2023, from: https://www.linkedin.com/business/marketing/blog/content-marketing/5-free-ways-to-build-your-personal-brand-on-linkedin

Do your homework

Greenberg, N. (2018, February 5). Finding and hiring top talent for your team: Five best practices to help you find the right hire. Retrieved on May 16, 2018, from: https://www.inman.com/2018/02/05/finding-hiring-top-talent-team/

Consider other staffing options

Rouse, M. (Date unknown). Gig economy. Retrieved on May 14, 2018, from: https://whatis.techtarget.com/definition/gig-economy

Thoroughly evaluate talent

Mercer Survey Panel: North American critical talent practices survey. (2014, February). Retrieved on May 8, 2018, from: https://www.mercer.com/content/dam/mercer/attachments/global/Talent/critical-talent-practices-survey-2014.pdf

Ulrich, D., Zenger, J., & Smallwood, N. (1999). *Results-based leadership: How leaders build and improve the bottom line*. Boston, MA: Harvard Business School Press, pp. 24–26, 181.

"Greenspoon Effect," (2019: copyright). Oxford reference. Retrieved on December 17, 2019, from: https://www.oxfordreference.com/view/10.1093/acref/9780199534067.001.0001/acref-9780199534067-e-3609

"Examples of Artificial Intelligence (AI) Uses," IESE Business School, LinkedIn posting. Retrieved on January 13, 2021, from: https://www.linkedin.com/feed/?trk=msn-top

Hire "A" players

Smart, B.D., & Smart G.H. (1997, Spring). Topgrading the organization. *Boards & Directors*.

A guide to hiring A-players. (2016, March 29). Retrieved on May 14, 2018, from: http://pronexia.com/blog/how-to-hire-incredible-employees/

Young Entrepreneur Council, the Blog. (2018, December 6). 11 interview questions that identify "A-players. Retrieved on May 14, 2018, from: https://www.huffingtonpost.com/young-entrepreneur-council/11-interview-questions-th_b_9742162.html

Character counts!

Weinstein, B. (2015). *The good ones: Ten crucial qualities of high-character employees*. Novato, CA: New World Library, p. 9.

Hire for intangibles

Davis, J.W. (2017, October 26). Creating a high-performance team: Finding talent & connecting the dots. Retrieved on May 16, 2018, from: https://theblog.adobe.com/creating-a-high-performance-team-finding-talent-connecting-the-dots/

Hire for talent AND experience

Bastien, S. (2006, September 20). 12 benefits of hiring older workers. Retrieved on May 14, 2018, from: https://www.entrepreneur.com/article/167500.

LaPonsie, M., Contributor. (2015, September 18). 5 reasons employers should hire more workers over age 50. Retrieved on May 14, 2018, from: https://money.usnews.com/money/retirement/articles/2015/09/18/5-reasons-employers-should-hire-more-workers-over-age-50

Williams, M.E. (2016, October 27). 8 reasons age is a giant plus for older job seekers. *Huffington Post*. Retrieved on October 28, 2016, from: http://huffingtonpost.com/eileen-williams/finding-a-job-after-50_b_12572796.html

Hire for diversity

Showers, R. (2016, March 17). 4 business benefits of diversity in the workplace. Retrieved on June 1, 2018, from: https://www.brazen.com/blog/recruiting-hr/benefits-of-diversity-in-the-workplace/

Positive candidate experience

Haefner, R. (2015, February 13). Finding top talent: 6 critical stats every employer needs to know now. Retrieved on May 8, 2018, from https://www.tlnt.com/finding-top-talent-6-critical-stats-every-employer-needs-to-know-now/

Check references

Why hiring A players should be your number one objective. (2018, May 14). Retrieved on May 14, 2018, from: https://www.icaew.com/en/technical/business-resources/hr-and-employment/recruitment/why-hiring-a-players-should-be-your-number-one-objective

If you get it right …

Davis, J.W. (2017, October 26). Creating a high performance team: Finding talent & connecting the dots. Retrieved on May 16, 2018, from: https://theblog.adobe.com/creating-a-high-performance-team-finding-talent-connecting-the-dots/

If you get it wrong …

Giving constructive feedback. (2018, August 15). Impraise, Inc: San Francisco, CA. Retrieved from: http://www.feedback.tips/give-constructive-feedback-to-employees-team-members/

Surround yourself with strong, opinionated people

Coach had many answers, but he did not have them all.

With a philosophy predicated upon, "the better your subordinates, the better the leader," Coach made it a point to listen to his assistant coaches through the years (including Jerry Norman, Denny Crum, Eddie Powell, and Gary Cunningham). These assistants collaborated with Coach by fulfilling many trusted duties such as running practices, handling key scouting assignments, mentoring players, recruiting, and consulting with Coach on matters of practice agendas, game preparation, and strategy.

These coaches were hardly "yes men." Case in point: Jerry Norman, who assisted Coach through the first four championship runs, had a relatively tumultuous relationship with him. Jerry played for Wooden at UCLA in the 1950s. Many would describe him as being a bit temperamental; others would say he had a firecracker of a personality. Apparently, not one to mince words, Norman frequently exhibited his thoughts and opinions with some animation, many of which were in contrast with Coach's relatively conservative style.

Many might think that their "oil and vinegar" approaches could be the cause of friction; rather, they were the basis of mutual respect and proved to be complementary. Coach made it work. Of note, Norman was largely credited with broadening UCLA's recruiting to a national scope, designing the team's trademark zone press, and being highly capable with his own knowledge of the game. In fact, it was Norman who suggested playing a "box and one" defense against Houston's Elvin Hayes in the 1968 championship game that led to a Bruin win.

Your coaching imperative: Participative management

The essence of participative management is best captured in this well-known quote from Steve Jobs: "It doesn't make sense to hire smart people and then tell them what to do. We hire smart people so they can tell us what to do."

Jobs was spot-on! Participative management is about inviting more (and the *right*) people to the table, to the extent reasonable and practical; thus, allowing a broader segment of employees to be actively involved in an organization's decision-making processes. Managers generally practice it to welcome and respect the opinions and ideas of all team members who deal directly with work processes and key organizational stakeholders. The practice is based on the premise that opportunities abound for change, leadership can be distributed, information and power can be shared, and all ideas are welcome. Employees closest to the work know it best and should "participate" in recommending and making improvements in quality, throughput, and cost.

DOI: 10.4324/9781003456902-7

Forms of participative management include process or product re-engineering committees, focus groups, employee involvement programs, self-managed teams, special projects, and suggestion boxes.

The decision to adopt a style of participative management tends to be a matter of managerial preference. It may also depend upon the organization's leadership preferences, culture, finances, or operational nature. Its intangible benefits include an enhanced sense of belonging, which helps promulgate a feeling of participant "ownership." This style also helps build collective and individual employee commitment, increases participants' sense of self-esteem, optimizes the sharing of intellectual capital and organizational knowledge, and heightens productivity.

Participative management is not without risks. If not carefully and appropriately managed, results may not come quickly; broadly sharing proprietary information can be a concern; some managers may confuse delegation and authority around this style; training time and related costs can escalate; projects can interrupt the day-to-day operations, and some managers have a hard time loosening their grip on the steering wheel. However, on balance, many companies have experienced positive direct and indirect outcomes.

There are several applicable management practices toward these ends of enhanced employee involvement and engagement in this principle.

Provide latitude

While there is no guarantee of results, many organizations have gone down this path of involving employees in information exchange, problem-solving, troubleshooting, opinion solicitation, and decision-making and realized the related benefits. For example, companies such as HSBC, British Gas, and Nokia Cellular have achieved profits and value creation through employee idea implementation. Other examples noted on ManagementStudyGuide.com include these well-known companies:

Toyota has been following suggestion schemes and employee involvement procedures for over a decade now. The management receives almost 2,000,000 suggestions and ideas every year and the company implements around 95% of these. Who is not aware of Toyota's success rate? About five thousand improvements per year have been made at Toyota, one of the fastest growing global organizations.

British Airways is another great example of participatory management. During economic troubles, employees' suggestions helped them cut the annual cost of their operations by 4.5 million pounds. This is just unbelievable. The company would have suffered from huge losses, had it not adopted employees' suggestions. It is a concern that to some extent employees can misuse industrial democracy, but with a proper management of HR functions, this problem can be solved, and the operations of the organization can be taken to the next level.

Satyam is another great example. It has been implementing a company-wide suggestion scheme, "The Idea Junction," since 2001. A real-time web-based portal was implemented in Intranet that can be accessed by all its employees across the globe. It is being used to support the entire life cycle of an idea right from its generation until its implementation. The main idea behind adopting this management style was to promote values and bring a sense of belongingness in the employees through ideas, suggestions, and complaints. The whole procedure is backed by a strong and comprehensive reward policy that encourages employees to perform better each time.

I would add one more example to this list. I worked at a company in the early 90s where, like other places, the cost of U.S. healthcare benefits was skyrocketing beyond our means. (Some things never change!) Fault could be pointed at our program management, a lack of employee education, inflation, and poor service providers relationships. In response, we formed a cross-functional, multi-site employee task force of a dozen members to help identify issues and raise concerns. Innovative for the time, we empowered that task force to assess the current state, determine gaps, oversee a request for proposals process, and recommend solutions. In parallel, the HR function was proactive with communications by keeping all employees abreast of timetables, related steps, and projected outcomes. By the time of annual benefits enrollment, with executive review and approval, we had a terrific new vendor, saving us 16% in our overall costs. By virtue of the task force process we used, we also had no employee relations headaches.

With some careful planning, adopting these types of programs may launch your team toward increased productivity and allow your team members to feel more committed with higher levels of job satisfaction.

Actively listen

In today's fast-paced world, with countless demands and distractions, effective listening can easily fall by the wayside. Yet, it would be at a leader's peril not to demonstrate a sincere willingness to focus on the matter at hand. Try to actively listen to ideas and suggestions sincerely and intently. The question is "How?"

We all like to think that we are effective listeners, but there is always room for improvement. To this end, Dianne Schilling has outlined some tips that would be useful at work (and home) including maintaining direct eye contact, avoiding distractions and interruptions, keeping an open mind, expressing empathy, and pausing before responding.

Create a psychological safety net

You must create an environment—a psychological safety net—where your team can responsibly and freely voice their opinions without fear of embarrassment, retribution, or water cooler backlash. A place that is "safe to say." When employees are free to express themselves, a unified team spirit grows. Employees actively engage with others. There is pride and a common purpose. Ideas are exchanged, voices are heard, and collective decision-making directs everyone down a better path. As a leader, you know what is going on, when, and who is involved.

How do you create this utopian workplace of free-flowing and open communication? Several steps can be considered.

Minimize their hesitation

We know that many people are fearful of public speaking, especially in front of their boss. Nerves lead to anxiety, which leads to avoidance. It is also not easy for everyone to knock on your door. In fact, it is likely that as you climb the corporate ladder, fewer employees will openly speak with you.

However, voices must be heard. It is incumbent on you to put your team members at ease about sharing their perspectives, needs, beliefs, emotions, and expectations. This often means leaving your job title outside of the conference room while speaking your own mind by example. No one will take a risk or be vulnerable unless you do.

To break the ice, you might tell a story where you struggled on central stage. For example, I once got a mechanical pointer stuck in my sweater when giving a benefits presentation in a cafeteria full of hundreds of employees. (I collapsed the pointer as I was speaking, but it somehow got caught and I could not gracefully "undo" it; therefore, I finished the presentation with the pointer hanging off my wooly sleeve.) A bit embarrassing to say the least and it made for a few laughs (and my blushing) afterwards.

Make the introverts comfortable

In some workplaces, meetings are a battlefront for voices. Employees seek to be heard, and it is acceptable to be aggressive with one's opinions. In other places, employees are not as forthcoming. This may be driven by the respect one has for their team members, a seniority system, personal introversion, social anxiety, culturaldistress, or an innate deference to authority. Silence may also be a derivative of different understandings of etiquette, language barriers, multi-cultural prejudices, or conflicting work styles.

Be aware of these many inherent influences and preferences, both individually and collectively, and how they may affect your team's sense of freedom to express themselves. It must be a "safe place." And remember, if you want to know how an extrovert is doing, simply listen; however, you must ask an introvert!

Ask for honesty

This can be tough. Someone may need or want to express an unpopular opinion or one that is non-conforming. Maybe the topic is uncomfortable, since it may involve being critical of a decision, process, or colleague. It is also possible that relationships could be strained across the organization if the truth is told. Maybe these thoughts are in boss' crosshairs.

Presumably, we are all adults in the workplace; therefore, while honesty may be messy and even painful, why not have an adult conversation?

Be fearless

In his inspirational remarks at the commencement exercise in May of 2018, Dr. Wallace Loh, president of the University of Maryland at College Park, discussed the characteristics of the school's mascot: The Terrapin.

This small turtle is found in coastal marshes of the eastern United States, and it must be constantly adaptable to the changes within and around its harsh environment. It has a hard shell, which makes it resilient. It has limited energy and, therefore, must be very deliberate and purposeful with each step. It can only walk in one direction—forward—and to do so, it must stick its neck out.

Maybe we all need a little terrapin inside. You should adopt this approach and invite others to do the same.

Welcome all ideas

Some may get a vote, but everyone should have a voice.

Differences of thought and opinion lead to better ideas and innovation. Ultimately, those team members with the most applicable knowledge base and skillset will likely determine the best path ahead. (Note: Diversity of people and ideas are covered in the next principle.) As a leader, encourage all team members to express their concerns, ideas, and suggestions—even at the cost of time and debate—and be prepared to act upon this input. It is possible that Jerry Norman could be sitting next to you at your next meeting.

React professionally

Encouraging participation, what happens when the opinion of one or more of your team members does not match yours?

As much as you may try to keep a calm demeanor, be careful. Everyone is watching. An inadvertent frown, raised eyebrow, or a subtle sigh will reverberate in the hallways and may potentially strain your relationships with other team members. A negative reaction will surely erode your attempts to encourage free expression.

Hear input, both compliments, and complaints, with grace and dignity. Keep your real-time and subsequent emotions in check and stay in control. Try to understand what is behind their message, even if it hurts. Someone is taking a risk and you should be grateful for their daring.

Let it go

Ethan Burns has conducted research that concludes leaders generally react quite poorly when challenged, even if their employees are well-intentioned and appropriate in their expression. It seems that their managers are more inclined to label these employees as substandard performers. Early findings of related research indicate that managers may even be abusive toward these employees with different points of view. They may be rude to them, ignore them, subject them to ridicule, or hold grudges.

I can cite a personal example of this—i.e., having a hard time moving forward. I was a member of the management team that was "locked in" during a work stoppage at a manufacturing site. The union was pressing for better wages and job security. The company was in no rush to meet their demands.

During the stoppage, salaried employees kept the facility running. I was assigned the task of driving a forklift 12 hours a day. Unfortunately, due to the site's unique layout, this meant that I was periodically driving through picket lines. Terribly angry picket lines.

I can assure you that I was not given a warm welcome. Despite knowing many of the workers on a first name basis, they had their role to play. My forklift's path was blocked, I was spit upon, eggs were tossed at me, and some rather unkind remarks were said about my mother. Still, one must turn the cheek and forge ahead.

I would like to tell you that when the labor agreement was settled that I forgot all. However, I could not shake it. As a professional, I never acted or spoke in an ill-advised way of that experience, nor did I seek retaliation; however, my opinions of a few colleagues were permanently changed.

Let ideas socialize

An idea surfaces and you, as the leader, have either mixed feelings about it or have no idea how to respond. When this happens, one option to consider is throwing the idea back at your team for their reactions and debate. It shows inclusion, will likely generate different approaches, and will give pause enough for you to form your own thoughts.

Provide constructive feedback

Feedback is one of the most powerful assets in a manager's toolkit. Effectively done, it creates learning opportunities, improves performance, and motivates individuals. It validates mutual understanding and accountability. It separates fact from fiction while clarifying perceptions. It also costs nothing, and it is always available to you.

Whether you are saying thanks or providing critique, use feedback early and often. Your comments should be given in a business context with clarity and forethought. Your team will appreciate your teaching intent and trust will be built.

Can employees really speak up without retribution?

Express the benefits for all participants

In addition to the benefits for you and, by extension, the organization, employees who freely express themselves in a professional manner (not too much, not too little—and stay on point) generally:

- Are more involved with their work, as discussion generates ideas and innovation through Groupthink.
- Earn reverence from others, especially when one's contributions are characterized as respectful, consistent, knowledgeable, and value-added. Speaking up requires some courage, especially if one's opinion is not conforming.
- Enhance their organizational impact as often these individuals are asked to take on additional responsibilities and broaden their sphere of influence.
- Generate unexpected opportunities, as one's thoughts and opinions may seem fit to be escalated in the organization.
- Establish a personal brand as others take notice.
- May experience career acceleration, having gleaned the admiration of others.

Lead with questions

According to Peter Drucker, one of the most well-known and influential management teachers, "The leader of the past was a person who knew how to *tell*. The leader of the future will be a person who knows how to *ask*."

As leaders, it is incumbent to create an environment where the truth can be heard and opinions may be openly expressed, thus providing a stage where insight and knowledge can be exchanged. To foster this, author Marvin Weisbord states that leaders should give information freely, tell the truth, and accept all input and feedback. They should not shoot the messenger, they should address the questions and rumors, and follow up on a timely basis. Jim Collins also echoes this theme in suggesting that leaders, among other activities, should lead with questions, not answers, and engage in dialog and debate.

What types of questions should be asked? To be a better manager, you want to get and keep employees engaged in the dialog, expressing their respective views. Start with questions that promulgate individual and organizational learning such as "What are the goals?" "What are the commitments?" "What would success look like?" and "What assumptions are we making?" These types of questions can bring optimism, show thoughtfulness, build community, avoid judgment, and provide clarity on the path toward a solution.

Seek the best solution

At the end of the day, you will be judged by the decisions you make. Therefore, it is important to use your time and resources wisely, embracing facts and logic.

Decision-making steps

The University of Massachusetts-Dartmouth outlines seven basic steps in effective decision-making. Each of these steps should be considered and reflected upon:

1 Identify the decision to be made
2 Gather relevant information
3 Identify alternatives
4 Weigh evidence and associated risk
5 Choose the course(s) of action
6 Act
7 Review the decision and its consequences

I would also add, as part of any decision-making process, it is also important to be cognizant of any assumptions, emotions, and biases. Such awareness, to the extent it is possible to recognize such, will lead to objectivity, and help avoid the tendency to oversimplify or amplify the challenge at hand.

We will take a closer look at decision-making later in this book; however, as a basic paradigm, following the above steps should help maximize your potential to move ahead.

Manage conflict

On the syndicated television show, "The Office," vulnerable and hypersensitive Phyllis anticipates a rough day at work around a party planning project with her coworker Angela. It seems that Angela has been downright hostile to Phyllis lately. To prepare for what will be an inevitable confrontation, Phyllis researches some strategies for dealing with difficult people. As the predicted battle later unfolds, Phyllis tries to diffuse Angela's condescending anger by asking questions such as "How do you feel … ," and stating, "I want to understand what you're saying, but it's difficult for me when you use that tone."

It was a terrific comedy, but not much of a cognitive study. Ultimately, Angela's sarcasm triumphed. Phyllis bravely licked her wounds and retreated. Their boss, Michael, seemed oblivious to all.

A certain level of natural workplace tension is normal and healthy. Yet, we have all witnessed the partial or even total collapse of a peer-to-peer and supervisory-subordinate relationship breakdown. Often these fissures may be attributed to a supervisor's failure to act. In these instances, excuses such as "If we confront her, she may leave" or "It's really not that serious of an offense" are blatant negligence of one's leadership responsibilities.

To resolve disparate views, Kenneth Thomas and Ralph Kilmann have identified specific strategies for dealing with conflict:

- Accommodating—When harmony is the desired outcome, one party may acquiesce to the other's desires without the battle, essentially giving the opposite party what they desired.
- Avoiding—While it may seem to be an attractive alternative to put your head in the sand and hope the problem goes away, it is more likely that time is not your friend and ignorance will not make the situation improve. In fact, if the related uneasiness around conflict festers, it can erode organizational and team effectiveness, as well as your credibility. Thus, while this may be one of the most significant personal challenges for any leader, try to address concerns *as they arise*.
- Collaborating—It takes time and personal investment, but solutions incorporate ideas from all parties. Often, this involves discussion around problem identification, input, priority setting, planning, and follow-up.
- Compromising*—You give; they give. Hopefully, there is an acceptable solution somewhere in the middle.
- Competing—There will be one winner and one or more losers in the competition for finite resources. This strategy brings out your inner aggressor. Decisions get made, and resentment is possible from those who feel short changed.

Choosing the best strategy is largely situationally dependent. Be particularly careful, if not deliberate, with your approach when issues are emotionally charged and people are invested. Remember that disagreement can be healthy; people just do not need to be disagreeable.

Respectful adult conversations with civil discourse are welcomed.

Note: As Bob Chell, Professor Emeritus of Psychology at Fairleigh Dickinson University points out, a compromised position is often viewed more as a "loss" than a "win." It may even set an expectation that since one party compromised, they should receive some additional consideration next time.

Don't manage conflict

But wait! You just said, "Manage it." There are occasions when letting your team sort through their own issues—without your intervention—is appropriate.

In February 1970, UCLA was undefeated and held the #1 ranking before losing a conference game to Oregon by 13 points. It was a stunning defeat.

Leading up to the game, there were some signs of unrest and dissension on the team. Losing this game brought this discord, which was along racial lines, into the forefront.

After the game, at their own initiative, all of the players ended up in a hotel room discussing what needed to change. It was an intense, painfully honest session, and uncomfortable things were said. In the end, the players were able to reconcile their differences—perhaps not all at the personal level—but at least to a place where there was going to be future harmony on the court.

One of the most powerful things Coach did about this dissension was ... nothing. He did not intervene. He did not chase after his players or follow up for details. He felt each player, whether they were a starter or the last man on the bench, was a leader in their own right. He trusted them to find the best way forward.

They did, later defeating Jacksonville in the 1970 NCAA championship game.
Using this approach is situational, but if you have trust, it may be a worthy early option.

"Yes, and ... "

"Yes, and ... ." is a foundational tool in the world of improvisation; however, author and subject matter expert Bob Kulhan will tell you that using this phrase can go a long way toward helping you manage conflict in a business setting (and maybe even at home).

In dealing with opposing views—and trying to come up with negotiated solutions—communication is our critical tool. We must be able to send and receive messages clearly and succinctly such that there is minimal room for misinterpretation. More art than science, employing a methodology like "Yes, and ... " may heighten focus, enhance the creativity of the discussion at hand, and lead to more solutions or hasten the path to appropriate forward.

While I cannot do justice to the worth of improvisation's benefits here, "Yes AND ..." may be used in response to an idea or opinion to spur further discussion and opinion gathering. It is constructive and reinforcing, and the words build bridges that may lead to the next level of thinking. It focuses on commonalities, not differences. It allows you to reframe issues and avoid being judgmental.

I believe that this is a topic worthy of your familiarity and practice.

How does this compare to conventional wisdom?

If I share leadership, won't my own stature be diminished?

Although job security in today's corporate environment can be fleeting, if your ego will not allow for the sharing of organizational power and decision-making (an extension of the Coach's view that leadership is a privilege and not an entitlement), then you may be, intentionally or not, placing personal gain or advantage ahead of your organization's best interests.

Endnotes for Principle 2: Surround yourself with strong, opinionated people

Wooden, J.R. (2002, August 22). Private conversation.
Bisheff, S. (2004). *John Wooden: An American treasure*. Nashville, Tennessee: Cumberland House Publishing, Inc., pp. 234–236.
Wooden, J.R. (2004). *They call me coach*. Waco, Texas: Word Books, p. 118.

Participative management

Guy. (2022, January 25). "'It doesn't make sense to hire smart people and then tell them what to do. We hire smart people so they can tell us what to do' —Steve Jobs." htts://businessfitness.biz/hire-smart-people-and-let-them-do-their-jobs/
McMillan, A. (Date unknown). Participative management. Revised by Debbie D. DuFrene. Posted at referenceforbusiness.com. Retrieved on May 31, 2018, from: http://www.referenceforbusiness.com/management/Or-Pr/Participative-Management.html

Provide latitude

Juneja, P. (2018). A basic understanding of participative management. Reviewed by Management Study Guide Content Team. Posted at ManagementStudyGuide.com. Retrieved on May 31, 2018, from: https://www.managementstudyguide.com/participative-management.htm.

Actively listen

Schilling, D. (2012, November 9). 10 steps to effective listening. Retrieved on May 30, 2018, from: https://www.forbes.com/sites/womensmedia/2012/11/09/10-steps-to-effective-listening/#1df8656b3891

Create a psychological safety net

Katzenbach, J.R., & Smith, D.K. (1993, March–April). The discipline of teams. *Harvard Business Review*, p. 291.

Let it go

De Cremer, D., De Schutter, L., Stouten, J., & Zhang, J. (2016, October 18). Can employees really speak up without retribution. Retrieved on May 23, 2018, from: https://hbr.org/2016/10/can-employees-really-speak-up-without-retribution

Provide constructive feedback

Dignen, B. (2014, March 17). Five reasons why feedback may be the most important skill. Retrieved on May 30, 2018, from: http://www.cambridge.org/elt/blog/2014/03/17/five-reasons-feedback-may-important-skill/

Express the benefits for all participants

Llopis, G. (2012, March 19). 6 reasons employees must speak up to thrive at work. Retrieved on May 23, 2018, from: https://www.forbes.com/sites/glennllopis/2012/03/19/6-reasons-employees-must-speak-up-to-thrive-at-work/2/

Lead with questions

Hesselbein, F., Goldsmith, M., & Beckhard, R. (Eds.). (1996). *The leader of the future: New visions, strategies, and practices for the next era*. San Francisco, California: Jossey-Bass Publishers, p. 227.

Weisbord, M.R. (1987). *Productive workplaces: Organizing and managing for dignity, meaning, and community*. San Francisco, California: Jossey-Bass Inc., Publishers, p. 351.

Collins, J. C. (2001). *Good to great: Why some companies make the leap and others don't*. New York: HarperCollins Publishers, Inc., pp. 74–80.

Adams, M. (2004). *Change your questions, change your answers*. San Francisco, California: Berrett-Koehler Publishers, Inc., pp. 32–33.

Decision-making steps

Carmela, S. (2017, July 4). Techniques and tools to help you make business decisions. Retrieved on May 30, 2018, from: https://www.businessnewsdaily.com/6162-decision-making.html

Manage conflict

"The Office" Television Show (2007). United States, Season 4, Episode 5/6, Production code: 4005/4006, Airdate: October 11, 2007. Retrieved on May 23, 2018, from: http://officequotes.net/no4-03.php

Dontigney, E. (2018, February 3). 5 conflict management strategies. Retrieved on May 23, 2018, from: http://smallbusiness.chron.com/5-conflict-management-strategies-16131.html

Chell, R. (2019, December 10). Private conversation.

Yes, and ...

Kulhan, B., & Chrisafullu, C. (2017). *Getting to "yes and," the art of business improv*. Stanford, California: Stanford Business Books, Stanford University Press, 2017, p. 8, 32–33.

Balance is everything

Coach was a firm believer in "balance" as it pertained to all aspects of his own life and the lives of those he taught.

On the court:

- His intention was for basketball to be a "pleasure," not a chore.
- Coach never scheduled a practice if it might interfere with class.
- Throughout the years, Coach liked to "mix" his starting five with seniors, as well as underclassmen.
- Even within his offense, he wanted players to "spread the court" and to be prepared for any eventuality.
- He cautioned players that too much off-season playing, training, or conditioning might deprive one of other worthwhile interests. In doing so, Coach was essentially underscoring the pyramid value of "self-control"—a warning to them to avoid burnout.
- In a vivid illustration of this principle, Coach insisted that Eddie Sheldrake, in spite of his protests, should miss a game in order to be with his wife during childbirth.

Off the court:

- Wooden balanced the books and basketball. At Purdue, he was a three-time All-American, two-time national champion, and the recipient of the Big 10 Scholar Athlete Award.
- He was a strong advocate and practitioner that balanced the three F's: *family, faith,* and *friends.*
- Coach tried not to "take games home."
- His wife, Nellie, accompanied Coach to all games and conventions. This was an unheard practice at that time.
- Coach professed that "love" and "balance" were the two most important words in the dictionary.
- He believed in moderation in all things.
- In his view, basketball was a part of life but not life. He did not want it to be defined this way.
- Coach was fond of saying, "Don't get so caught-up in making a living versus having a life."

DOI: 10.4324/9781003456902-8

Your coaching imperative: Embrace diversity, equality, and inclusion ("DEI")

In the minds of many business professionals, the word "balance" usually conjures up images of a corporate setting with cultural, generational, and gender representation from all corners of the globe. Worse yet, "diversity" connotes quotas or statistically driven hiring mandates.

What some business leaders fail to appreciate is that balance, i.e., diversity around their table, should not be embraced solely because of legal requirements or public relations concerns. Rather, it has been shown to yield a proven competitive advantage from blending and including different thoughts in this ever-changing global environment.

Diversity

Diversity is about "who" someone is; not "what" someone is.

Each of us has a point of view that has been shaped by the unique lens through which we view the world. That lens has been and continues to be influenced by a variety of factors—gender, race, ethnicity, age, disabilities, religious views, various cultural exposures, economics, political opinions, personal values, role models, relationships, work experiences, education, and key life experiences. Our generational markers alone, from "Matures" to "Millennials," have given us dramatically different exposure to and attitudes about local and world events, social causes, social justice, technology, institutional trust, medical advancements, and globalization, among other subjects.

Diversity is a mix of differing people with their varying perspectives. It is the physical and cognitive representation of your team of different genders, ages, races, backgrounds, thinking styles, personality types, education levels, employment levels, and work functions.

Equality

Simply, without true equality in all comparable terms and conditions of employment for all (i.e., treat all with respect, respond to everyone's needs, provide equal opportunities, equal pay for equal work, comparable benefits, etc.), the rest is just lip service. It is where the rubber hits the road; action over words.

Inclusion

In his book of essays, "All I Really Need to Know I Learned in Kindergarten," author Robert Fulghum describes his early life lessons about sharing, fairness, and accountability. He also mentions that holding hands and sticking together is a good thing to do when you go out in the world.

In this same vein, on the iconic children's television show, "Mister Rogers' Neighborhood," the daily message was about the value of each child and how every child deserves abundant and unconditional love.

Both the author and beloved television host recognized the value of inclusion. You should too.

Inclusion ensures that everyone's ideas are invited and that viewpoints are represented, welcomed, and valued. It allows for the sharing and exchanging of these various perspectives, ideas, and knowledge. Through interaction, it generates opportunities for workplace creativity, innovation, and success.

And then there is "belonging"

"Diversity," "equality," and "inclusion" are the words that get most of the attention in corporate settings (and we will focus upon them here); however, there is another attribute worthy of your managerial attention: belonging.

When someone feels as though they belong, they are in the right place. They feel good. They are comfortable, secure, confident, and safe. Most importantly, their self-esteem is high.

A sense of belonging is a basic human need. It prompts transparency and openness. It promotes candor, honesty, and even risk-taking. Most importantly, it encourages participation and authenticity. It makes one feel accepted by their coworkers, and they feel a part of something bigger than themselves. It is the basis for community and psychological safety.

(Note: It is my belief that you cannot have DEI without "belonging.")

The benefits of diversity

The starting line-up of UCLA's 1964 championship team was comprised of individuals from all walks of life. It included: Fred Slaughter, an African American from Kansas; Keith Erickson, a California beach kid; Jack Hirsch, a scrappy Jewish kid from Brooklyn; Gail Goodrich, a native of the San Fernando Valley; and Walt Hazzard, an inner-city kid from Philadelphia.

Coach reached the pinnacle of success with this on-the-court diversity, and you can, too.

Diversity is good for your bottom line

Investors take note. Twenty years ago, there was little evidence to support the correlation between diversity and profitability. Fifteen years ago, there were a few studies. Since 2015, the causal link is indisputable as multiple studies prove that diversity boosts a company's bottom line.

For ethnicity:

- The top quartile of ethnically diverse companies is 35% more likely to outperform the national industry median (McKinsey, 2015).
- Companies with above-average total diversity had both 19% higher innovation revenues and 9% higher EBIT(Earnings Before Interest & Taxes) margins, on average (Boston Consulting Group/HBR, 2018).
- The 50 companies on the 2016 Best Workplaces for Diversity list average 24% higher year-over-year revenue growth than non-list winners (Bush and Peters' research into the 2016 Best Workplaces for Diversity).

For gender:

- Gender-diverse companies are 15% more likely to have better financial returns (Bush & Peters citing Fortune, 2015).

- Companies with at least 30% female leaders had net profit margins up to 6% higher than companies with no women in their senior ranks (McEvoy citing The Peterson Institute for International Economics and Ernst & Young, 2016).
- Gender-diverse business units in the retail industry have 14% higher average comparable revenue than less-diverse business units (5.24% versus 4.58%) (Badal citing Gallop, 2014).
- Gender-diverse business units in the hospitality industry show 19% higher average quarterly net profit than less-diverse business units (Badal citing Gallop, 2014).
- *Fortune 500* companies with the highest representation of women board directors performed better financially than those with the lowest representation of women on their board of directors (Showers citing Catalyst, 2016).
- Teams where men and women are equal earn 41% more revenue (Woolf, 2017).

Conclusively, diversity is a driver of enhanced business performance and profitability.

Diversity brings you closer to your customers

A diverse team knows your local marketplace and can help monitor your customer demographics. This leads to better business connectivity and enhanced marketing, improving your competitive stature. A diverse team may also have insight into the differentiation of the products and services you offer. Case in point: 73% of all household spending in the United States is controlled by women, whose earning and buying power increase each year (Catalyst).

If you are in a consumer-driven business, that statistic should catch your eye and prompt you to be sure that you have women on your team.

Diversity attracts more qualified employees

Recruiting from a diverse pool of candidates means a more qualified workforce, regardless of local economics. According to the Center for American Progress, when companies source candidates intentionally, including those with diverse backgrounds, they maximize the scope of their search. In doing so, businesses capitalize on the growth of women and people of color, increasing the probability of hiring the best, most qualified talent for their positions.

Diversity fosters creativity

Groupthink is conformity in thought and behavior without challenge. It becomes less likely when diversity is present.

As noted in the previously cited Boston Consulting Group study, research shows that socially diverse teams are consistently more innovative than their homogeneous peers. People with unique perspectives and backgrounds, when actively involved in sharing and exchanging, have the potential to provide beneficial thoughts and opinions. Thus, a robust dialog with everyone's contributions will bring enhanced creativity, "outside of the box" thinking, new and fresher ideas, and real-time feedback.

If innovation is one of the keys to your team's success, you would be foolish not to send out invitations to a diverse audience for your next brainstorming session.

Diversity leads to better decisions

A recent *Forbes* article by Eric Larson noted that inclusive teams make better business decisions 87% of the time. They also found that teams that follow an inclusive process make decisions twice as fast as half the meetings. Decisions made by these diverse teams also yield 60% better results.

Diversity makes sense in a changing world

Today's diverse candidates might not be tomorrow's. Demographics are changing in the United States and across the globe. The current and upcoming shifts, if they continue, will alter the landscape of our neighborhoods, as well as our local and global workplaces. For example, the share of adults living in middle-income households has fallen in several countries in Western Europe, millennials are now the largest adult population in the United States, and 20% of the U.S. population is expected to be 65 or older by 2050.

Issues such as healthcare, health awareness, the local quality of life, the politics of refugees, border disputes, wars, asylum applications, and economic plight are also causing shifts in populations.

From a business perspective, you need to monitor these trends and events. Diversity is here, now. It will be more pronounced tomorrow!

It is the right thing to do

Morally and ethically, diversity and inclusion belong!

May 2020 was a tipping point as passionate protests unfolded in the streets of the United States over the horrifying and wrongful death of George Floyd in Minneapolis. These protests, and others from similarly disturbing occurrences that followed (and seemingly continue to follow), reflected the unanswered sadness, pain, frustration, and outrage that Black Americans have systemically experienced for generations—socially, economically, and politically. Injustice personified.

Racism, inequality, unfair treatment practices, and discrimination have no place in our communities, nor should these practices be tolerated in our workplaces. Many of us naïvely thought these topics were a thing of the past; however, there is still so much, much more to do. Corporations and their respective leadership teams must do better.

Why traction is missing

Excuses. Mistakes. Ignorance. Words, not actions.

For every success story in corporate diversity, there is another of either inactivity or failure. In fact, despite financial allocations and intentions, research shows that most workplace diversity programs fail to produce intended outcomes, and some have actually increased bias among individual employees. This may be a result of executive ignorance, slow adaptation, miscast perceptions, or even the view that diversity is a threat. There are also legacy challenges. For example, in the fields of science, technology, engineering, and mathematics (STEM), both the private and public sectors continue to struggle with recruiting and retaining a diverse workforce. Case in point, as of 2017, nearly 75% of those in computing and mathematical fields were men and fewer than 15% were Blacks or Hispanics.

Also, according to a study published in the *Journal of Personality and Social Psychology,* the number of workers from a specific group can be a gauge for the effectiveness of a diversity program. If there are very few workers from a specific group, programs stressing differences are likely to be ineffective.

Diversity is in the eye of the beholder

I worked for a large Japanese holding company. In 2017, I was invited to our annual General Manager meeting in Tokyo. This was (and I certainly considered it to be) a great honor. For the first time in the company's 400-year history (or at least for as long as they had been having these meetings), I was one of three non-Japanese members of senior management who were invited.

Picture an exceptionally large meeting room (hotel ballroom size) stuffed with tables and chairs. Now picture it populated with approximately 247 Japanese males and three middle-aged, white American males—the senior management team of the company.

To my eye, I was shocked. This was a new paradigm for me, at least visually, and I felt really awkward. Of note, my fellow Japanese colleagues viewed our attendance as a significant first step toward diversity and seemed pleased.

To be fair, you have to start somewhere, even if some belated catching-up (by my standards) is involved.

Today, I am pleased to report that the company has since moved forward with more aggressive staffing and inclusion efforts, but this was an important lesson for me. DEI is all about perspective. My definition and expectations about workplace diversity may not be the same as yours, especially on a global stage.

Open minds are needed

With challenges and complexities, open minds are needed.

Your organizational mindset

Forget the preconceived notions. Get away from thinking that diversity is about mandates, compliance, statistics, or some flavor-of-the month.

In multi-national, multi-cultural, and multi-generational organizations where diversity has been unleashed, management has implemented programs that generate employee engagement, causing increased contact, involvement, and communication between different groups. In other words, as noted by Dobbin and Kalev in a recent *Harvard Business Review* article, these companies have moved away from control and mandates. Instead, they have countered by enabling employee measures such as voluntary training, self-managed teams, cultural cross training, college recruiting for women and minorities, mentoring, diverse task forces, and diversity management placements. (More on this to follow.)

These prescribed practices will help make diversity and inclusion institutionalized for the right reasons. Your shareholders will also likely approve.

Your personal mindset

Are you biased? Despite your best intentions or beliefs, there is a high probability that your subconscious has influence.

Have you ever assumed that a working mom must have her work life as a second priority? Have you ever assumed that an older worker is technology-challenged? Have you ever assumed that someone without kids should carry more weight at work? Have you ever assumed that someone is less intelligent because they are less articulate with their language skills? Have you ever assumed that younger workers lack drive? Have you ever assumed that "she" got the promotion because of her gender or race?

Assumptions can be dangerous. In Malcolm Gladwell's book, *Talking to Strangers*, the best-selling author proves this point with an over-arching premise that we are generally ill-equipped in our human experience to deal with and interpret cues from others—and our shortcomings have potentially harmful consequences. To this end, Gladwell cites numerous case studies as evidence, from judges determining incongruent criminal sentences to the Central Intelligence Agency falsely trusting key operatives.

If the CIA(Central Intelligence Agency) can be deceived, what chance do the rest of us have?

We all experience the world in our unique manner. That manner has filters, biases, labels, categories, fears, assumptions, barriers, emotions, and expectations—derived from heredity and environment. If that is not enough, throw in religious views, politics, economics, social perspectives, cultural roots, Yankees versus Red Sox, and cat versus dog lovers. It is amazing that we are not in a continuous verbal food fight.

It is not easy to cast all of this subjective baggage aside. It may even be uncomfortable at first. Yet we must do so, with patience, kindness, trust, grace, and humility. And you—and I— can and must manage to do this correctly with empathy and understanding.

A blueprint for DEI

Title VII was enacted in 1964; however, if your company is just initiating a diversity and inclusion program (or yours is a bit slow to get out of the gate), you need not be a multi-national corporation to get started. And you can personally help in many areas.

The buck starts here

Simply stated, in order for any diversity and inclusion strategy to succeed, it requires full executive and senior management commitment, sponsorship, and support. If this active commitment—and a "lead by example" behavior and attitude—does not exist at your workplace, it may be time to update your resume.

Know your current state

Before you can take steps to realize your ideal state, you must know where you stand. Collect the demographic information about your workforce—age, gender, gender identification or expression, ethnicity, languages, race, disability, veteran's status, and any other pertinent data. As the next step, examine the diversity of hiring placements, compensation awards, promotional moves, succession candidates, training opportunities, and performance review comparisons.

Once the data are collected, analytics can determine demographic areas that are under-represented. This typically starts with the three general areas of gender, age, and ethnicity. Look for patterns that might reflect concerns. Try to obtain and understand any reasons behind the voids or gaps. Could the company's culture, employment policies, politics, systemic practices, nepotism, or biases be a root cause or barrier preventing you from where you want to be?

Take the pulse

Much as retailers chase you for feedback on your shopping experience, you want to know if your employees are having a favorable experience working with and for you. Whether it is focus groups, informal discussions, blogs, lunch meetings, pulse or broader surveys, or roundtables, you should understand the real-time mindset of your team and the broader organization—for DEI, engagement, and other workplace climate matters.

This climate check provides critical insight. Hopefully, the findings are not too much of an eye-opener. At a minimum, this input will identify some areas where attention and managerial intervention is required. It will also establish a baseline from which progress can now be measured.

Caution is urged here. If you are going to ask people their opinions on this or other workplace topics, *you must be prepared to share the feedback and act upon it*. Not to do so would be irresponsible and might cost you significant managerial credibility.

Develop a policy statement

Diversity and inclusion are not a fad. They should be a continuous effort and be deeply rooted in your institutional core. Making it policy highly assures these ends.

A diversity policy statement should be simple, concise, and meaningful. It must be consistent with your organizational culture, be supported and practiced by management, and be both pragmatic and directional. It should be along the lines of closing any real or perceived gap between "us" and "them." It should state that differences are valued.

Check the Internet. There are some good examples out there that you can tailor to your needs. Remember that this is about actions, not just words.

Appoint a diversity officer

Need a spotlight on this issue? If your company does not have a diversity officer (or a like designee), it is time for such consideration. This role can act as the chair of a DEI steering committee and help provide oversight to related task forces (i.e., for communications, HR practices, policies and procedures, and development and support initiatives).

A steering committee's primary responsibilities may include enhancing efforts to become an "Employer of Choice" by embedding DEI into your business philosophies and practices; developing pragmatic DEI strategies, identifying tactics, providing program guidance, and communicating accordingly; building and sharing DEI knowledge; engaging leadership about DEI initiatives; and using a data-based approach to define what success looks like—with correlating goals and key performance indicators.

Get others involved

Everyone needs to be responsible.

DEI are not the sole responsibility of the CEO, your diversity officer, or the head of talent management. It is everyone's responsibility. However, our colleagues often cannot build the bridge between what they do on a daily basis and how it connects to organizational diversity and inclusion efforts. In fact, there can even be resistance from those who lack this understanding.

For a DEI strategy to move ahead, you need champions, cheerleaders, and articulate advocates. This requires keeping this topic front-of-mind for all beyond basic optics.

Across your population, identify parties of interest and regularly inform, educate, and engage them about diversity and inclusion initiatives and progress. As mentioned, use task forces. Also consider coalitions, affinity groups, committees, councils, succession planning implications, and mentoring and shadowing programs. Make DEI part of your organizational fabric.

Consider best practices

In a recent article in *Fast Company*, Gwen Moran highlights some terrific examples of what some companies are doing to make employees feel like valued, inclusive members of their organization.

At Johnson & Johnson, the conversation about diversity and inclusion starts on the first day of work and continues throughout the employee's life cycle. The topic is built into their training programs, as well as their talent management system. They are proactive with their communications to internal and external stakeholders—and back up their words with related actions.

Diversity and inclusion is about community at AT&T. They try to ensure that every voice is heard by establishing a multitude of employee teams and networks that provide support, training, mentoring, and advocacy to diverse groups. This allows people with common interests to connect in a comfortable environment. Leadership is also involved in these efforts.

Unilever has a Global Diversity Board, chaired by their CEO, which provides overarching vision, governance, and target goals for diversity and inclusion across their broad businesses. Over a ten-year journey, they have reached significant milestones with female representation in their management ranks.

Finally, Ernst & Young has always been an early and staying leader in the field of diversity and inclusion. EY holds managers accountable for making diversity and inclusion part of daily life. With full executive support, the EY performance management scheme emphasizes diversity and inclusion in a manner that rewards the best practitioners. With this broadened perspective, they are serious about diversity and inclusion and believe that they reap significant benefits on a global scale.

Assess your talent sources

At the macro-level, barriers must be removed for the entry of diverse candidates. You should target and partner with specific schools, referral programs, recruiting firms, and professional associations for minorities and women. Appropriately steer your social media and branding for the same. Also, you can expand your labor pool in light of today's flexibility around remote and hybrid working.

Bottom line … a diverse slate of candidates should be identified for every position at every level in the organization. Period.

Assess your selection procedures

Recalling the "Greenspoon effect" from our first principle when an interviewer inadvertently gives positive reinforcement to a candidate with head nods and expressions, the opposite is also true. An interviewer might unknowingly reveal a bias through negative signals (i.e., the interviewer stops taking notes, glances at their watch, yawns, or looks bored), thus causing the candidate to alter their responses. For example, if the candidate senses from the interviewer that their answer is going down the wrong path, the candidate might alter their response midstream or for future exchanges—telling the interviewer what they may want to hear versus what the truth or reality may be. The candidate's responses become phony.

In another scenario, an interviewer and candidate may "connect" well beyond the niceties of their initial exchange and end up spending 45 minutes discussing some of the personal things they share in common—their hometown, their school, their love for pickleball, their children, or a mutual acquaintance. When this happens, questions about the candidate or the position's job description do not receive proper attention as the personal topics have derailed an otherwise fair interrogatory process. Research points out that this "similar to me" effect results in flawed higher interview ratings.

Another possibility might be that the interviewer makes certain face value assumptions about the candidate based upon certain stereotypes. For example, the interviewer might assume that a candidate with a certain degree from a certain school must be highly proficient in a certain subject matter, when a few pointed questions might draw different conclusions.

In order to minimize these possible pitfalls, interviewers should be professionally instructed and be part of a diverse panel, if appropriate. They should prepare for each exchange. Interviews should be highly structured. "Unconscious bias" training should be engrained into the process. Scripts should be utilized to keep evaluations about candidates on a more level playing field. In addition, technology is developing in this area that enables companies to screen candidates more effectively.

Examine your management practices

Is yours one of the companies where African American workers are still offered 65 cents to the dollar compared to white workers or perhaps your hiring practices are reflective of the bigger picture where women make up a mere 18.75% of software engineers?

The time to act is now. If diversity and inclusion are not part of your management practices, then you are complicit with the problem. This must be addressed.

- In your HR world, gather and examine information regarding current recruitment sources and selection practices, career development programs, advancement determinants, compensation practices and criteria, and retention practices. Identify and understand any reasons behind current voids or gaps. Could your company's antiquated policies, politics, systemic practices, nepotism, heritage, or biases be a root cause of or barrier preventing you from your aspirations?
- Gather and analyze policies directly or indirectly related to DEI. Are your paid time-off/ flexible-time policies fair, equitable, and competitive? Can those with child or elder care issues be comfortable? What about parental leave? Do you encourage work/life balance?

Do you need a revised "Remote Working" policy? What about looking at holidays through a DEI lens?

- Try to drive DEI awareness, branding, and related employee engagement through promotion and publicity across your organization. Bring in speakers. Share stories, presentations, and metrics. Hold cross-cultural exchange events like food gatherings and book clubs. Discuss headlines. Use social media. Get a website established. Related to this, organizational leadership should take every opportunity to reference and be actively engaged with any new or on-going effort. This can be in the form of lunches, newsletters, team, and one-on-one meetings, workshop sessions, and town hall gatherings. Publicize success.
- Look at your culture and how it is lived. Where do you want to go? Do you walk the talk? How do your values, corporate culture, processes, systems/tools help or hinder the advancement of DEI practices? Do you have now, or do you ensure an "open door" policy, and what does that really mean? Do employees feel comfortable reporting problems? How do you prevent any biases in overall employment practices? How do you ensure that diverse voices are heard on substantive matters? How do you guarantee that people are treated fairly? Do you embrace and practice participative management and inclusive decision-making? If not, why?
- Establish and socialize DEI metrics for attracting candidates, selecting employees, developing employees, and retaining employees. Track progress. Hold management accountable for bringing these measures to life. Make targets part of the business plan, as well as management performance goals.

Provide cross-cultural training for your team

As your local workforce becomes more diverse, cross-cultural training for your team members will help promote understanding and improve communications.

Laura Kriska, a preeminent consultant and author of *The Business of We*, noted in this growing field:

> The goal of cross-cultural training is to narrow gaps between any "us" versus "them" dynamic that is causing damage in order to limit liability, lower complaints, and create a more welcoming work environment. It is not necessary to like or even agree with the behaviors and backgrounds of people who you might consider a "them," but it is absolutely necessary to gain some basic level of information and basic interpersonal experience in order to get along without causing damage.
>
> Social science, as the foundation of this training, helps us understand that seeking the affiliation in one's own perceived identity group (whether than is a gender group, racial group, ethnic group, etc.) is a common and human response to a diverse community, especially when a person experiences themselves as a minority. But social science also teaches us that our advanced cognitive capabilities enable us to re-draw the lines quickly and easily around the identity of who is "us" and who is "them." By focusing on common goals and shared identity factors through training and education, we are able to both acknowledge our differences (no need to pretend to be "colorblind") and build affiliations that are more inclusive and based on factors of identity that are not visible (like gender, race, and ethnicity).

Kriska further added a personal observation:

> After 30 years working in this field among international professionals, I know that the one factor that stops people from taking action to bridge gaps in our lives is fear, the hesitancy that our gestures or actions might be unwelcome or unnecessary. We all know how to make others feel more welcome and safer, yet we are not always willing to take steps to do it. There must be metrics to track process and progress.

Laura is spot-on. When designing a DEI training program—for all employees—your targeted outcomes should include raising general awareness about diversity (i.e., "gap" awareness"), promoting workplace practices that support sensitivity and understanding, giving examples of behaviors and attitudes that are inconsistent with diversity, and teaching management and peers how to act and intervene when bias is evident in workplace discussion or practices.

Provide cross-cultural training for those "on assignment"

As the world has become smaller and companies continuously extend their global reach, your ability to be successful is largely predicated upon your awareness and understanding of cultural differences. To this end, employers dispatching employees "on assignment" into other countries should offer extensive cross-cultural training. This should include mentorship programs that will enable the assignee to speed through their learning curve for absorbing new traditions, customs, symbols, and ways of interaction. Of note, they will also become familiar with the nuances of how to conduct business in their new surroundings. This might include the presentation of the business card, the proper salutation, positioning of meeting participants, communication styles, or the meaning of the word "yes." This knowledge will also lead to enhanced business development, management skills, and operational understanding.

Of note, similar cultural orientation and training should also be considered for the family members of the "assigned."

These offshore assignments—usually limited to trainees, functional specialists, or executives—tend to be exorbitantly expensive and should only be pursued if the investment is deemed worthy of the time and risk. Otherwise, companies in multiple geographies should hire and trust local talent wherever possible.

Use suppliers with diversity commitments

As part of your company's emphasis on diversity and its overall importance to your business paradigm, a natural extension of this is to advise your procurement team to give extra attention to suppliers who practice diversity as a core value.

If you receive a complaint

If you receive a complaint of alleged harassment, discrimination, or bias, thoroughly investigate the matter without haste. Use trained and objective parties (like your HR or legal team). Use outside counsel if the matter is too close to home or has the potential to become wide in scope.

Bringing diversity home

While diversity—its attitudes and actions—is critical to the success of your workplace, let us not forget that it has meaning in your personal life as well.

Identify your 3 F's

As mentioned at the beginning of this principle, Coach believed in life balance through moderation. Never too high, never too low. Three square meals a day. His time was largely divided among his 3 F's: family, faith, and friends. Related personal practices like exercise, eating right, and getting to bed early were his routine.

So often in our chase for "success," we become consumed with our job title, money, and material goods. As a practical matter, "success" should also consider having a good relationship with your boss and coworkers, being engaged, feeling fulfilled, nurturing others, and enjoying what you do. As personal factors, you should also consider how "success" includes your needs for rest, recreation, and time for outside interests. To these ends, periodically, carve out time to contemplate this professional purpose and attainment strategy, in order to make course adjustments. Putting such dedicated "self-time" on your calendar may sound awkward, but some solitude or time shared with a small circle of trustees is a requirement for personal growth.

My balance is not your balance

We have all worked with people who worked crazy hours or juggled endless commitments. This is either their happy place or they have fallen into the trap of pretending that they can endure endless stretches of work and only work. But it may come at a cost. For example, skipping or losing sleep causes cognitive performance to decrease in a near linear manner and they will likely not even realize it. Meanwhile, their coworkers must endure their irritability, short-temper, and oscillating levels of engagement.

Balance does not mean equal time toward work endeavors and life interests. In today's world, "integration" is probably a better description of the blended space between the two ends. Try to find where your fulcrum is and defend it, recognizing that there will be occasional exceptions. Your mental well-being depends on this.

I have seen far too many cases where bosses have held their direct reports to their own non-stop work standards. It has not been pretty and usually does not end well. Hopefully, this practice is starting to abate.

Another aspect

The boundaries of work/life balance have been stretched, if not shattered during the recent pandemic. Many employees start their days sooner and stretch the workday well beyond what was the norm in 2019. In many cases, it seems like working from home has morphed into living at work.

If you are a leader, empathy is important here.

While the "new" home-hybrid-worksite normal is still evolving, you must be sensitive to the real-time needs and direction-pulls of all of your team members. Some are juggling children needs; others have aging parents. Some are experiencing personal and financial stress. There are family tensions, neighbor versus neighbor politics, generational friction, and divisiveness about our institutions.

Simply, you cannot possibly know all of the pressures and pain points that your team may be experiencing. Thus, to the extent possible, make sure that you keep in personal touch with and understand each party's dynamics and circumstances. Respect timelines; respect boundaries. Safety is paramount. As mentioned, fostering a sense of belonging is crucial.

Harry said it best

In Harry Chapin's song, "Cat's in the Cradle," (1974), the singer laments that time passed too quickly before he realized he had not paid due attention to what should have been his priority, his child.

If we are fortunate, we will experience about two billion heartbeats over a lifetime. Let's use them wisely.

How does this compare to conventional wisdom?

The sum of the parts really can exceed the value of the whole.

Be cognizant of the many different aspects of individual perspectives. Leverage the strengths and differences of each person so that balance and synergy are achieved. You will find, as did Coach Wooden, that populating your teams with diversity and having inclusive management practices builds a productive conduit within organizational walls, and profitable bridges to the outside.

Endnotes for Principle 3: Balance is everything

Wooden, J.R. (2002, August 22). Private conversation.

Embrace diversity and inclusion

McEvoy, O. (2017). Diversity—is it good for business? Ernst & Young. Published in Ireland. Retrieved on June 1, 2018, from: http://www.ey.com/Publication/vwLUAssets/EY-diversity-is-it-good-for-business/%24FILE/EY-diversity-is-it-good-for-business.pdf

Inclusion

Fulghum, R. (1986). All I really need to know I learned in kindergarten. Retrieved on June 8, 2018, from: https://www.scrapbook.com/poems/doc/842.html

Walsh, K. (2018, June 8). 'Won't you be my neighbor?' celebrates humanity's gentle champion. *The Star Ledger*, Entertainment Section, p. 9.

Diversity is good for your bottom line

Hunt, V., Layton, D., & Prince S. (2015, January 1). Why diversity matters. McKinsey.com. Retrieved on February 3, 2021, from: https://www.mckinsey.com/business-functions/organization/our-insights/why-diversity-matters

Bush, M., & Peters. K. (2016, December 5). How the best companies do diversity right. *Fortune.com.* Retrieved on June 1, 2018, from: http://fortune.com/2016/12/05/diversity-inclusion-workplaces/

Showers, R. (2016, March 17). 4 business benefits of diversity in the workplace. Retrieved on June 1, 2018, from: https://www.brazen.com/blog/recruiting-hr/benefits-of-diversity-in-the-workplace/

Badal, S.B. (2014, January 20). The business benefits of gender diversity: How hiring a gender-diverse workforce can improve a company's bottom line. *Gallop Business Journal.* Retrieved on June 11, 2018, from: http://news.gallup.com/businessjournal/166220/business-benefits-gender-diversity.aspx

Lorenzo, R., & Reeves, M. (2018, January 30). How and where diversity drives financial performance. *Harvard Business Review.* Retrieved on June 11, 2018, from: https://hbr.org/2018/01/how-and-where-diversity-drives-financial-performance

McEvoy, O, (2017). Diversity—is it good for business? Ernst & Young. Published in Ireland. Retrieved on June 1, 2018, from: http://www.ey.com/Publication/vwLUAssets/EY-diversity-is-it-good-for-business/%24FILE/EY-diversity-is-it-good-for-business.pdf

Woolf, S. (2017, October—posted/updated). 10 diversity statistics that will make you rethink your hiring decisions. *Clear Company.* Retrieved on June 1, 2018, from: https://blog.clearcompany.com/10-diversity-hiring-statistics-that-will-make-you-rethink-your-decisions

Diversity gets you closer to your customers

Showers, R. (2016, March 17). 4 business benefits of diversity in the workplace. Retrieved on June 1, 2018, from: https://www.brazen.com/blog/recruiting-hr/benefits-of-diversity-in-the-workplace/

Diversity gets you more qualified employees

Kerby, S., & Burns, C. (2012, July 12). The top 10 economic facts of diversity in the workplace. Center for American Progress. Retrieved on June 1, 2018, from: https://www.americanprogress.org/issues/economy/news/2012/07/12/11900/the-top-10-economic-facts-of-diversity-in-the-workplace/

Diversity fosters creativity

Showers, R. (2016, March 17). 4 business benefits of diversity in the workplace. Retrieved on June 1, 2018, from: https://www.brazen.com/blog/recruiting-hr/benefits-of-diversity-in-the-workplace/

Diversity leads to better decisions

Larson, E. (2017, September 11). New research: Diversity + inclusion = better decision-making at work. *Forbes.com.* Retrieved on June 15, 2018, from: https://www.forbes.com/sites/eriklarson/2017/09/21/new-research-diversity-inclusion-better-decision-making-at-work/#68eabaaa4cbf

Diversity makes sense in a changing world

Cilluffo, A. (2017, April 27). 10 demographic trends shaping the U.S. and the world in 2017. Pew Research Center. Retrieved on June 13, 2018, from: http://www.pewresearch.org/fact-tank/2017/04/27/10-demographic-trends-shaping-the-u-s-and-the-world-in-2017/

Kotkin, J. (2010, August). The changing demographics of America. *Smithsonian Magazine.* Retrieved on June 12, 2018, from: https://www.smithsonianmag.com/travel/the-changing-demographics-of-america-538284/

Why traction is missing

Scott-Pruitt, A., Brinkworth, C., Young, J., & Aponte, K.L. (2018, March 30). 5 things we learned about creating a successful workplace diversity program. Retrieved on June 1, 2018, from: https://hbr.org/2018/03/5-things-we-learned-about-creating-a-successful-workplace-diversity-program

Woolf, S. (2017, October—posted/updated). 10 diversity statistics that will make you rethink your hiring decisions. *Clear Company*. Retrieved on June 1, 2018, from: https://blog.clearcompany.com/10-diversity-hiring-statistics-that-will-make-you-rethink-your-decisions

Harts, M. (2019). *The memo: What women of color need to know to secure a seat at the table.* Seal Press.

Your organizational mindset

Dobbin, F., & Kalev, A. (2016, July-August). Why diversity programs fail. *Harvard Business Review*. Retrieved on June 1, 2018, from: https://hbr.org/2016/07/why-diversity-programs-fail

Showers, R. (2016, March 17). 4 business benefits of diversity in the workplace. Retrieved on June 1, 2018, from: https://www.brazen.com/blog/recruiting-hr/benefits-of-diversity-in-the-workplace/

Your personal mindset

Gladwell, M., (2019). *Talking to strangers*. New York: Little, Brown and Company, pp. 342–343.

Know your current state

Society for Human Resource Management. (2017, April 25). How to develop a diversity and inclusion initiative. Retrieved on June 1, 2019, from: https://www.shrm.org/ ... /how-to-develop-a-diversity-and-inclusion-initiative.aspx

Get others involved

Society for Human Resource Management. (2017, April 25). How to develop a diversity and inclusion initiative. Retrieved on June 1, 2019, from: https://www.shrm.org/ ... /how-to-develop-a-diversity-and-inclusion-initiative.aspx

Scott-Pruitt, A., Brinkworth, C., Young, J., & Aponte, K.L. (2018, March 30). 5 things we learned about creating a successful workplace diversity program. Retrieved on June 1, 2018, from: https://hbr.org/2018/03/5-things-we-learned-about-creating-a-successful-workplace-diversity-program

Best practices

Moran, G. (2017, January 23). How these top companies are getting inclusion right. *Fast Company*. Retrieved on June 1, 2018, from: https://www.fastcompany.com/3067346/how-these-top-companies-are-getting-inclusion-right

Assess your selection procedures

Lottie S. (2011, December 8). Interviews—the interviewer bias effect. Field Research in Organizational Psychology, Fall Edition. Retrieved on June 15, 2018, from: https://psyc450.wordpress.com/2011/12/08/interviews-the-interviewer-bias-effect/

Examine your management practices

Showers, R. (2016, March 17). 4 business benefits of diversity in the workplace. Retrieved on June 1, 2018, from: https://www.brazen.com/blog/recruiting-hr/benefits-of-diversity-in-the-workplace/ (African American and Women stats).

Dobbin, F., & Kalev, A. (2016, July-August). Why diversity programs fail. *Harvard Business Review.* Retrieved on June 1, 2018, from: https://hbr.org/2016/07/why-diversity-programs-fail

Lorenzo, R., & Reeves, M. (2018, January 30). How and where diversity drives financial performance. *Harvard Business Review.* Retrieved on June 11, 2018, from: https://hbr.org/2018/01/how-and-where-diversity-drives-financial-performance

Krawcheck, S. (2018, October 19). Everything you think you know about promoting diversity is wrong. Here's how to do it. *CNN.com.* Retrieved on October 19, 2018, from: https://www.cnn.com/2018/10/19/perspectives/sallie-krawcheck-ellevest-gender-diversity/index.html

Provide cross-cultural training for your team

Kriska, L. (2018, June 19). Private conversation.

Scott-Pruitt, A., Brinkworth, C., Young, J., & Aponte, K.L. (2018, March 30). 5 things we learned about creating a successful workplace diversity program. Retrieved on June 1, 2018, from: https://hbr.org/2018/03/5-things-we-learned-about-creating-a-successful-workplace-diversity-program

Provide cross-cultural training for those "on assignment"

The Commisceo Global Blog—Perfect for Culture Vultures. (2016, April 19). The four benefits of intercultural training. Retrieved on June 15, 2018, from: https://www.commisceo-global.com/blog/the-four-benefits-of-intercultural-training

Bush, M., & Peters. K. (2016, December 5). How the best companies do diversity right. *Fortune.com.* Retrieved on June 1, 2018, from: http://fortune.com/2016/12/05/diversity-inclusion-workplaces/

Identify your 3 F's

Aschwanden, C. (2019, January 20). The walking tired. Parade Magazine, supplement to *The Star Ledger*, p. 8.

Teamwork is not a preference; it is a necessity

Coach Wooden understood the term "synergy" long before the term appeared in any MBA textbook. Stressing team needs ahead of individual interests:

- No UCLA player's number was retired while Coach was there.
- Coach had only three team captains in 27 years at UCLA.
- Without question, Lewis Alcindor (later known as NBA great Kareem Abdul Jabbar) could have led the nation in scoring; however, Coach felt it would be at the sacrifice of the team's potential.
- Sidney Wicks, then a future All-American and arguably the most physically gifted all-around athlete to play for the Coach, sat on the bench at times during his sophomore year until he could get his game "under control."
- Other than the lodgings on the night before a game, there were no special accommodations made on campus that might differentiate the players from the balance of the student body. There were no athletic dorms; the players were "student-athletes," in that order.
- Coach appreciated all working parts of the team. He knew that it took the effort of five people (or "ten hands" as he was in the habit of saying), for one individual to make a basket. After all, someone threw in the ball or got the rebound, someone else likely brought it up the court, a third person ran the play and set a pick, and someone delivered the ball to the open man for the shot.

Emphasizing this point of teamwork, UCLA All-America Bill Walton once noted, "… It was more important for people to come and be part of the team than go off in their own direction."

Your coaching imperative: It's about performance

We have all been part of a team. In a corporate setting, they are critical for getting things done. They are charged with trying to create, introduce, improve, or reinvent a product, process, or service.

Sometimes things go smoothly, and the team's goals are attained; other times they do not. To the latter point, Stanford's Behnam Tabrizi found in his research that 75% of cross-functional teams, those teams with members from multiple organizational disciplines, were dysfunctional due to a myriad of reasons and conditions. Your challenge as a leader is to ensure the former outcome, not the latter.

DOI: 10.4324/9781003456902-9

What is a team?

According to Katzenbach and Smith, teams are "a small number of people with complementary skills who are committed to a common purpose, a set of performance goals, and approach for which they hold themselves mutually accountable."

What is teamwork?

A team's ability to function effectively and efficiently will spell the difference in mission realization, productivity gains, and improved quality. Teamwork is a group of individuals working through and supporting each other, subjugating individual or parochial interests for the greater good. It is essential in an organizational setting where there are cross-dependencies. It is predicated upon many factors, including common values, open communication, mutual trust, healthy professional relationships, and mutual cooperation.

Who should be on your team?

Team composition in the workplace is a tough task. The ideal number of direct reports, also known as your "span of control," should be between six and eight. As a practical matter in today's flattened global world spanning multiple time zones, as few as eight might be envious. More members make decision-making unwieldy, cause fewer voices to be heard, and allow more interests and politics to creep in.

While we touched on this topic when discussing staffing, it is worth reiterating. As "basic" people considerations, when looking at potential team candidates, evaluate complementary skills and attitudes. What does each individual bring to the table? Are they accountable? Do they take ownership for their work? Do they have the needed energy to persevere through any given tests? Are they team-oriented? Are they respected in the organization, and are they role models for your values? How do they manage conflict? Do they know their stuff? Will the team have proper diversity?

To take your team to peak performance, be sure you assemble your team's roster carefully. Ensure that participants currently (or will soon) share your beliefs about the direction the organization is taking and the team's role to assist toward that end. This will help foster an environment of trust and open communication and will instill a willingness to manage conflict in a healthy manner. In addition, people will feel energized with new learning and achievement potential.

Remember, this is your team. Everyone on it, and the way they conduct their business, is a reflection upon you.

What is team building?

Team building includes the activities associated with identifying roles, relationships, and accountabilities among team members in pursuit of goal realization. It has both tangible and non-tangible components. When done well, it contributes toward employee engagement, morale, and increased productivity. Return on Investment is difficult to measure, but it is there. It is not an activity performed in a vacuum; it is the combination of many of the Coach's principles.

Stages of team building

Research models abound; however, there are generally four or five stages through which teams pass in their growth and evolution. *I will cite five stages here, blending the research in this area (with due apologies for and a grateful tip of the hat to this subject's pioneers, Bruce Tuckman and Thomas Quick):*

Wassup?

At this stage, team members come together for the first time, with management sponsorship, to discuss the challenge at hand. While most participants are friendly and cordial to each other, there is likely to be some early confusion about charter and roles. Accordingly, members should agree upon desired goals, respective assignments, communication channels, and frequency, and team ground rules. Typically, a leader or facilitator has been appointed or one may emerge from the team's ranks to help define processes and guidelines. A commanding leadership style is best at the onset.

Grinding

Remove the sharp objects from the room. This is when team members bump into each other as they try to work their way forward. Role clarity may be evolving. Trust, self-interests, and influence are issues. Individual ethics and attitudes are exposed; standards are tested. The project's scope may be shifting. Communication may be inconsistent and feedback loops are slowly being defined. Chaos may even be present as ideas are generated; some are adapted, while others crash to the conference room floor. Egos may be bruised.

This is a turbulent and necessary stage, and an easy one for teams to get mired in. Tolerance, consideration, and patience are generally required to smooth things out. The leader must call for mutual respect and steer the team toward its goals, providing further detail around accountabilities as required.

Beyond baby steps

Forward on! In this stage, team members are being far more productive. They have settled upon the agreed rules. Communication is flowing. Trust is now growing and being earned by fulfilled commitment delivery. Differences of opinion are maturely discussed and resolved. Teammates feel committed and are focused on the accomplishment of common goals. Confidence is building. Enhanced professionalism and mutual respect are further evolving.

Kum Ba Yah

It is rare to reach this performing utopia, but at this stage, the team shows the highest levels of commitment and loyalty to each other. Group decisions are the norm. The team is largely self-driven and motivated. They are completing their "to-do" lists quickly and with utter confidence. Collaboration is foundational. Conflict is minimal and managed. Team members are comfortable with each other. All parties are experiencing personal growth and professional development. A leader's role at this point is mostly maintenance and fallback prevention.

Pulling the plug

In a stage that corporations often forget, with goals having been accomplished, there should be a formal winding down of the team. Closure is reached and, if appropriate, there are both reflections about key leanings, as well as celebration. Members are moving on. It is time for recognition and celebration.

Not all teams will make it through all five stages, and some stages may take (much) longer than others. Timing may well depend upon the challenge at hand, as well as the motive and experience of the team members around the table.

Team building as part of your culture

A team can only operate successfully as team members see and feel themselves as part of the team. Therefore, the more effective and efficient team members become at related skills of communication, role understanding, cooperation, collaboration, and trust, the more cohesive—and productive—the unit will become.

It starts with trust

This cannot be overstated. Trust is the glue that holds all professional and personal relationships together. You will go nowhere without it.

Trust is earned, not given. You have absolute control over it. Its presence or absence is a fundamental personality trait. It is built over time. Its characteristics are simple and straightforward: be honest, show you care, be true to your words, and maintain a steady and predictable behavior and demeanor.

Your team needs to trust you. It is an essential leadership competency. Without it, your ability to lead and inspire is seriously jeopardized.

Team first

Coach did not play every player in every game. However, he did make it a point to play every player as often as he could. This meant that the players who were not starters or part of the regular rotation got into games when UCLA was ahead (or rarely behind) late in the game. However, they got in.

You want your team members to experience and share every win and loss to the extent possible; therefore, be sure that all are included and appropriately acknowledged. Some may do heavier lifting than others, but all are important.

Everyone plays an important role

Dr. R. Meredith Belbin studied team dynamics and found that team members naturally tend to assume certain "roles" or exhibit certain behavioral tendencies. Balance among these roles leads to enhanced team outcomes. Using Belbin's model, you can ensure that team roles are fulfilled and deficiencies addressed, to the extent possible. These roles are aligned into three categories:

Action-oriented

• Shaper—Keep positive attitude despite the challenges. Can motivate and inspire others.

- Implementor—Practical, well-organized, structured, and pragmatic.
- Completer/Finisher—Detail-oriented, highly conscientious, and deadline-driven.

People-oriented

- Coordinator—Mature, confident, and have good listening skills. Guide team activities.
- Team Worker—Strive for team unity, resolve conflicts, and lend team member support. Place team cohesion ahead of their individual concerns or voice.
- Resource Investigator—Inquisitive, enthusiastic, and extroverted in nature.

Thought-oriented

- Monitor-Evaluator—Critical thinkers, serious-minded, and prudent in their approach.
- Specialist—Have expertise and required knowledge in a specific area.
- Plants—Sources of new ideas and innovation. Problem-solvers. Sensitive in nature.

What role do you gravitate toward in a team setting and why?

Create a unified team spirit

Coach frequently defined team spirit as, "the eagerness to lose oneself for the good of the group." He knew that unity among and between team members could spur productivity.

There are some ongoing, everyday ways you can foster this type of team mindset:

- Be clear with your mission statement and purpose.
- As previously discussed, highlight your team's values at every opportunity and be THE role model for such.
- Leadership is a privilege. Demonstrate your commitment. Actions are far more significant and meaningful than words.
- Be clear with expectations.
- Start with the low-hanging fruit in setting goals that are attainable and can be broken into individual parts. Build momentum.
- Identify the enemy and go after it. Have a sense of urgency. Attack where and when you can. An "us against them" attitude can be inspirational.
- Be aspirational. Challenge your team to do something not tried before or go where others have failed. Encourage daily growth.
- Celebrate the accomplishments. Nothing builds team spirit more than a well-deserved reward for crossing the finish line. This is why sports teams have champagne ready in the locker room.
- Show energy and sincerity in all you do.
- Eat, drink, and play together. Spending time together helps forge bonds and a sense of family, and it costs relatively little.

In an example of team building (going back several years), my boss shut down our department early on Christmas Eve and took us all to the Knights of Columbus hall down the street. Here, we played shuffleboard, darts, and billiards; we had some drinks and plates of appetizers. There was no pomp and circumstance; rather, it was a terrific (and surprising) gesture that genuinely touched us all.

Acknowledge an assist

If you watch the television clips of UCLA basketball during the Wooden years, you will notice that if the basket was made as the result of a pass from a teammate, the player who hit for the score always pointed at the man who fed him the ball. It was his way of saying thank you and publicly acknowledge the assist.

Was this acknowledgment done at the Coach's insistence or perhaps a ritual handed down from the last graduating class? Neither. Simply, this was an embedded philosophy of UCLA basketball. Team play was their mantra.

Be sure to acknowledge the contributions of all. It nurtures cohesion and team pride.

Foster engagement

People want to feel good about what they are doing, for whom they are doing it, and for what their organization stands. Engagement is a means to these ends.

Engagement has two "connectivity" components: psychological and behavioral. If you get the first, the latter should follow. *(Note: Organizations have traditionally looked at the macro-level construct of engagement as one's over-arching sense of connectivity to their organization; however, there is a shift underway to look at engagement with a more granular perspective: engagement to one's coworkers; engagement to one's job; engagement to one's boss; engagement to oneself; and engagement to one's organization. I think this area of research will expand in the near future, particularly as it applies to retention strategies.)*

For psychological engagement to occur, team members should feel fully committed and absorbed by their work. They feel physically and psychologically safe. They have unbridled energy and enthusiasm. They are goal-oriented, take inspiration from their work, and their personal values scheme is aligned with the organization. They possess vigor, passion, and resilience. Their work is a natural extension of who they are and who they want to be. They are organizational champions and articulate advocates. They have found meaning.

For behavioral engagement, team members are your good corporate soldiers, leading organizational citizens, and identifiable role models. They will go well beyond the language in the job description (by doing something innovative or creative, not just more) in order to drive success. They take on new assignments, volunteer as needed, and get desired outcomes. They build relationships. They learn and grow. They embrace continuous improvement.

Research tells us that engaged employees give discretionary effort that leads to higher levels of customer service and satisfaction, sales and profits, and shareholder returns.

Unfortunately, recent statistics tell us that a vast majority of our teammates are checked-out!

In their best-selling and pioneering book, *First, Break All the Rules*, authors Buckingham and Coffman discuss what the world's best managers do to attract, select, retain, and develop talent. Their findings, proven over time, are based upon years of in-depth interviews conducted by the Gallup Organization with over 80,000 managers in over 400 companies. Conclusively, the authors submit that by analyzing employee competence (having the relevant training, tools, education, and equipment), expectations (knowing what is expected of them), and confidence (in the future, the leadership, and the team), there is a casual link between employee engagement and profit, productivity, and customer satisfaction.

The ten questions posed by Buckingham and Coffman from this classic study that gauge individual employee engagement are:

- Do I know what is expected of me at work?
- Do I have the materials and equipment I need to do my work well?
- At work, do I have the opportunity to do what I do best every day?
- In the last seven days, have I received recognition or praise for doing good work?
- Does my supervisor, or someone at work, seem to care about me as a person?
- Is there someone at work who encourages my department?
- At work, do my opinions seem to count?
- Does the mission/purpose of my company make me feel my job is important?
- Are my coworkers committed to doing quality work?
- Do I have a best friend at work?
- In the last six months, has someone at work talked to me about my progress?
- This last year, have I had opportunities at work to learn and grow?

The above model has been tweaked by others since its inception in order to provide more balance between the psychological and behavioral aspects of engagement; however, its roots remain strong.

Giving people an opportunity to build a personal bridge with the organization, thereby experiencing a sense of enhanced belonging and engagement, helps create the aforementioned unified team spirit. Seize any and every opportunity to do so. "Stay interviews" might be a good starting point to establish your baseline and areas for attention.

Deal with the naysayers

You know (or one day, will know) these people. No matter how much you cajole, push, incentivize, attempt to persuade, or rationalize, some naysayers will not convert to your team's agenda. They cannot move beyond their limited mindset of skepticism, pessimism, inertia, self-interest, jealousy, status protection, blind ambition, or lack of confidence or ability.

To my eye, naysayers generally fall into four categories: the minimalists, the squeaky wheels, the passive-aggressive types, and the snakes.

First, the minimalists.

When I was an undergraduate at Rutgers College, my ultra-wise economics professor had a unique view of my cohort group. It was his theory that college students were the only consumer group on the planet that wanted the least amount for their money. Unfortunately, many of these students went on (and still do) to the real world, carrying their "let me do just enough to get-by" attitude. These are the minimalists. They may not say "nay" with their words, but their actions speak volumes.

The squeaky wheels are loud and boisterous; bully-like in approach. They tend to have all the answers and are closed-minded. New ideas and unwanted facts slide off their backs. The status quo is most important, as change is a potential threat to their organizational standing. If they did not come up with the idea, it could not possibly be a good one. They mumble and complain. They like putting down others to seemingly elevate themselves. They believe, through their exaggerated view of self-importance, that they are opinion molders, but most people see them for what they are.

The passive-aggressive types are a bit more dangerous. To them, it's about self-preservation. Like chameleons, they can change colors frequently and fast. They support the change initiative in one conversation and privately oppose or undermine it in another. They start their conversations with phrases like, "Do you have a few minutes?" "Just between us … ," or "I just thought you should know … " Before you know it, time has passed that you cannot get back. They make you feel emotionally drained. Parasitic in nature, they also zap you of your energy and enthusiasm.

Lastly, there are the snakes. They are selfish in perspective and are motivated by career advancement. It's all about them. Be very, very careful with the snakes. They are hard to distinguish, and they may be solid performers. They disguise their words and behaviors, and you might unknowingly trust them. The problem is that they will stab you or your reputation in the back, and you will not even notice the knife. They are political, self-absorbed, self-prioritizing animals.

Who needs these exhausting subplots and disruptive theater? Certainly, you don't. Nor do your team members who are believers and supporters.

While easier said than done, lose the drama. Quickly removing these detrimental cancers when their colors first show is to everyone's advantage. Try to weed them out for performance. Lacking that, a discussion about their attitude becomes the focal point. Either they shift gears to your heightened level of expectations or be gone. A good labor attorney could be your friend here.

Admittedly, with hindsight over a 40-year career, I was probably more tolerant of these four types than I should have been. It is likely responsible for some of my gray hair. Be forewarned.

Lead toward high performance

Every manager wants a high-performing, highly skilled, highly motivated, highly adaptive, agile, and high-velocity team. They are nimble, lean, fast, boundary-less, inspirational, innovative, and can leap tall buildings in a single bound. They go the extra mile.

The challenge, of course, is bringing this to life. A recent study completed by Joseph Folkman concluded that there are five key leadership "dimensions" toward bringing out the best in others, and you will need to check all of these boxes. These include:

- Inspiring more than driving—Leaders need to pull more than push. Creating energy and enthusiasm about the team goals is paramount.
- Resolving conflict and increasing cooperation—Conflict tears teams apart. Significant differences of opinion must be addressed and resolved in a timely fashion. Leaders may need to intervene accordingly. Likewise, cooperation should be stressed over competition.
- Setting stretch goals—By setting reasonable stretch goals, you are encouraging the team to do something extraordinary.
- Communicating the vision and direction—Focus; stay on message; keep desired outcomes as part of the conversation.
- Being trusted—Lack of trust slows everything down. Build relationships; stay credible in your field of knowledge; and be consistent with your words and behaviors.

Do team building exercises work?

There are countless examples of team building events and activities geared toward stimulating unity and bonding among all. In fact, there is an entire industry devoted toward helping you escape and bond with your coworkers by climbing ropes, participating in a group intervention, or going whitewater rafting together.

Certainly, these exercises have their time and place; however, my personal bias would be to try an internal fix first. If there is a team fracture, as a leader, you should make every effort to determine the root cause. Among dozens of possible variables, it could just be role confusion or lingering conflict in the air that is causing a breakdown.

You may not be fully equipped to tackle the issues that surface, but an initial try is in order before giving out the life jackets.

The more evident warning signs

Your team seemingly has top-notch educational pedigrees, relevant experience, professional mastery, diverse backgrounds, and good chemistry. They seem perfectly aligned with your culture. Yet, there is one thing: Why can't they be more productive?

The answer may be that they have never had to work as a team together. They may clash over egos, brash personalities, politics, culture, toxic alliances, bad behavior, questionable judgment, selfish motives, and bad habits. These can all derail a team's efforts from accomplishing the greater good. In addition, you may have fault. Perhaps you unintentionally played favorites, did not confront a tough issue, or were inconsistent with your words and actions.

To minimize the potential for team inefficiency or ineffectiveness, there are early warning signs that should stay on your radar as outlined in Patrick Lencioni's noteworthy book, *The Five Dysfunctions of a Team*. These deserve your time and continuous attention:

• Absence of trust—unwilling to be vulnerable within the group
• Fear of conflict—seeking artificial harmony over constructive, passionate debate
• Lack of commitment—feigning buy-in for group decisions creates ambiguity throughout the organization
• Avoidance of accountability—ducking the responsibility to call peers on counter-productive behavior which sets low standards
• Inattention to results—focusing on personal success, status, and ego before team success

Individual warning signs

We have all been there. Exhaustion. Depression. A sense of being overwhelmed. Dreading meetings. Fear of missing out. Trouble at home. A feeling of loss. Loneliness. Insecurity. Excessive stress. Financial problems. Draining family matters … At or when brought to work, these simmering issues may cause an individual's withdrawal, behavioral change, or eroding attitude. Eventually, these ills and burdens come to light and manifest in disruptive ways.

To the extent possible, monitor the physical and mental well-being of your team members respectfully and constantly. Their health in these areas—and your ability to respond—is a critical lever toward their satisfaction, happiness, engagement, and retention.

And if it starts to derail

The wheels may not have fallen off the cart yet, but they are wobbling. How do you get things back on track?

Meet with your team. Respectfully ask questions. Engage them in two-way dialog. Start with discussing the targeted results that the team should be accomplishing. Discuss what is preventing you from attaining the results. Discuss the required mindset and supporting behaviors for success. If this fails to get desired traction, bringing in an outside facilitator may be a last, but worthwhile investment.

When Andy and I worked together, we were part of an executive team that had its bouts with dysfunction. Roles bumped into each other, direction and accountability were lacking, and strong personalities were in the mix. As the HR guy, I had days where I felt like a battered referee. Ultimately, we brought in an outside facilitator to help us sort out our differences. Appropriately dubbed the meeting in the "Basement of the Sheraton" (in midtown Manhattan), ten of us gathered around a conference table in a windowless room on a December morning.

It was freezing outside; it seemed colder inside.

The day's agenda called for us to begin with a brief discussion of our warts, with the majority of our session to be spent focusing upon a harmonized path forward.

From the meeting's kick-off, it was a brutal, contentious discussion. Guardrails came down. Anger, frustration, and desperation were on full display and at high volume. People were honest; perhaps, too honest. Wounds were exposed and salt was applied.

The airing of our dirty laundry, scheduled to take 90 minutes, took the entire morning. And while it never got personal (or, at least, not too personal), it was three of the most uncomfortable and unpleasant hours I have spent in any professional setting. Yet, in some respects, it was also a relief. Things had to be said.

During lunch, I privately met with our facilitator. We quickly reviewed our tactical options. Fortunately, he did a great job in getting us back on track and aiding our afternoon recovery. We were able to begin some of the needed healing and focus upon corrective measures. Over time, trust was (slowly) rebuilt, caring was demonstrated, and mutual appreciation emerged. To my surprise, participants actually expressed gratitude for the opportunity to participate. Morale may have even improved a notch by the end of that day. There was much work to be done, but things were on the way to a better place.

How does this compare to conventional wisdom?

There is no "I" in team; nor should there be.

Endnotes for Principle 4: Teamwork is not a preference; it's a necessity

Introduction

Walton, B. (2000, March 2). Andy Hill notes. Private conversation.

Your coaching imperative: It's about performance

Tabrizi, B. (2015, June 15). 75% of cross-functional teams are dysfunctional. *Harvard Business Review*. Retrieved on January 3, 2020, from: https://hbr.org/2015/06/75-of-cross-functional-teams-are-dysfunctional

What is a team?

Katzenbach, J.R., & Smith, D.K. (1993). The discipline of teams. *Harvard Business Review*, March-April, p. 112.

What is teamwork?

Bennis, W.G., & Thomas, R.J. (2002). *Geek and geezers: How era, values, and defining moments shape leaders*. Boston, Massachusetts: Harvard Business School Press, pp. 130–136.
Katzenbach, J.R., & Smith, D.K. (1993, March-April). The discipline of teams. *Harvard Business Review*, p. 112.

Who should be on your team?

Keller, S., & Meaney, M. (2017, June). High-performing teams: A timeless leadership topic. McKinsey & Company, *McKinsey Quarterly*. Retrieved on August 9, 2018, from: https://www. mckinsey.com/business-functions/organization/our-insights/high-performing-teams-a-timeless-leadership-topic

What is team building?

Davies, S. (2017, October 30). What is the point of corporate team building? TalentCulture.com. Retrieved on August 9, 2018, from: https://talentculture.com/point-corporate-teambuilding/

Stages of team building

Lee, S.F. (Date unknown). Five stages of team development. The Team Building Directory. Retrieved on August 9, 2018, from: http://www.innovativeteambuilding.co.uk/five-stages-of-team-development/
Team building 101: The four stages of team development. (2016 estimate). Championship Coaches network.com. Retrieved on August 9, 2018, from: https://www.championshipcoachesnetwork.com/public/329.cfm

It starts with trust

Julien, R. (2019, May 17). Private conversation.

Team building as part of your culture

Why team building should play a central role in corporate culture. (Date unknown). Strayboots.com. Retrieved on August 9, 2018, from: https://www.strayboots.com/blog/teambuilding-play-central-role-corporate-culture/

It starts with trust

Kouzes, J.M., & Posner, B.Z. (1995). *The leadership challenge: How to get extraordinary things done in organizations*. San Francisco, California: Jossey-Bass Inc., Publishers, pp. 165, 220–223.

Everyone has a role

Merchant, P. (2019, February 14). What are the nine types of team roles? Reviewed by Jayne Thompson, LLB, LLM. *Smallbusiness.chron.com*. Retrieved on December 17, 2019, from: https://smallbusiness.chron.com/nine-types-team-roles-15566.html

Create a unified team spirit

Feuer, M. (2013, March 8). How to create esprit de corps in your organization. *Smart Business*. Retrieved on August 9, 2018, from: http://www.sbnon-line.com/article/michael-feuer-how-to-create-esprit-de-corps-in-your-organization-2/

The secrets to creating a culture of esprit de corps within your business. (Date unknown). Euro Projects Blog, United Kingdom. Retrieved on August 9, 2018, from: http://www.europrojects.co.uk/nine-secrets-to-creating-a-culture-of-esprit-de-corps-within-your-engineering-or-manufacturing-business/

Scudamore, B. (2016, May 9). Why team building is the most important investment you'll make. *Forbes.com*. Retrieved on August 9, 2018, from: https://www.forbes.com/sites/brianscudamore/2016/03/09/why-teambuilding-is-the-most-important-investment-youll-make/#6182ccc9617f

Foster engagement

Pulley, M. (May 12, 2023). "Culturally Responsive Systems," a presentation for the SHRM faculty at Rutgers University.

Castellano, William G. (2014). *Practices for engaging the 21st century workforce: Challenges of talent management in a changing workplace*. Upper Saddle River, NJ: Pearson Education, Inc. ISBN 13:978-0-13-308637-9

Kruse, K. (2012, June 22). What is employee engagement. *Forbes.com*. Retrieved on August 13, 2018, from: https://www.forbes.com/sites/kevinkruse/2012/06/22/employee-engagement-what-and-why/#4986c1d37f37

Mautz, S. (Date unknown). 7 ways to make work more meaningful. Lead Change Group, Retrieved on August 15, 2018, from: https://leadchangegroup.com/7-ways-to-make-work-more-meaningful/

Buckingham, M., & Coffman, C. (1999). *First, break all the rules*. New York: Simon & Schuster, jacket cover.

Coffman, M. (2003, October 8). One thing you need to know. Presentation notes from the New Jersey Human Resources Planning Group at The Headquarters Plaza Hotel, Morristown, New Jersey.

Deal with the naysayers

Wakeman, C. (2019, June 19). Keynote remarks at the Evanta CHRO Conference at the Roosevelt Hotel, New York, New York.

Lead toward high performance

Davis, J.W. (2017, October 26). Creating a high-performance team: Finding talent & connecting the dots. Retrieved on May 16, 2018, from: https://theblog.adobe.com/creating-a-high-performance-team-finding-talent-connecting-the-dots/

Folkman, J. (2016, April 13). 5 ways to build a high-performance team. *Forbes.com*. Retrieved on August 9, 2018, from: https://www.forbes.com/sites/joefolkman/2016/04/13/are-you-on-the-team-from-hell-5-ways-to-create-a-high-performance-team/#457bc59a7ee2

Do team building exercises work?

McDuffee, S. (2016, February 3). 6 reasons why leaders choose team bonding ideas that work. *Teambonding.com*. Retrieved on August 9, 2018, from: https://www.teambonding.com/reasons-for-teambuilding/

Ryan, L. (2016, September 22). The ugly truth about team building, *Forbes.com*. Retrieved on August 9, 2018, from: "https://www.forbes.com/sites/lizryan/2016/09/22/the-ugly-truth-about-teambuilding/#344fe3825605

Scudamore, B. (2016, May 9). Why team building is the most important investment you'll make. *Forbes.com*. Retrieved on August 9, 2018, from: https://www.forbes.com/sites/brianscudamore/2016/03/09/why-teambuilding-is-the-most-important-investment-youll-make/#6182ccc9617f

The more evident warning signs

Schwartz, R. (2013, November). Get a dysfunctional team back on track. *Harvard Business Review*. Retrieved on August 9, 2018, from: https://hbr.org/2013/11/get-a-dysfunctional-team-back-on-track
"The five dysfunctions of a team," Wikipedia. (Date unknown). Retrieved on August 9, 2018, from: https://en.wikipedia.org/wiki/The_Five_Dysfunctions_of_a_Team (Patrick Lencioni)

Individual warning signs

Pfeffer, J. (2018). *Dying for a paycheck: How modern management harms employee health and company performance—and what we can do about it*. New York: Harper Business.

And if it falls off the tracks

Schwartz, R. (2013, November). Get a dysfunctional team back on track. *Harvard Business Review*. Retrieved on August 9, 2018, from: https://hbr.org/2013/11/get-a-dysfunctional-team-back-on-track

Cultivating culture
Defining how people should interact

The topic of culture, discussed in the upcoming principles, deserves some introductory comments.

What is culture?

Whether you have inherited a new role or are trying to shift your team in a new direction by injecting new drive and energy, chances are that you are confronting a cultural challenge in your organization.

Defining "culture" can be daunting as it is complex, dynamic, subjective, and in constant flux. It generates multiple perspectives and opinions, even in the same workplace.

For our purposes and in its broadest terms, culture is the personality and character of your organization. It is described with a list of adjectives about your work environment. It surrounds you; it permeates everything and everyone. It shapes your attitudes, relationships, and work enjoyment (or not). As the foundation of your team's morale, motivation, and individual engagement, culture takes the form of shared values, policies, traditions, symbols, beliefs, myths, stories, ceremonies, celebrations, defeats, assumptions, norms, and rites.

Where does culture come from?

Leadership, individually and collectively, defines culture.

As the boss and role model, you have significant influence over and are responsible for your team's structure and controls, ability and willingness to collaborate, patterns of communications, and how problems are solved. You organize priorities, manage performance, hold people accountable, and govern reward and recognition systems. You designate how decisions are made, who participates in decision-making, who has access to whom and what, the language used, the design or enforcement of policies and procedures, and the determinants of the dress code. You make choices about talent selection, deployment, development, and retention. You decide what behavior is acceptable and by whom, as well as what rules get bent. You can draw out your team's potential or squash it. Succinctly, you determine the threshold and tolerance for the poorest attitude and the weakest performance link.

Why culture matters

The "strength" of an organization's culture can be a valuable indicator of individual loyalty and commitment. A strong culture has consensus about common values and behaviors that drive the company. It has a degree of intensity visible to outsiders.

DOI: 10.4324/9781003456902-10

Great companies are built with a strong foundation of mission and values. It is your employment brand. Your team members, through their respective words and actions, bring your company culture to life in a manner consistent with your mission and values.

It is worth keeping in mind that social media now places your organization's culture in a very visible public eye.

As a leader, you want your organizational culture to be as positive as possible. A positive culture attracts talent, drives engagement and retention, impacts happiness, and drives financial performance. In fact, 92% of leaders believe there is a high correlation between culture and profits. Thus, how employees anticipate, encounter, adapt to, socialize, and extend or modify the culture is therefore critical.

Why the "right" culture can be elusive

One of the biggest mistakes organizational leadership can make is to let the culture take care of itself. Go ahead ... bide it little or no attention. Let it naturally evolve, allowing the dust to settle as it may. Besides, other things are more important—like attention to the bottom line or getting financing from that impatient venture capitalist. No single individual can influence culture anyway.

Wrong!

A well-defined, positive, and productive workplace culture needs constant nurturing. It must be carefully defined and refined. Its desirable elements are to be taught and handed down. It requires focus from day one and each day beyond, and a misstep can shift the winds. When you have the "right" culture, especially one predicated on growth and innovation, hang on tight. Observe it, measure it, have team discussions about the topic, and conduct internal interviews. Do not let it slip away due to distractions. It is much harder to build than to lose.

Can culture be changed?

Changing a culture is not easy. It tends to be deeply rooted. People may come and go, but culture remains. Try to change it and you will likely bump into selfish interests, complacency, a lack of interest, a lack of urgency, and competitive mindsets. Resistance will come from those who feel threatened, are disenfranchised, or have the need to protect the status quo. Embedded attitudes do not transform overnight, if at all.

To shift an organization's culture takes a tremendous amount of work, time, and commitment. You will have to confront and overcome challenges of all shapes and sizes. Many organizations fail in this endeavor, especially around mergers and acquisitions; yet some succeed.

On February 4, 2014, Satya Nadella was appointed CEO of Microsoft, succeeding Steve Ballmer. Nadella became only the third leader in the company's 39-year history. At the time, Microsoft was already well-established as an industry leader and was consistently one of the world's top five firms for market capitalization. It had lived up to Bill Gates' original vision of a "computer on every desk" and had successfully gone through and led technological transformations. Nadella could have put the company on cruise control and reaped its continuing benefits, but he did not. He has led several notable acquisitions and shifted its business focus from "devices and services" to "mobile and cloud." Microsoft has also shifted away from proprietary hardware and operating systems to subscription products with regularly recurring revenue. More importantly, he started to shift the company's culture from products to people.

Coach Wooden understood culture. He knew that for the team to advance and accomplish its goals, individual sacrifice was required. This meant building an esprit de corps with a shared purpose, common energy, heightened enthusiasm, commitment, and loyalty to and for each other. With this philosophical underpinning, he embraced and practiced the following principles about cultivating culture:

5 Fairness is giving all people the treatment they earn and deserve
6 Make your "yes" mean yes
7 Be quick, but don't hurry
8 The team with the most mistakes ... wins!
9 Rules are made to be followed, not broken

Endnotes for cultivating culture

What is culture?

What is a workplace culture really? (2020, June 30). Sidekicker.com Blog. Retrieved on September 10, 2020, from: https://sidekicker.com/au/blog/workplace-culture-really/

Where does culture come from?

Workplace culture: What it is, why it matters, and how to define it. (2019, February 1). ERC consulting. HR insights blog. Retrieved on April 12, 2019, from: https://www.yourerc.com/blog/post/workplace-culture-what-it-is-why-it-matters-how-to-define-it
Hassell, D. (Date unknown). 10 questions to create a workplace culture that employees love. 15Five.com blog. Retrieved on April 12, 2019, from: https://www.15five.com/blog/10-questions-to-create-a-workplace-culture/

Why culture matters

Workplace culture: What it is, why it matters, and how to define it. (2019, February 1). ERC consulting. HR insights blog. Retrieved on April 12, 2019, from: https://www.yourerc.com/blog/post/workplace-culture-what-it-is-why-it-matters-how-to-define-it
What is a workplace culture really? (2020, June 30). Sidekicker.com blog. Retrieved on September 10, 2020, from: https://sidekicker.com/au/blog/workplace-culture-really/

Why the right culture can be elusive

Workplace culture: What it is, why it matters, and how to define it. (2019, February 1). ERC consulting. HR insights blog. Retrieved on April 12, 2019, from: https://www.yourerc.com/blog/post/workplace-culture-what-it-is-why-it-matters-how-to-define-it

Can culture be changed?

Stolzoff, S. (2019, February 1). How do you turn around the culture of a 130,000-person company? Ask Satya Nadella. Quartz at work. Retrieved on September 12, 2019, from: https://qz.com/work/1539071/how-microsoft-ceo-satya-nadella-rebuilt-the-company-culture/

Fairness is giving all people the treatment they earn and deserve

As much as Coach was a man of consistency and routine, he believed that each team member deserved respect, and each should be dealt with or managed the way they deserved. His view was that each player contributed to the team in unique and valued ways, and therefore warranted individualized and differentiated treatment.

The best example of this principle in action was the Coach's oversight of Lewis Alcindor. Coach, from time to time, excused Lewis from practice. He allowed Lewis to have his own room for away games when other players shared. In addition, Lewis was given a bit more latitude when it came to mealtime.

More than once, the media would note such "preferential treatment" of Lewis. What the media did not know, ignored, or did not appreciate was that Lewis, at seven-foot, two inches tall, required special accommodaitons for sleeping, necessitating his own room. In addition, Lewis also suffered from migraine headaches, prompting the need to be excused from occasional practice. In addition, despite being a generous autograph provider, he was often the subject of vicious racial slurs and verbal abuse, causing him to shun the spotlight.

Your coaching imperative: Treat everyone fairly

The critically acclaimed AMC television series *Mad Men* (2007–2015) focused upon the high-pressure stakes of working in the field of advertising in the 1960s. Based on Madison Avenue in New York City, the fictional series depicted real societal themes of drinking, womanizing, sexism, ruthless behavior, and adultery (among others).

With the television show "Mad Men" as a backdrop, 20-plus years into our new millennium, do you think any of these workplace scenarios could happen today?

- *A marketing executive taking his entire department to a strip club to celebrate the close of a successful business conference.*
- *A man weeping and speaking gibberish under his desk, psychologically broken by a hyper-Machiavellian-style supervisor.*
- *A business trip. A hotel room. Some drinks. He is the boss; she is the subordinate. He said it was consensual. She said it was rape.*
- *A female technician having to deal with the adolescent pranks of her coworkers such as leaving condoms and sexually explicit materials on her desk.*
- *A company's high-performer driven to alcoholism in an effort to deal with what he deemed to be an inordinate amount of workplace stress.*
- *Dirty jokes told by an executive at an after-work cocktail hour.*

DOI: 10.4324/9781003456902-11

- *An employee who had a gun shipped to work because the delivery required a signature.*
- *Employee DUI's (plural) after company-sponsored events.*

The answer is a definitive and unfortunate "yes." And I was involved in sorting through the pieces, none of which were pretty.

On the personal front, people lost jobs, reputations were tarnished, individuals and families were in utter turmoil, legal proceedings were launched, jail time was served, and once-promising careers were derailed. In one of these terribly sad and unfortunate stories, a funeral was held.

On the organizational front, leadership's credibility from either not knowing, turning a blind eye, or inappropriately handling these situations was dramatically eroded. Common sense was thrown to the wind; policies had been violated; and in some cases, laws had been broken. Certainly, had any of these issues become public, the organizations' otherwise good names would have suffered loss.

The root causes for the above vary, but respect and fair treatment were certainly missing in each scenario.

Employees ARE your most valuable resource

Just about all company credos suggest that their employees are their most valuable resource. It is the motherhood and apple pie of organizational philosophy. You need this underpinning to build your brand, attract would-be employees, and maintain a positive public perception. Yet too few companies and managers translate those words into actions.

An often-cited example of erred managerial judgment in this evolving time of the hybrid work environment is the boss who claims that he or she does not know if they can trust those team members who are remote or virtual. Are they really working?

I simply reply, "If you do not trust them, why are they on your team?"

It is about respect

Treating EVERYONE with genuine respect and dignity should be the standard. Doing onto others as you would have them do onto you should be the basis of ALL interactions. This attitude should be authentic and run through your personal and organizational veins.

Bringing this intangible of "respect" to life comes naturally for some. Others need to work at it. Lolly Daskal has some good tips:

- Stop judging people by their past. Stand by them and help them take steps forward.
- Be honest with your words and act with integrity.
- Nurture relationships by giving them time and attention as fuel to help them grow.
- Give care and kindness with no expectation of its return.
- Everyone has a story. Listen. Empathize. Respond. Move forward.
- Stop trying to fix everyone's problems.
- Do not look down at anyone unless you are helping them up.
- Maintain professional relationships and keep the personal topics "light." Stay away from politics, religion, and other sensitive areas.
- Forgiveness may not change the other party, but it may change you.

It is about fairness

Everyone is composed of unique attitudes, experience, skills, and abilities. Accordingly, each team member should be individually evaluated based upon circumstance and his or her respective contribution. Democratic notions must fall by the side as you recognize and appreciate your employees' distinct qualities and characteristics. One size does not fit all when it comes to treatment.

Pay is a perfect example. It is the great differentiator. You pay more for greater contribution and heightened performance. You pay more for experience and a record of accomplishment. You pay more for subject-matter expertise, particularly if it is a rare and needed commodity. Two employees may be working side-by-side, but based upon their contribution levels, their W-2s may be different at the end of the year.

Another differentiated area is praise. Some employees relish the bright lights; others, not so much. You need to know what works on an individual basis in order to maximize the impact of recognition.

Providing direction and guidance also varies. To some, you need to give detailed instruction. Others just need general parameters to get them off and running. The same holds for setting performance goals and objectives. You need to know, perhaps by asking, which approach works best.

Providing ongoing performance feedback needs to be an individualized exchange. Some people welcome direct evaluation and criticism, others may be sensitive and need some massaging. A misstep here can be a distasteful managerial experience.

As a final example, note that individual training experiences and outcomes vary by personalized styles. (We discuss this later in the book.) Know your students.

Treat everyone fairly but customize your approach. Be thoughtful. Your goal is to make each team member feel valued and appreciated.

It is about being nice

Everyone has a rough day from time to time. We get emotional. We act out ways to displace or wash away our frustrations and stress. We become short, cranky, and irritable with those around us, who likely do not deserve such treatment. Think about the last time this happened to you. What was the cause? Did you handle it appropriately? How did your reaction affect others? What did you learn? Could you handle a similar situation differently going forward?

When things come off the tracks at work, pause. Resist the temptation to lash out or use sarcasm. Reflect upon the entire situation and its implications. Calmness can be a hidden virtue. Perhaps, as an option, you could consider a different response: supportive words, comments of encouragement, or a smile.

Being nice is a strength, not a weakness. Your team members will notice the difference.

It is about putting employees first

Throughout this book, I have written (and will continue to write) about the need for you to keep your teammates connected, satisfied, generally happy, and engaged. These factors are all important, but what you are really after is their passion*. You want to surround yourself with people who have a fire in their belly and who will advance the cause. Passionate people crave and exude excitement. They actively seek out challenges and want to be part of the solution. The hair on their arm raises with excitement when they think about the work they are doing and the difference it makes. They give their hearts and minds, even when you thought they had no more to give.

These people are your pillars. You will make demands of them, push them, put them in difficult spots, debate them, and give them your toughest assignments. They will love every minute of it. They will give your customers a positive experience. They will also protect your brand with vigor as if it is their own because they feel it is.

Building this type of passionate culture takes significant intent and execution. It is based upon a philosophy that if you treat employees as if they make THE difference in the organization, they will work hard to make the difference FOR the organization. It means putting "employees first."

You can bring out your team's passion in a few ways.

First, believe in your team. Support them. Work with them. Bring nothing but wild optimism. Show your unbridled pride about having them as teammates. Discover and explore their talents. Invest in them. Nurture them to the next level of performance with your unconditional faith in them. You are their cheerleader extraordinaire!

Second, make engagement a priority. Take a chance. Ask your team members what they want from their work experience and deliver. Weed out apathy and complacency. You want your team to enjoy coming to work and channeling that positive energy into innovation, creativity, and results. This constructive spirit will also become the fabric of your customer interactions.

Last, treat people as ... people. They are not commodities. They are not interchangeable parts. They are not disposable. They do not have "best if used by" dates. They are people with strengths and weaknesses, with hopes, limitations, and struggles. They deserve to be treated as individuals, with your recognition of their needs. Know, to the extent, it is appropriate or volunteered, who is dealing with a sick child, addiction issues, healthcare concerns, or eldercare challenges. Knowing that one person's balk at something in the office could really be a cry for help. Adapt as needed.

Note* If you can get their *love* of job and company, even better. That is considered the Holy Grail of the employee/employer experience.

It is about helping others

During the summer of my junior year of college, I worked at the headquarters of a major pharmaceutical company as a custodian on the second shift. Not having a clue about what I wanted to do in life, I made it a point to get to work early and "aimlessly" wander down the halls of the ivory tower with a mop in my hand. My hope was that a nearby executive might engage me in small talk, and, if I carefully steered the conversation, ask me into their office where I might politely pepper him or her with questions about what they do. Fortunately, a few executives were kind enough to oblige me. I left this summer experience with a macro-view of the accountabilities for some corporate functions, to the extent that I could understand such at the time.

In hindsight, I am truly grateful to those individuals who shared their stories and perspectives with me—a youthful stranger. Accordingly, I try to "pay it back" whenever possible. You never know where a conversation may lead.

(Note: If our paths ever cross, ask me how this how this approach allowed me to meet the CEO and how he later helped me with a school paper on succeeding in business!)

It is about care

Companies like the Virgin Group, SAS, Southwest Airlines, and HCL Technologies, among others, had and have visionaries as leaders who understand that if you want your customers taken care of, you should prioritize the care of your employees. To this point, Harvard researchers found a direct correlation between favorable employee treatment and increased customer brand loyalty, suggesting that companies could consequently realize significant gains in profitability from just a nominal increase in customer satisfaction ratings.

Remember, your employees directly influence your customers' experience. Treat your colleagues well, and they will share their passion about your organization with your customers.

Love your teammates

Webster's II New College Dictionary defines "love," among other descriptions, as a "feeling of kindness and brotherhood toward others."

Coach always said that he did not necessarily like all of his players the same, but he loved them all. He viewed life to be a journey and that, as common travelers trying to find our way, we have an obligation to help and assist each other, and to see and accept each other as we are—not as we want others to be.

Appreciate the individual

Every part of a car serves a purpose and has an important role to play in order to get you to your destination. The engine may be the most expensive and complex component, but the sight of a tow truck is an absolute blessing when you are on the side of the road with "just" a flat tire.

Employee appreciation counts for everyone. It is linked with job satisfaction and both employee happiness and morale. It can also boost engagement, motivation, loyalty, and productivity. Studies further show that appreciated employees have better attendance, feel more invested, pay more attention to detail, and are more willing to take on expanded responsibility.

Every position has its own measuring stick of progress. Acknowledge those who are hitting their marks. They are the backbone of all of your success.

Teach others how to treat you

You want respect. You want people to care. Your title deserves it. You personally deserve it. Yet, if you are not mindful, respect can be fickle. Inevitably, people will treat you the way you allow them to treat you.

To teach others how to treat you, begin with self-awareness. As a parent does with a child, be cognizant of the impact your words have upon others. This touches all aspects of your communications—your audience, your intent, your tone. Be cognizant about where and with whom you spend your time. Notice situational clues and actively seek feedback to be most effective.

Next, behave in the manner you wish others to behave. You cannot control the behavior of anyone else, but you can change the way you react to the person. Be positive.

Be inclusive. This may include being early if not punctual, answering your own phone, promptly returning phone calls, and being prepared for meetings. You should also honor deadlines, keep people abreast of project progress, dress appropriately, maintain your professionalism at all times, interact with purpose, and not engage in water cooler hearsay.

Another consideration includes respecting yourself. Display confidence. Do not allow others to somehow belittle you or demean your efforts. Do not let others make their problems your problems. Stand up for yourself when required. Your efforts, contributions, and reputation warrant your defense. This is your integrity at stake.

Last, you should have some guidelines and common understanding for interaction. We will touch on those further below.

Embodying these responsive and proactive practices will show your care for your coworkers (and yourself). Accordingly, people should reciprocate. If dissonance should arise, call them out on it.

Make your own commitment

I have a section in my syllabus for each class I teach entitled, "My Commitment to You." It reads, "To accomplish the learning goals associated with this course, I will do my best to:

- *Prepare for helpful and interesting course materials*
- *Lead meaningful lectures and discussions*
- *Treat each student with respect and dignity*
- *Encourage everyone's voice*
- *Be an active listener*
- *Appreciate and learn from our differences*
- *Provide developmental and timely feedback to help students to monitor and make progress in this course*
- *Evaluate students' performance with fairness*
- *Make this a "safe to say" environment*

Something like this could be customized by you for your team.

Express empathy

There is a sign that hangs over my favorite bar, McSorley's Old Ale House in New York City's fabled Greenwich Village. It reads, "I had no shoes and I complained until I met a man with no feet." Talk about changing one's perspective.

Research tells us that emotional empathy—the ability to understand, relate to, and share feelings—is a critical management skill, highly correlated with coaching, engaging, and driving performance. Yet, a study conducted by DDI found that "only 40% of frontline leaders" were "proficient or strong" with this skill.

Empathy is a strength. It helps us build closer and deeper relationships with our coworkers. It provides insight into team issues and performance matters. It shows awareness and understanding. It puts others' needs ahead of your own, which is consistent with servant leadership. Empathy helps you know, appreciate, and be sensitive of others' emotions and attitudes. (Note: *Cognitive* empathy, as the next step of reflective understanding, involves appreciating the other's mindset and thought processes as to how they have reached their opinions and conclusions.)

To practice emotional empathy requires work and intentness. You must be open and attentive to your team's needs. It requires listening, openness, and responsiveness. *Of note, it is my observation that those entering the workforce today may require special attention as the pandemic has pushed mental health issues around communication, a sense of belonging, and socialization (among others) to the forefront. Accordingly, training (and coaching and counseling) around topics such as stress management, conflict resolution, giving and providing feedback, having difficult conversations, dealing with adversity, self-expression, and team building are paramount.*

Make reasonable accommodations

Organizations must make reasonable accommodations to the extent possible for employees with special needs or limitations. No question.

The challenge for management is when employees, citing special or limited circumstance, seek accommodations for an out-of-policy change in hours or days, shared and alternative workspaces, working from home, or extended time-off requests.

You want to accommodate these requests in order to gain some managerial goodwill. However, you must walk the fine line of not jeopardizing your team's productivity, playing favorites, or setting in motion coworker grumbling and resentment. When weighing your options, there are a few key cautionary factors to consider in consultation with your HR partner:

- Not every position lends itself to bending rules.
- If exceptions are to be made, try to find a mutually beneficial solution. Generally, you must ensure that your team productivity levels are maintained, if not enhanced.
- Do not set an unwanted precedent. You will have to defend your decision to your other team members.

Most importantly, under no circumstances should you place individual accommodations ahead of your organizational requirements. Business needs must always take and be the priority. Trust me.

Leave them alone

It is called vacation or sabbatical for a reason. Allow your team to unwind and recharge. A physical and psychological break has broad benefits. Do not chase after your teammates when they are out of the office unless it is critical to do so.

Manage to the expected behavior of the best

Regardless of size or objective, for optimal productivity and results, you need your team to perform at its peak. This means creating and raising the bar for behavioral norms. These norms, or expected behaviors, should be universal in their appeal, self-defining, and easy to understand and live. They should also be consistent with the culture within the broader organization.

Lisa DiTullio has written extensively on this subject. She has identified these essential team behaviors as:

- Treating others with respect and dignity
- Supporting and promoting intra- and inter-departmental teamwork
- Understanding and considering the needs and impacts of your own work on others
- Demonstrating an ability to problem-solve and make timely decisions
- Actively seeking and receiving feedback for improvement
- Consistently sharing knowledge and information

Team members' expectations should be introduced and discussed at an early stage (i.e., "Grinding," as discussed in the previous principle).

How to interact

In getting a bit more granular, DiTullio further identifies and provides some definitions for the ways that people should interact and treat one other. As extensions of "treating others with respect and dignity," these rules should be part of your team's fabric, understood with consensus, and given whatever weight you deem appropriate.

Of special note, be sensitive to those working remotely or in virtual environments, as you may have to contend with time zone differences, language challenges, and technology shortfalls and limitations.

- Basic courtesies—Listen and respect other people's opinions; be focused and on time.
- Operating agreements—Publish a team calendar; have agendas and keep minutes; post minutes.
- Problem solving and decision-making—Gather all relevant information; identify and confront issues, not people; be timely; have a defendable business rationale; combine team facts, experience, and judgment.
- Accountability—Articulate roles and deliverables; be clear and concise; no finger pointing, constructive comments; total team support.
- Conflict resolution—Engage everyone; focus on the topic, not the people; stay on topic; use a facilitator; if unsolved, move the discussion off-line; evaluate processes throughout the journey.
- Leader's role—Take responsibility for task completion; be accountable; ensure all team members have your full support.

With whom to spend your time

Time is a valuable and finite resource. How you utilize such in terms of shepherding your group is a critical factor toward success.

Just as Coach spent most of his time and attention with the players in his rotation, good performers deserve the majority of your attention. In considering this model, differentiate your oversight whereby:

- High performers who are generally high maintenance should receive correlating attention. Presumably, these are your "rainmakers." They get additional dispensation based upon their respective contribution.

- High performers who are low maintenance deserve appropriate space to let them create and innovate to their own drumbeat. They get attention with less frequency, but the exchanges are deeper and have more meaning. Occasionally compare notes, timetables, and alignment. Discover what motivates them (i.e., recognition, challenging work, or compensation), and push their buttons. These will be your early adapters in times of change.
- Solid contributors get whatever time and attention you can afford. Do so in a way that promotes encouragement and positive reinforcement. Invest in those with the most potential.
- Low performers, whether high or low maintenance, are not worth priority. Coach to improve and consider other training or remedial actions. Do not become consumed in attempting to correct their shortcomings.
- Low performers who bring down the morale of the rest of the team need stricter rules. You should proceed with documenting problems on a path toward eventual separation.

How does this compare to conventional wisdom?

Treat everyone the same.

Notwithstanding your legal obligations or those associated with a collective bargaining agreement, differentiate as needed. However, be hesitant to initiate anything that might be considered as unwarranted, preferential, or discriminatory treatment.

Endnotes for Principle 5: Fairness is giving all people the treatment they earn and deserve

Your coaching imperative: Treat everyone fairly, but not equally

"Mad Men," Wikipedia. (August 2020, Last edited). Retrieved on September 10, 2020, from: https://en.wikipedia.org/wiki/Mad_Men

Employees ARE your most valuable resource

Crispin, J. (2012, July 26). Our employees are our most valuable asset. ERE. Retrieved on January 18, 2019, from: https://hbr.org/2011/10/valuing-your-most-valuable
Amabile, T., & Kramer, S. (2011, October 10). Valuing your most valuable assets. *HBR.org*. Retrieved on January 18, 2019, from: https://www.ere.net/our-employees-are-our-most-valuable-asset/

It is about respect

Watson, C. (2017, September 6). Treat everyone with respect and dignity. Clint Watson—Blog. Retrieved on January 18, 2019, from: https://clintavo.com/blog/124479/treat-everyone-with-respect-and-dignity
Daskal, L. (2016, April 25). 9 valuable principles that will make you treat people better. *Inc.com*. Retrieved on January 18, 2019, from: https://www.inc.com/lolly-daskal/9-important-ways-that-will-make-you-treat-people-better.html

It is about fairness

Nicholson, N. (Date unknown). Why treating employees fairly is important. Sparkhire.com. Retrieved on January 18, 2019, from: https://hr.sparkhire.com/talent-management/why-treating-employees-fairly-is-important/

Bacal, R. (Date unknown). Common leader mistake—trying to treat everyone the same. Leadertoday.org. Retrieved on January 18, 2019, from: http://leadertoday.org/faq/mistakesame.htm

Salgado, S.R. (2014, October 29). Why you shouldn't treat all employees the same. *Inc.com*. Retrieved on January 18, 2019, from: https://www.inc.com/susan-salgado/why-you-shouldn-t-treat-all-employees-the-same.html

Theriault, M. (2014, January 10). Why managers shouldn't treat all employees the same. *Foxbusiness.com*. Retrieved on January 18, 2019, from: https://www.foxbusiness.com/features/why-managers-shouldnt-treat-all-employees-the-same (thoughtful)

It is about being nice

Garst, K. (2014, April 9). Treat everyone with kindness and respect. Not because they are nice, but because you are. Philosiblog. Retrieved on January 18, 2019, from: https://philosiblog.com/2014/04/09/treat-everyone-with-kindness-and-respect-not-because-they-are-nice-but-because-you-are/

It is about putting employees first

Weir, J. (2018, July 13). For first-class customer service, put your employees first. *Business.com*. Retrieved on January 18, 2019, from: https://www.business.com/articles/put-your-employees-first-for-first-class-customer-service/

It is about care

Nayar, V. (2010, June 18). Why I put my employees ahead of my customers. *Forbes.com*. Published on June 18, 2010. Retrieved on January 18, 2019, from: https://www.forbes.com/2010/06/18/employees-first-vineet-nayar-leadership-managing-hcl.html#2a527f584e81

Schurenberg, E. (Date unknown). Richard Branson: Why customers come second at virgin. *Inc.com*. Retrieved on January 18, 2019, from: https://www.inc.com/eric-schurenberg/sir-richard-branson-put-your-staff-first-customers-second-and-shareholders-third.html

Weir, J. (2018, July 13). For first-class customer service, put your employees first. *Business.com*. Retrieved on January 18, 2019, from: https://www.business.com/articles/put-your-employees-first-for-first-class-customer-service/

Appreciate the individual

Why employee appreciation is important in the workplace. (Date unknown). *JobMonkey.com*. Retrieved on January 18, 2019, from: https://www.jobmonkey.com/employer-insights/employee-appreciation/

Blitsein, G. (Date unknown). Make every day employee appreciation day. *NevadaSmallBuiness.com*. Retrieved on January 18, 2019, from: https://nevadasmallbusiness.com/the-benefits-of-appreciating-your-employees/

Teach others how to treat you

Tartakovsky, M. (2018, July 8). What it means to teach people how to treat you. *Psych Central*. Retrieved on January 18, 2019, from: https://psychcentral.com/blog/what-it-means-to-teach-people-how-to-treat-you/

Dickerson, D. (2015, March 31). Best advice: top 8 ways you teach others to treat you. *LinkedIn*. Retrieved on January 18, 2019, from: https://www.linkedin.com/pulse/best-advice-top-ways-you-teach-others-how-treat-debbie-dickerson/

Express empathy

Lipman, V. (2018, February 24). How important is empathy to successful management? *Forbes.com*. Retrieved on January 18, 2019, from: https://www.forbes.com/sites/victorlipman/2018/02/24/how-important-is-empathy-to-successful-management/#323650fa46d7(40%)

Pressley, D. (2012, November 16). The importance of empathy in the workplace. Smart Business Network, Inc., Cleveland, Ohio. Retrieved on January 18, 2019, from: http://www.sbnon-line.com/article/the-importance-of-empathy-in-the-workplace/

Behavioral norms

DiTullio, L.A. (2009). Expected behaviors for project team performance: road rules, not road rage. Paper presented at PMI® Global Congress 2009—North America, Orlando, FL. Newtown Square, PA: Project Management Institute. Retrieved on January 18, 2019, from: https://www.pmi.org/learning/library/project-team-performance-expected-behaviors-6759

How to interact

DiTullio, L.A. (2009). Expected behaviors for project team performance: road rules, not road rage. Paper presented at PMI® Global Congress 2009—North America, Orlando, FL. Newtown Square, PA: Project Management Institute. Retrieved on January 18, 2019, from: https://www.pmi.org/learning/library/project-team-performance-expected-behaviors-6759

Make your "yes" mean yes

Coach led by example and actively and visibly demonstrated the behavior he wanted his players to emulate. He embraced self-discipline through punctuality, preparation, and a tireless work ethic. He never demanded that standards be set or met beyond which he could hold himself accountable.

Wooden was also a man of his word.

In 1948, Coach wanted the then-available University of Minnesota coaching job. In fact, he had been offered the job, but wanted to bring his assistant coaches with him. This was a bit of a sticking point for Frank McCormick, the athletic director at Minnesota, as this meant getting permission from the University of Minnesota President, Lotus Coffman.

It took a few days for the approval. When McCormick went to convey the news, a snowstorm had knocked out the phone lines in South Dakota where he was staying. He could not contact Wooden by the agreed-upon time. Thus, with this prolonged silence and the deadline having passed, Wooden assumed that Minnesota had a change of mind. He accepted the UCLA position with a three-year commitment.

The next day, McCormick did get a call through to Wooden with a more attractive offer, but to no avail.

If a snowstorm had not intervened, the greatest coach in college basketball history might have been a Golden Gopher.

Your coaching imperative: It is your name

Integrity, defined as being honest and upholding the highest moral principles, is always at or near the top of every survey when it comes to the most desirable personal characteristic for a leader to possess. A deficiency in this area, in a business world full of temptations, will quickly erode your reputation and leadership effectiveness. It should never be compromised.

I once worked with a C-level executive who was "over-served" at a holiday party. Over-served is the term we use in the corporate world to say he was drunk. (When you say over-served, it sounds like the fault lies with the party or facility hosting the event. After all, it could NEVER be the fault of one of our corporate executives.) Anyway, upon having one too many, our male executive proceeded to "hit upon" one of our newly hired female employees. He was out-of-control with his comments before someone had the good sense to send him home in a taxi. However, the damage had been done.

On Monday, word of his behavior spread quickly as gossip. As you might also guess, the female employee was in my office, still quite upset, telling her version of that night's events. By the way, did I mention that she had been just brought on-board as an attorney in our legal department?

DOI: 10.4324/9781003456902-12

All of this put the company in a terrible position from a variety of perspectives. Ultimately, the CEO and board of directors had to weigh in. It was decided, quite leniently in my judgment, to slap the executive on the wrist and write the attorney a sizeable check as a parting gift for her short tenure and bruises.

The executive's reputation never recovered. Ultimately, he crashed and burned.

Here are some other head-scratching examples of behaviors in corporate settings that I have witnessed where an individual's lack of integrity led to their termination. Unfortunately, I could make this list much longer. A lot longer.

- *The facilities manager who thought he could shield his identity from the surveillance camera as he occasionally removed small change from a vending machine.*
- *The office manager who figured out a way to sell unused company N.Y Knicks basketball tickets on social media for personal gain.*
- *The finance manager who colluded with one of his clerks and an outside vendor to create a scheme to process false invoices. (They were fired and prosecuted, only after $200,000 had been taken.)*
- *The sales manager who went to lunch at the same bar everyday claiming to take a customer. This was uncovered when a clever accountant noticed that the receipts were consecutively numbered over time.*
- *A vice president of HR (Yes, HR!!!) who made an inappropriate sexual comment to a colleague.*
- *A customer service leader who used profanity as naturally as you and I breath, and could not understand why it offended his coworkers.*

Then, there was the senior executive in the electronics industry who wore shorts and flip-flops to work, arrived at work at 10:00 each morning, often with a hangover. He also misappropriated a significant amount of company funds, shared pornography with coworkers, publicly asked for details about coworker's sex lives, entertained customers at lavish weekend retreats where alcohol was the main feature, and encouraged ill-advised games of horseplay in the company's warehouse. There was more.

Integrity is not situational or fleeting. It does not have an "on" and "off" switch. When decisions and behavior choices present themselves, do the right thing. Do not let your thinking wander or sway. Also, do not allow your integrity to be compromised by bias, personal allegiances, politics, a desire to please others, greed, ambition, blind loyalty, or a desire to protect the status quo. Short-term gains are not worth any long-term tarnish. Remember, you are always in the limelight, and you and your business benefit when you:

- Stay true to your word.
- Be appropriately transparent.
- Are honest at all times.
- Are consistent with your behavior and attitude.
- Respect everyone.
- Build and maintain trust.
- Are not afraid to face the truth.
- Go the distance to please customers.
- Stress compliance.
- Build integrity into your corporate culture.

Remember, your name was a good one when your parents gave it to you. Protect it with vigor!

What goes around ...

With some apprehension, Coach and his wife Nellie headed to Los Angeles to assume his new role. He was appalled with what greeted him upon arrival. The facilities were inadequate, the "required" social climate involved what he deemed to be an exorbitant amount of fraternizing with boosters and alumni, and he had to share the gym with the school's gymnastics team. The school also did not have a retirement program.

With this bumpy backdrop, at the end of his second season, Coach yearned to return to the Midwest. He asked if UCLA would accommodate his desire by releasing him from the last year of his contract. In response, school officials reminded him that he was the one who insisted upon the original three-year deal and that Coach should honor his word. He did.

A man of integrity, Coach knew deep down and understood—even if he needed a reminder—that credibility is a currency easily spent, not but easily earned.

Your handshake is your word

Back in the day, your handshake *was* your word. It mattered. It was all that mattered. It was the basis of relationships, the foundation of one's reputation, and it was how business was done.

Your handshake represented closure. It did not mean "yes," until something better came along. It had meaning and honor. It was a bond between people, your signature. It was not fluid nor fleeting. It was firm and of confidence. It memorialized an agreement. Written words and lawyers were not necessary.

It almost sounds dated by today's standards. In fact, how many of us would have called UCLA back and taken the Minnesota job? In your organizational life, you want to surround yourself with trusted colleagues. Liars have no place; they stall progress, create obstacles, and waste team energy. You need to exude and have integrity all around you.

Limit the use of "maybe" in your vocabulary

In organizational life, you handle questions and choices each day involving various levels of detail and complexity. Sometimes, our answer to these decisions or questions is "yes" sometimes it is "no." Sometimes, we hesitate or pause. We might lack confidence, second guess our intuition, or fear making a wrong turn. When these possibilities arise, "maybe" tends to be our choice.

If "maybe" cannot be avoided, reflect appropriately, gather needed information, sift through alternatives, ward off impulsive tendencies, and find the best answer. And be sure to follow-up with all involved parties in a timely matter. This shows that you listen, take the input of others seriously, and appreciate their concerns.

No means no

"No" is such a short, powerful word. Its definition is clear. Its intentions are not subject to interpretation. Heck, as parents, we use the term all the time.

At work, using "no" is a little trickier. In fact, it can be difficult. Pragmatically, you want to be a team player, take the stretch assignment, and otherwise demonstrate your commitment, but it is not always possible. By implication, "no" can bring on correlating feelings of guilt, fear of missing out, or the potential of disappointing others.

Stay strong. If the request is not in the best interests of you or your team, say "no," and mean it.

Strive for consensus (when it makes sense to do so)

Consensus means finding an agreeable position (more or less) with all team members.

There are several ways to seek consensus with your team members. Informally pooling ideas, listening to pros and cons, and discussing differences are ways to drive toward a common solution. Other ways that have a bit more formality include judgment-free brainstorming sessions, multi-voting where participants cast votes to whittle down options, and a pseudo-combination of these methodologies that involves idea-generation and forced ranking voting with facilitation.

Consensus does have its drawbacks. First, it can lean more toward the status quo, as many people are happy leaving things just the way they are. Selfish motives might lead the team not to rock the boat or even raise a finger. Second, your cynics, pessimists, and naysayers can prove to be disruptive, as they may actually steer the team toward a less-than-desirable outcome. Third, mediocrity tends to rule in the land of consensus, as the majority tends to skew toward the middle. Conservative views trump moderate and liberal thinking, potentially squashing innovation. Fourth, people may compromise to avoid debate or not disrupt team harmony, leaving unresolved conflict behind. Lastly, your dreamers and "big picture" thinkers may be suffocated.

If a major decision is causing you concern, particularly one that significantly affects your employees or operations, try consensus as a means toward that end.

I had just started with a company and was eager to make a fast and favorable impression. Accordingly, I tackled the performance management system first. Its redesign was fairly progressive for that time, in that it involved 360-degree feedback and a cross-sectional management review process. When my CEO asked with whom I had shared the project, I proudly said that it was my sole work product.

He did not like that response. He wanted every executive to opine prior to rollout.

We discussed the matter at length. Ultimately, he pointed to a painting on the wall above my desk that was of a country landscape with a river. He suggested that it was my job to bring my peers from one side of the river (theirs) to the other (mine).

It was a graceful and powerful analogy. He was right. I had been so caught-up with my "ready, fire, aim," approach that I neglected the view of others. Their later input helped make our system better and it also made for a smoother implementation when the time was right.

This was a most valuable lesson. I think of it often.

Watch out for Abilene

In the context of management practices, Abilene, Texas is not a place you want to visit.

Jerry B. Harvey introduced the term "Abilene Paradox" in 1974. The paradox is based on an anecdote he used to describe the decision-making process undertaken by a group of family members who collectively agreed upon a course of action that no one preferred.

Go back in time. Picture a blazing mid-afternoon sun over the flatlands of Texas. It is hot, scorching hot. The thermometer is over three figures Fahrenheit. A family is sitting on their shaded front porch. They are playing dominoes to pass the slowly-moving time. They are as comfortable as you can be in this desert-like environment. Throwing a verbal dart at the wall, the father-in-law suggests that they go to Abilene for dinner. It is a 53-mile drive. The wife says, "Sounds like a great idea." The husband, who has significant reservations, but does not want to rock the boat, says, "Sounds good to me. I just hope your mother wants to go." The mother-in-law chimes in, "Of course I want to go. I haven't been to Abilene in a long time."

They go to Abilene. It is a long, dusty drive in their 1958 Buick—without air conditioning. When they arrive, they have an awful meal, reflective of the day and the unfolding mood. They get back home four hours later, much worse for the wear.

Now the fun begins. One of them insincerely says, "It was a great trip, wasn't it?" In response, the mother-in-law says that she really wanted to stay home, but did not want to go against the others' wishes. The husband says, "I wasn't delighted to be doing what we were doing. I only went to satisfy the rest of you." The back-pedaling continues. Each now admits that they only went along to satisfy what they thought were the desires of everyone else.

The truth is that no one wanted to go, but they were team players. Silence of honest opinion prevailed and the individuals acted contrary to their actual wishes, leaving negative feelings and somewhat strained relations about the outcome. Don't let this happen to you.

How does this compare to conventional wisdom?

If you live in the corporate world, you may have seen this happen: the "integrity two-step."

An edict comes down from the corner office stating that, effective immediately, all departments are to freeze all non-essential spending and tighten their budgets in order to realize a 10% reduction in general and administrative costs. Everyone panics. Projects come to a screeching halt, capital expenses are put on the back burner, recruiting is forgotten, vendors are pressured, and inventory is dramatically reduced. Field offices and factories do everything they can think of to squeeze a dime.

This is all fine and dandy until the same corner office executive comes to visit your site and does so by taking the corporate jet. Not to mention the limousine service and the five-star hotel with fine dining that are part of the trip.

"Ouch" for the worker bees!

When your actions do not match your words, your ability to lead an organization will be dramatically undermined. If you make the rules, play by them. You must walk the talk. It's your name.

Endnotes for Principle 6: Make your "yes" mean yes

Walk the talk

Hartman, S. (2010, June 5). Wooden missed the chance to coach at U. *Star Tribune*. Retrieved on March 25, 2019, from: http://www.startribune.com/wooden-missed-chance-to-coach-for-gophers/95702419/

It is your name

Zwilling, M. (2012, March 30). 5 ways to see if your business integrity is showing. *Forbes.com*. Retrieved on February 7, 2019, from: https://www.forbes.com/sites/martinzwilling/2012/03/30/5-ways-to-see-if-your-business-integrity-is-showing/#357903d52421 (Eisenhower quote, first five bullets)

Tracy, B. (2016, December 7). The importance of honesty and integrity in business. *Entrepreneur.com*. Retrieved on February 7, 2019, from: https://www.entrepreneur.com/article/282957

Cairns, B. (2017, November 6). The importance of integrity in business. *Business.com*. Retrieved on February 7, 2019, from: https://www.business.com/articles/importance-of-integrity/

Sheppard, D.L. (2018, May 7). Ways integrity can improve your business. *Businessknowhow.com*. Retrieved on February 7, 2019, from: https://www.businessknowhow.com/manage/business-integrity.htm

Your handshake is your word

Densley, S. (2019, April30). When a handshake was your word of honor. Herald Extra. Retrieved on March 20, 2019, from: https://www.heraldextra.com/news/community/steve-densley/steve-densley-when-a-handshake-was-your-word-of-honor/article_3291762c-ce5d-5117-ad9c-9d15b31e29a4.html

Day, P.E. (Date unknown). Is your handshake your word? Academy of Financial Literacy, Inc. Retrieved on March 20, 2019, from: https://www.academyoffinancialliteracy.net/archived-articles.asp?i=6003

Limit the use of the word "maybe"

Pundir, R. (Date unknown). What to do when you just can't make a decision. Lifehack. Retrieved on March 20, 2019, from: https://www.lifehack.org/591444/what-to-do-when-you-just-cant-make-the-decision

Strauss Cohn, I. (2017, November5). 7 tips on how to kick the habit of indecisiveness. *Psychology Today*. Retrieved on March 20, 2019, from: https://www.psychologytoday.com/us/blog/your-emotional-meter/201711/7-tips-how-kick-the-habit-indecisiveness

Strive for consensus

The United States Office of Personnel Management. (Date unknown). Effective teams strive for consensus. Retrieved on March 20, 2019, from: https://www.opm.gov/policy-data-oversight/performance-management/teams/effective-teams-strive-for-consensus/

Morgan, T. (2017, July). 5 reasons not to strive for consensus. The Unstuck Group. Retrieved on March 20, 2019, from: https://theunstuckgroup.com/2017/06/making-decisions-reaching-consensus/

Cherry, K. (2019, March16). How to recognize and avoid groupthink. Very well mind. Retrieved on March 20, 2019, from: https://www.verywellmind.com/what-is-groupthink-2795213

Quick Books Canada Team. (Date unknown). When (and when not) to strive for company consensus. Retrieved on March 20, 2019, from: https://quickbooks.intuit.com/ca/resources/managing-employees/when-to-strive-for-company-consensus/

Watch out for Abilene

"Abilene Paradox," Wikipedia. (Date unknown). Retrieved on March 29, 2019, from: https://en.wikipedia.org/wiki/Abilene_paradox

Be quick, but don't hurry

Coach was not one to waste time or effort. He wanted his teams to play at the fastest pace possible yet be able to change speed or direction if circumstances required it. Waste no time, no motion, or no effort. Lose the hesitation and stay balanced. Yes, to quickness, control, and effectiveness.

The best example of UCLA's penchant for speed was their full-court press, pressuring the opposition from the time they inbounded the ball. This full-court defense increased the tempo of the game, thereby taking the opposition out of their comfort zone. As a by-product, it also caused frenzied turnovers. The press became a notable trademark of Wooden-coached teams.

Beyond the press, there was a more subtle example: the UCLA fast break.

The fast break, as the term implies, is a play where the team with the ball races down the court and tries to get a shot off ahead of the pursuing defenders. UCLA's fast break had surgeon-like precision. It was disciplined and structured, part poetry and part grace. It was an important ingredient of their offense, and it had subtleties that even the most ardent fan might miss.

The play began as the other team was taking its shot. With the ball in the air, two concurrent activities were taking place. First, unlike other teams that "boxed-out" their man, Wooden coached his defenders to make contact with the offensive player, stop him, and then release toward the basket to get the rebound. They were in motion, aggressively seeking the opponent's errant shot versus maneuvering for position under the basket. Second, the Bruins' big men, the ones most likely to grab the rebound, glanced over their shoulders as the ball released in order to anticipate where they would pivot and throw their outlet pass.

Once the fast break was underway, lay-ups were the goal, but often a 15-foot jump shot from the side of the court was the result. It was common to "settle" for that shot. (Andy noted that his teams took "thousands" of those bank shots in practice; thus, it was not "settling.") The shooter was also instructed not to follow his shot; rather, go to the area in front of the foul line. Coach felt that missed shots were more likely to come that way.

No battle or pushing match under the boards. Get after it. Anticipate the outlet pass. Hasten the transition. Constantly forward movement. Pulling-up for an unconventional 15-foot banker. Not following your shot, but head to the foul line!

The perfect blend of speed and execution worked like no other.

Your coaching imperative: See the frog; eat the frog

You find yourself at a fancy restaurant attending a high-society function, and the waiter has presented you with a fresh out-of-the-kitchen plate of frog legs. You do not like frog legs.

DOI: 10.4324/9781003456902-13

Maybe you have tried them before, and the taste was not in your favor. Maybe you just do not like the look of them. Maybe they conjure up memories of a high school biology class experiment gone bad. Whatever the reason, frog legs are akin to Sam-I-Am's early encounter in Dr. Seuss' *Green Eggs and Ham*. Not for you!

Staring at them will not make them go away. Neither will pushing them around on your plate. Bartering with your neighbor does not look promising, nor does covering them with a napkin. There is no pet dog available. Having no choice, you pick-up your utensils and put this behind you—quickly. Procrastination will not change the circumstance or save you. Just get it done!

Have a sense of urgency

In the business world, everything you do is a series of interconnected, non-stop decisions and actions.

Getting things done and being agile in this high-speed environment requires urgency. Urgency creates momentum, pushes people's comfort zones, sparks motivation, and combats the status quo. It is a spirit, not a state of heightened anxiety or stress. It gets things done.

There are several ways to inject, project, or nurture urgency:

- Start with yourself—Do you honor deadlines? Are projects on time and on budget? Are decisions promptly made? Do you return calls and e-mails quickly? Are directions clearly given?
- Communicate—Be open, honest, and consistent. Show passion! Radiate energy! Keep meetings and conversations on point.
- Set high standards—Kill complacency. When there is an attitude of "good is good enough," raise the bar. Aim high. Create opportunities to improve service, quality, and productivity. Make it a shared accountability.
- Focus on results—Encourage a culture where outcomes, as appropriate, are rewarded over process and tasks.
- Act—Push, pull, and otherwise motivate your team to give their best effort.
- Streamline—Be smart. Wastes of time and energy are your enemies. Wherever possible, minimize or eliminate overhead, bureaucracy, and excess administration. Get rid of any obstacles.
- Increase your visibility—Having multiple "touch points" throughout the day helps keep you in contact with your team. Use this time to show your support of their efforts. Be careful not to appear too Big Brother-like.
- Listen more—Your team members are in the trenches, closest to the action. Gather opinions and seek ways to innovate! Stress continuous improvement. Employees will appreciate that you asked and likely be more engaged in the "fix" process.
- Remove the skeptics—Separate from the fence sitters, skeptics, and naysayers (see Principle 4). They are destructive to your culture and too concerned about how their role or status might be impacted by any change.
- Simulate and stimulate-Postulate to your team that a fierce new, well-financed competitor is entering the market tomorrow morning with the goal of eating your lunch. How would your team react?

Avoid analysis paralysis

There is some merit to the saying that he who hesitates is lost.

I once worked with a woman who, true to her love for analytics and technical training, waited until all of the data was collected and analyzed to the finest detail, allowing the findings to dictate her course of action. While this attribute served her extremely well in her functional role, it proved to be her Achilles' heel as a leader. Her staff gradually abandoned her, frustrated and weary over her laborious nature and tedious avoidance of making decisions. She was "paralysis by analysis" exemplified.

Perhaps you feel more information is required in order to move ahead. This is becoming more the rule in our evolving world of increased analytics; however, it is also possible that you are "over-thinking" the dilemma.

Do not agonize, falsely or otherwise. Analysis paralysis can be lonely and personally disruptive. Handle the decision process effectively and approach it with a flexible style that involves appropriately challenging yourself. Smaller steps work better than large ones if there is the potential for things to become paralyzing.

Some tips include:

* Keep a proper queue. Know which decisions need to be made and when. Keep moving forward.
* Perfection is elusive. Unless the decision could crater the company, stay the course. Be sure that your decisions stay aligned with your company's desired strategic outcomes. Keep your perspective.
* Separate your needs from your wants. Emotions tend to cloud perspective.
* Set a time limit and honor it.
* Stick to a calendar.
* If you can delegate the decision as a learning opportunity for someone you trust, do it.
* Listen to the voice of others. Seeking advice is a wise path to follow, especially if the subject matter is not in your area of expertise.
* Write down the pros and cons. Toss out the less-then-optimal options. Less clutter equals clearer thinking.

Avoid avoidance

Leading a team at work, as on a basketball court, is an ongoing journey of decision-making. Yet, we have all seen managers who, rather than make or communicate a difficult decision, assume that time and unforeseen future circumstance will somehow remedy the issue.

In such cases, time is rarely an ally and the absence of action usually amplifies the matter's gravity.

These managers are neglecting or abdicating their responsibilities. They do not need more information to decide a matter; they are just uncomfortable with the pending decision—and perhaps more. They deem the task or decision to be unpleasant. Procrastination sets in. Emotions become unregulated, and anxiety may even result. Avoidance may lead to dread, stress, fear, and a failure to cope. Intentional or not, indecision becomes the decision.

If procrastination becomes chronic, it can lead to longer-term destructive effects on our mental and physical health.

Here are some tips to consider when you feel like putting your head in the sand:

* Conduct root cause analysis
* Ask someone for advice
* Seek out your support system
* Remember recipes from past successes
* Control what you can control
* Do not be afraid to make changes
* Take a baby step and build upon it

Why quality matters

Every leader wants quality. Every leader wants speed. And then there's cost control.

In the business world, you must continuously triangulate each of these factors in order to be competitive with your industrial adversaries. Harmonization is the challenge.

Quality is paramount

Robert Winship Woodruff, President of Coca-Cola (1923–1939), was a pioneer for quality and continuous improvement in the workplace. In 1928, the company had the foresight to create a training program to ensure that all employees who serviced soda fountains were knowledgeable about the product and other company offerings. At the same time, he introduced universal quality control and assurance standards at all of the bottling facilities, along with a standard operating manual.

When is the last time you had a sip of Coke that did not taste like the last?

Quality is paramount. It is not to be sacrificed. I do not know of any organization's business plan or values proposition that states imprecise work is the encouraged norm. When quality standards are lowered or take an ill-advised shortcut, risk is taken. The probability of errors occurring increases. Some of those errors will need prompt fixing; others may come back to haunt you. Progress and processes become slow and delayed since resources must now be devoted to problems, not innovations. Time and money may be lost. Customers may lose confidence. Your brand can suffer damage. In most cases, it would certainly be best to correct the missteps earlier then later.

When you strive for the highest quality standards, start by seeing the world through your customers' eyes. They want their expectations and demands realized. They want products and services that last, solve a problem or deliver on a promise, meet their budget, and are easy to use. They want to be safe and comfortable using the product, knowing that it is also efficient and effective.

Fulfilling the above will help set you apart from the other market offerings. It will enhance customer appreciation and trust, increase the chance for return business, and further establish your company's reputation, as social media might pick up on quality-fueled recommendations. Profits will likely be nearby.

Speed: Be quick

Speed OR quality? How about speed AND quality?

In business, as much as you want to do things faster and more efficiently (and that should always be a goal), do things at the pace at which they are supposed to be done without affecting quality. Go as fast as possible, *under control*, able to pivot, and without avoidable miscues. Be mindful of the costs and benefits around standardization versus customization.

Speed: But don't hurry

Readers of a certain age will recall the television show, *I Love Lucy*. In the premier episode of 1952, "Job Switching," Lucy and Ethel are moved from job to job in a candy factory—apparently failing miserably at each spot—only to be assigned to the "wrapping department." In this role, they must keep up with the ever-increasing speed of the candy-filled conveyor belt. They became quickly overwhelmed, and a timeless comedy scene was born.

Lucy and Ethel's supervisor saw "hurry" as a means to increase results as the duo "hid" their mistakes; yet it ultimately led to their undoing.

What was true in that television classic remains valid today. "Hurry" is the world we live in. It is the razor's edge of "get it done now." As a consequence, planning is often an afterthought or minimized. We make things up as we go along. Unintended chaos often ensues.

Hurry generally has a price associated with it. In careers, progressive ladder-climbers may sacrifice their time, energy, health, home, character, and happiness in their hasty quest for status and the almighty dollar. For your bottom line, hurry's costs—returns, waste, quality compromise, cut corners, processing errors, inventory mismanagement, eroding customer service, unrealized sales, and misallocated resources—are to be avoided. Short-term gains are not worth their trade-offs.

Everything worthwhile in life is generally a product of personal investment, time, and growth. If you are going to do something, it is worth doing something right.

Build quality into your culture

Quality is not what it used to be. It is much more. Today, a prospective buyer need only refer to *Consumer Reports*, J.D. Power, *Good Housekeeping*, *MotorTrend*, Amazon, or any one of a multitude of related websites for reviews covering just about any consumer product or service. To this end, quality must be a fundamental building block of your team's culture.

A "quality culture" is not a corner office edict. It is created when employees follow quality guidelines, take quality-focused actions, discuss quality as part of their natural regimen, and encourage continuous quality improvements. It is a culture where governance exists, metrics are embraced, and continuous improvement is emphasized, resulting in satisfied customers and a healthy bottom line. A quality culture has a spirit and practice that is adaptive rather than prescriptive.

Inculcating such a culture takes intention and direction. Of note, management has several levers at its disposal to make this happen:

- Leadership emphasis—Managers need to "walk the talk" about quality. It is a priority. It should be part of the performance evaluation. There must be a prevailing mindset that quality is everyone's responsibility.
- Message credibility—Messages about quality should state the business imperative (cost, rework involved, waste generated, or customer satisfaction impact) and why people have a stake in making sure that high standards are attained.

- Peer involvement—Quality is part of the regular discussion on the shop floor and in the office. Peers can go to each other to discuss quality matters and should hold each other accountable for such.
- Employee ownership of quality issues—Team members have the required resources and are empowered to make quality decisions, feel comfortable to raise questions or concerns, and have a clear understanding of how quality fits into their role.
- Learning experiences—Ensure decisions are made, and actions are taken based upon the experience, information, and understanding at the time. Share the lessons.
- Long-term perspective—Ensure sustainable solutions.
- Measurement—There may be tangible value in systematizing and bringing discipline to any organizational process. This will allow for measurement, repetition, and improvement. Explore programs such as "Six Sigma," "process re-engineering," "Kaizen," and "quality circles."

Motion versus progress

Coach always sounded a cautionary note about having activity without accomplishment.

We have all worked with a certain type of "busy" person. This individual never seems to have enough hours. Their schedule is full of non-stop meetings and appointments. They participate on task forces and raise their hands for every committee. Their desk has piles of the latest references and work materials. They give the impression that they are slaves to their work. They are overwhelmed and their overbearing drama about their self-importance is exhausting. In addition, they typically have some politician in their veins, name-dropping at key opportunities in an effort to raise their own "indispensable" profile and image of grandeur, while creating (real or illusional) allies at higher levels for cover.

Chances are that this person is not your best performer. In fact, while they may experience some short-term contribution, I have seen them quickly plateau and stumble beyond that.

When you bump into or manage this type, listen carefully. Is progress really being made? There is a major difference between motion and progress. Do not be sucked into having this line blurred by those with selfish motives. These are not your "A" players. And if they report to you, lean toward micromanaging these types, potentially on the path to weeding them out.

"Let's go" versus "go" or "get going!"

Whether far along into navigating a challenging road or just taking the first steps on a project's journey, be the leader who through *example and pace,* is a mentor, a caring enabler, a builder, and an inspiration to your team. This approach creates bonding, camaraderie, learning, and participation. It will differentiate you from the rest. People will want to follow.

How does this compare to conventional wisdom?

You do not have to trade-off speed for quality or cost.

Endnotes for Principle 7: Be quick, but don't hurry

See the frog

Dr. Seuss. (1960). *Green eggs and ham.* New York: Penguin Random House.

Have a sense of urgency

Armstrong, W. (2002, July 22). Communicating a sense of urgency. *Smart Business Magazine*. Retrieved on March 4, 2018, from: http://www.sbnon-line.com/article/communicating-a-sense-of-urgency-4419/

Clark, T. (2013, May 22). How to create a sense of urgency with your team. The Liquidplanner Blog. Retrieved on March 4, 2018, from: https://www.liquidplanner.com/blog/team-urgency/

Advanced Leadership Consulting. (2019: copyright). 5 ways to create a necessary sense of urgency. Retrieved on March 4, 2018, from: http://leadershipconsulting.com/5-ways-create-necessary-sense-urgency/

Llewellyn, R. (2015, September 24). 20 ways to create a sense of urgency. The Enterprisers Project. Retrieved on March 4, 2018, from: https://enterprisersproject.com/article/2014/8/20-ways-create-sense-urgency

Zwilling, M. (2012, July 28). Many confuse sense of urgency with sense of emergency. *Forbes.com*. Posted on July 28, 2012. Retrieved on March 4, 2018, from: https://www.forbes.com/sites/martinzwilling/2012/07/28/many-confuse-sense-of-urgency-with-sense-of-emergency/#1af5c79b1988

Avoid analysis paralysis

Greenberg, J., & Baron, R. (1995). *Behavior in organization* (Third edition.). Englewood Cliffs, New Jersey: Prentice-Hall, Inc., p. 501.

Hoekstra, R. (2019). Should I get back on the horse? Two ways to approach your fear that won't work. renee.hoekstra.co. Boston DBT Group. Retrieved on March 11, 2019, from: https://reneehoekstra.com/get-back-horse-two-ways-approach-fear-wont-work/ (overwhelming)

Rodriguez, M. (2015, November 12). 9 tips to avoid paralysis by analysis. bsci21.org. Retrieved on March 11, 2018, from: https://bsci21.org/9-tips-to-avoid-paralysis-by-analysis/

Avoid avoidance

Scott, E. (2018, October 27). Avoidance coping and why it creates additional stress. Very Well Mind. Retrieved on March 20, 2019, from: https://www.verywellmind.com/avoidance-coping-and-stress-4137836

Lee, T. (Date unknown). Practice facing the small things: 11 ways to avoid avoidance. The body is not an apology. #NoBodiesInvisible. Retrieved on March 20, 2019, from https://thebodyisnotanapology.com/magazine/practice-facing-the-small-things-11-ways-to-avoid-avoidance/

Star, K. (2018, October 1). How to reduce your panic-related avoidance behaviors. Very Well Mind. Retrieved on March 20, 2019 from https://www.verywellmind.com/how-to-reduce-your-panic-related-avoidance-behaviors-2584148

Lieberman, C. (2019, March 25). Why you procrastinate (It has nothing to do with self-control). *The New York Times*. Retrieved on March 27, 2019 from: https://www.newyorktimes.com/2019/03/25/smarter-living/why-you-procrastinateeit-has-nothing.

Quality

Bennis, W.G., Brown, T., Champy, J., Crainer, S., Davis, S., Edwards, H., Goleman, D., Gottlieb, A., Heller, R., Larreche, J.C., Leyden, P., Meyer, C., Norton, B., & Rayport, J. (Advisory Board), (2002). *Business: the ultimate resource*. Cambridge, Massachusetts: Perseus Publishing, p. 1161.

Jeffries, R. (2019, February 1). Quality-speed tradeoff—you're kidding yourself. RonJeffries.com. Retrieved on March 4, 2018 from: http://ronjeffries.com/xprog/blog/quality-speed-tradeoff-youre-kidding-yourself/

Alton, L. (2016, July28). Why quality is the most important thing to your customers," Mycustomer.com Community Blog. Retrieved on March 14, 2019 from: https://www.mycustomer.com/community/blogs/larryalton/why-quality-is-the-most-important-thing-to-your-customers

Business.com Editorial Staff. (2018, April 11). Elevating expectations: 5 ways product quality impacts your brand. Business.com Writer. Retrieved on March 14, 2019 from: https://www.business.com/articles/5-reasons-why-product-quality-matters/

Speed: be quick

Lynch, B. (2012, December 20). quality vs. quantity: why faster is not always better. Geautomation.com. Retrieved on March 4, 2018 from: http://www.geautomation.com/blog/quality-vs-quantity-why-faster-not-always-better

Speed: but don't hurry

Jordan, W.G. (1900). *The majesty of calmness: Individual problems and possibilities.* San Bernardino, CA: Publisher unknown. Republished September 20, 2016. p. 7–11.

Build quality into your culture

Srinivasan, A., & Kurey, B. (2014, April). Creating a culture of quality. *Harvard Business Review.* Retrieved on March 4, 2018 from: https://hbr.org/2014/04/creating-a-culture-of-quality (leadership, message, peer, ownership)

El Safty, S. (2012, August30). Five essential ingredients for a quality culture. Process Excellence Network. Retrieved on March 4, 2018 from: https://www.processexcellencenetwork.com/lean-six-sigma-business-performance/articles/key-ingredients-for-quality-culture-development

Lesmeister, F. (2018, March14). How to Create a Culture of Quality Improvement. Boston Consulting Group. (2019). Retrieved on March 4, 2018 from: https://www.bcg.com/en-us/publications/2018/how-to-create-culture-quality-improvement.aspx

Stoop, E. (2017, November 6). 7 habits of a mature quality culture. Beacon Quality Blog. Retrieved on March 4, 2018 from: https://www.beaconquality.com/blog/7-habits-of-a-mature-quality-culture

Chickadel, J. (2017, February 15). The 'speed to market vs. quality' conundrum. Decisivedge.com. Posted on February 15, 2017. Retrieved on March 4, 2018 from: https://www.decisivedge.com/blog/speed-market-vs-quality-conundrum/

Let's go

Geist, S. (2018, May 11). Why a leader says "let's go." *The Globe and Mail.* Retrieved on March 11, 2019 from: https://www.theglobeandmail.com/report-on-business/careers/leadership-lab/why-a-leader-says-lets-go/article15929284/

The team with the most mistakes ... Wins!

How can making mistakes be good for your team or business? Unlocking the key to this principle involves three intertwined constructs.

The first is trust. Not earned trust; *given* trust. Coach understood the need to trust his players. He would recruit the best players, define what was important, coach them, discipline them, stress and practice fundamentals, and challenge them to push their boundaries. He would teach them to understand what needed to be done, help place them in the best possible position to be competitive in and drive them toward making maximum productivity and related results happen. However, once the ball was in play, he wanted his team to execute – with execute—with minimal sideline guidance. He trusted the players—and expected them to trust themselves—to execute the game plan.

The second is risk. Coach was fond of saying, "Those who are afraid to risk failure seldom have to face success." This principle is about moving beyond the real or psychological limitations and obstacles that could sabotage your success.

Third, this principle is about experiential learning. Coach encouraged aggressive play. He wanted players who would look at the scoreboard and want a bigger lead. If players made a mistake, they might catch an earful if they deviated too far from the Coach's desires; however, he used mistakes of "commission" (trying to do something positive) versus "omission" (repeating an unacceptable behavior) as learning opportunities. He did not allow the fear of failure to stop group or individual progress.

Your coaching imperative: Fear not

In Principle 4, we touched upon how critical it is for your team to trust you (i.e., upward trust). In looking at this attribute through a broader lens, trust has multiple directions in a healthy organization.

Instill trust in your team members

Trust is difficult to establish and even more difficult to maintain. It takes time and daily effort to build mutual relationship stock and shared experiences. We are often not sure how much of our "true" self to reveal in a workplace, and trust can quickly vanish with one false move.

You have a stake in having your team trust you, and you must reciprocate.

Extending trust to your team members can be challenging and complex. As leaders, we tend to want to control situations and people, especially since their work reflects upon our

DOI: 10.4324/9781003456902-14

supervision. Micro-managing is an all-too-common example of pulling the leash too tight, as it demonstrates a lack of faith and confidence in your team and generally results in sub-optimal outputs.

With that in mind, let us consider some ways to instill trust in others:

- Hold people accountable—When people do not trust each other and something goes wrong, fingers get pointed. Let people take responsibility from the start for deliverables. Accomplishing goals yields pride and helps set the bar for future and peer efforts.
- Be honest—Sugar-coating a response may seem polite and expedient, but if the message is lost, the intent is at best ambiguous. Visibility and transparency are assets.
- Grant autonomy—If people are to grow and develop, there must be an acceptable degree of independence and empowerment. Provide "distance right" guidance, schedule project "check-ins," and keep the course.
- Start small— Begin by assigning smaller tasks and build from there.
- Share stories—Exchange stories that show empathy and break down barriers between people. Talk about wins and losses. This will foster connections.
- React positively to mistakes—Easier said than done, but to the extent possible, try to be encouraging.
- Encourage others—Show your optimism and belief in them.

Bear with me for an on-court example of this last point ...

When I was a senior in high school, I played basketball on a conference-winning team. I started several games, but was largely first-off the bench. I could handle the ball pretty well and got my minutes when the other team cranked-up their ball pressure. In one particular game against Cranford, the score was tight with seconds remaining, and I was going to the foul line to hopefully give us a hard-fought victory on their court.

Before I stepped to the line, the coach of the other team called "time-out" to give me a little more time to think about the gravity of the situation. When you are 17 and the gym is full of the opposition's heckling fans, there is a lot of gravity!

In that time-out's huddle, my coach gave instruction to all of us, but he started his comments by saying, "After Billy makes these shots ... " With those five words, my coach had instilled an invincible confidence in me that was previously unknown. He trusted me.

When the whistle blew, I calmly and confidently went to the line and knocked down the pair of shots, securing our win. While I remember the shots, I more so recall the uplifting feeling that the coach had provided with his belief in me. What a great feeling that was!

Can a leader trust too much?

There is a school of thought that you should trust others from the start, wholly and completely, until they give you a reason otherwise. While it is great to be optimistic about human nature, do not be naïve.

There are times when affording unlimited trust can backfire. You may have blind spots caused by your own work absorption, inattention to detail, or unconscious biases. These and like circumstances and traits can cause you to overlook or make excuses for someone's shortcomings. You might miss a team member's indications of dishonesty, lack of loyalty, a breach of confidentiality, or heightened self-interests. Trust, but be cognizant of people's motives.

I have been burned by this twice in my career when I extended blind trust, rationalizing away the self-serving and undermining behaviors of subordinates. Keep your eyes open.

Ways team members can develop trust among and between themselves

Mutual trust is critical in an organization for optimal performance—not only up and down but also across. Colleagues must depend on each other for task completion and deliverables. Teams cannot function unless all parts are dependably synched.

Mutual trust develops in teams when there is a high degree of respect for each other, people are treated fairly, and colleagues have shared accountability for results. Trust takes a hit when colleagues take an inordinate amount of time on long lunches, waste productivity on the phone with personal calls, or miss project deadlines.

Establishing and maintaining trust among colleagues has both pragmatic and emotional elements. It is a derivative of three behaviors and attributes, all of which are in your control. First, as a team member, you must earn personal *credibility*. Telling the truth, admitting your limitations, and admitting when things are your fault are ways to demonstrate this competency. Second, you must be accountable and *reliable*. Your colleagues must know that your word is true. If you say it, do it. There should be no disconnect between your words and actions. Explain why you are doing things in a transparent manner. Lastly, be *inclusive* and give others the benefit of the doubt. Mutual trust comes from collaboration. Exchange ideas with others and encourage their input. Listen attentively and respond accordingly.

Build back trust

You lost someone's trust. Your credibility is damaged.

Assuming this is something from which you can reasonably expect to recover and that you have a desire to do so, you can initiate some actions to move the practical and emotional healing along. Clearly, admitting the fault and taking responsibility for it is at the top of the list. Do so with genuine sincerity and regret. Use this as an opportunity for learning, sharing, and raising self-awareness.

Going forward, you will need to make conscious decisions about your behavior and attitude. Being honest, transparent, and authentic are steps in that direction. Other measures toward rebuilding integrity and reputation include keeping your word, making amends to reconcile the past, and intently demonstrating action over words.

Fight fear

Atychiphobia.

You may not recognize the word, but you know its meaning. Atychiphobia is the persistent fear of failing. It can stop you dead in your tracks. You will not make a mistake because you will not do anything. It will hold you back from any possible success.

Do not let this happen to you! There are multiple strategies to become more comfortable with putting yourself "out there."

- Understand what is keeping you from moving ahead. Is it potential embarrassment, rejection, mockery of others, or perhaps avoidance of certain people or situations?

- Learn from your disappointments. What were the key learnings? Have you applied those lessons? What were the benefits that arose? Are you actually better at or more proficient at a skill today—better organized, more careful, or more analytical, because of what happened?
- Instead of looking at the road ahead as a potential for failure, consider it as a challenge. This may help with your outlook, as well as your ability to manage stress. To do this, view the challenge as a project manager might. Bring objectivity to the front of your mind and leave the emotional elements of your hesitation behind.
- Visualize success. What will success look like? Focus on the positive rather than all of the possible pitfalls or psychological obstacles. Maybe the challenge is not as insurmountable as originally thought.
- Pay attention to your feelings. If fear does arise, do not ignore it; face it. Call timeout. Analyze its roots. Take steps to handle stress. Sit quietly and reflect. Manage your breathing and any tightness you may be experiencing. Trigger your body's natural defense mechanisms to bring on calm.
- As your challenge unfolds, and the "to do" list appears overwhelming, reflect on what has been done and the related progress and pride. Get some of the low-hanging fruit tasks done first in order to gain momentum and build confidence. Do not let panic crop up, as it will cloud your judgment.
- Self-esteem matters. Be kind to yourself. Mistakes are not a time to wallow in self-pity. Find a way to grow from the experience. There are upsides to mistakes and rebounding is possible. Your attitude remains most important for the next challenge.

Scar tissue lessons

We all make mistakes. They come in all shapes and sizes. The key is to learn from these challenging times—yours and others—and attempt to prevent a recurrence.

Have fortitude

Thomas Edison received hundreds of patents in his lifetime. Of course, he is most noted for his invention of the incandescent light bulb.

His success did not come overnight. He experimented with thousands of different material combinations before finding the best and most durable filament. Suffice it to say that less patient individuals may have been discouraged; however, Edison was not. His contrarian and ever-optimistic view was that he wanted negative findings: "They are just as valuable to me as positive results. I can never find the thing that does the best job until I find the ones that don't."

Edison knew that failure—or failures—were the precursor to success.

Trust your instincts

Akio Morita was a risk-taker and a global visionary. He left his family business in 1946 in order to start an electronics company (Tokyo Tshushin Kyogu/TTK)—with virtually no experience. He changed the name of the company to "Sony" in 1958 to give it more universal appeal. His products became known for their innovation and ingenuity, such as the world's first pocket radio (1957), all-transistor TV (1960), and home videotape recorder (1968).

He emigrated to the United States in 1963, moving the company's headquarters in the process. He launched the Sony "Walkman" in 1980 with NO market research, as he trusted his instincts based upon his own observations of young people and music. Even though Betamax was a failure to VHS, it helped in making home video a mainstream technology.

Take a chance

Henry Robinson Luce was a 1920 graduate of Yale. He was voted the "most brilliant student" in his class. He enjoyed writing and went on to do so in the newspaper industry. Eventually, he launched his own weekly news magazine, *Time*, to be distributed in March of 1923 at a cover price of 15 cents.

The magazine's first distribution was a disaster, as only 9,000 of the printed 25,000 copies were distributed. Three years later, circulation exceeded 100,000.

Challenge the status quo

A leader should cringe when he or she hears the phrase, "but that's the way we've always done it."

In the 1990s, Louis V. Gerstner, CEO of IBM, had to make unpopular decisions challenging the status quo of the company in order to speed its turnaround. These included disbanding the Management Committee, building a new board with a reduced number of participants, re-engineering the company toward a new customer orientation, thus "breaking up the fiefdoms," and breaking out the service unit of the company. All were tough decisions, which surely the entrenched incumbents, pessimists, or IBM traditionalists did not welcome.

Gerstner recognized that today is the time to prepare for tomorrow. You must constantly adjust your strategy, people, and processes in order to keep up or ideally get ahead of the latest business wave or technological avalanche.

Persevere

In addition to struggling with math in his youth, Albert Einstein was unemployed for two years after college. Oprah Winfrey's Network suffered from poor initial ratings. Mark Cuban was a bartender, a short-order cook, and a carpenter before starting MicroSolutions. Jay Z's second album fell short of his commercial hopes. J.K. Rowling, the author of *Harry Potter*, was at one time an unemployed single mother who considered herself a failure. The first company that Bill Gates and Paul Allen formed, Traf-O-Data, closed with a loss.

Obviously, there are countless examples on all scales. The key message is simple: when one door closes, stay positive and knock on another.

Be relentless

Michael Jordan was told that he was not tall enough to play high school basketball. When cut from the team, it deeply imprinted his life. He felt ashamed, snubbed, and embarrassed. Fortunately for Tar Heel fans, his wise mother told him that he should focus his efforts on proving the coach wrong. He left his disappointment behind and concentrated on improving his level of play. He refused to give up and used what another viewed to be his shortcoming as the basis of his unbridled motivation. The seeds for his future stardom in the National Basketball Association were sown.

Fight back

In 1927, Walt Disney created the animated character Oswald the Lucky Rabbit, which helped turn his struggling studio toward profitability, allowing him to expand his operations and staff. In the spring of the next year, Disney traveled to New York to meet with his producer, Charles Mintz. Disney thought they were going to discuss an increase to his budget. Instead, Mintz informed Disney that his budget was to be slashed and that Mintz was starting his own firm having hired many of Disney's animators behind his back. To add insult to injury, Mintz told Disney that the copyright for Oswald the Lucky Rabbit also belonged to him.

Disney was determined not to give up. On his return train trip, he got the idea for a new character, Mickey Mouse, With his new creation, the origins of what would one day be a "Kingdom" were born.

Your best guess may or may not be good enough

To slightly modify a quote from hockey great Wayne Gretzky, "Wouldn't it be great to always know where the puck is going?" Unfortunately, such a crystal ball does not exist. No one knows what lies ahead in the business world or elsewhere. If this were the case, Excite would have bought Google, Daimler-Benz would not have merged with Chrysler, and Blockbuster would have bought Netflix.

When we consider the future of our business, we are making a calculated guess about market trends, technological advances, supply and demand curves, economic factors, trade wars, and the like. Illustrative of this point, prior to the pandemic, we were starting to see consumer attitudes shift about material goods and sustainability. Renting goods and services for real-time and/or one-time use was becoming more attractive. Neighbors were sharing lawn mowers, ladders, and other garage equipment. Automobile makers were tailoring ownership and rental programs around consumer needs, and Uber (and others) had made it easier to forget about car ownership altogether. Vacation homes and boats were nice, but why take on full-time ownership risk and worry when you can share, rent, or swap with others?

The pandemic rocked some of these trends, highlighting that predictive analytics has its limitations.

When you are making decisions today that involve a strategic shift and/or significant risk, throw a wide net for information and gather and listen to the relevant voices of others. Information is power and you want the most of it in these key decision situations.

Encourage "appropriate" risk-taking

In most organizational circles, the thought of change and its related processes such as re-engineering, "rightsizing," and organizational redesign is greeted with a sigh, cynicism, or reluctance. We are generally not prone to embrace variance outside what we have come to know as expected or customary.

Every organization has a different threshold of tolerance for undertaking change and risk-taking. It is best to identify such tolerance, i.e., granting "permission" to fail, within the context of the organization's strategy and values, and to communicate it *ahead* of time.

Allow people to fall (not fail)

Bill Walton once noted that Coach "was willing to let us fail, to teach us a lesson."

This is not an easy thing for a coach or manager to do. Perhaps some topical reframing might help.

In *Leaders Eat Last*, Simon Sinek makes the very compelling case that the word "failure," with all of its negative connotations, is a label worthy of closer examination. After all, failure generally means that it is over. It is dead-end; a stop sign. Pull the plug. The fat lady is singing. Someone has an "F" on their forehead.

Failure can mean some or all of these things. Depending upon its magnitude, it may put your career on life support. The trick is not to allow it to become fatal.

To this end, Sinek, in line with the spirit of Thomas Edison, uses the term "falling" to describe those less-than-career-ending mistakes. Falling is an iterative step. It is an opportunity for shared and transformative learning. It allows you to say, "Good try, now let's try it again." It implies getting up, brushing off, and moving ahead. Falling may even turn out to be the impetus to propel you to greater heights, as there is an education to be had here.

Falling is far more preferred and digestible compared to failing. It might even be considered a badge of honor for those who rebound onto bigger and better.

Hold hands

In the aftermath of a mistake, an individual might experience a wide range of reactionary emotions. These include numbness, denial, irritability, or resistance. Getting over a mistake can take time.

As boss, you should remain cognizant of how individuals internally process and react to adversity, recognizing there are limits to what can be absorbed. Extending empathy will individually and collectively support the transformation and minimize any initial drop in productivity. In the long run, it is hoped that the situation allows for the mistake to be forgotten, less its learnings, such that all may move ahead.

Cut the cord quickly when you have to

After careful consideration and trial, he or she may not be the right hire. The project may be the wrong investment. A competitor is eating your lunch. Promises made simply cannot be kept.

When the signs are becoming more frequent and obvious that your hoped-for success is slipping away, cut the cord and move on. Do so quickly. The bleeding must be stopped.

A miscue by Coach

Funny thing about spoken words. Once "out there," they cannot be taken back. Coach once learned this lesson the hard way.

During the 1967–68 season, UCLA traveled to the Astrodome to play the Houston Cougars. Referred to as the "Game of the Century" due to its elite pairing of top teams, the game was also the first nationally televised regular season match-up. Houston upset the Bruins, 71–69, behind 39 points from Elvin Hayes.

As the game unfolded, Coach Wooden benched Edgar Lacy after 11 minutes of disappointing play. Coach never put him back in and was critical of Lacy to the media after the game. Damage done, three days after Wooden's poorly directed comments, Lacy quit the team.

That was the last time Wooden ever was critical of a player in a public forum.

My bad!

Early in my career, I worked as a shipping manager for a large chemical company. I was responsible for the scheduling of all in-and-outbound bulk freight, truck and rail.

One night, I mistakenly instructed that tank car containing raw material "A" be placed in an unloading spot meant for raw material "B." Now in most cases, there are a series of safeguards and quality checks—even back then—to ensure that all is in good order. Such should have been the case here; however, the mistake was only caught after the unloading had begun. This led to cross-product contamination and a total plant shutdown for system sterilization.

I got the call in the wee hours. As you might suspect, there was no sleep thereafter. I thought this was curtains for me.

Throughout the next morning, my boss was in closed door meetings. Not a good sign. After what seemed an eternity, he called me into his office before lunch. I nervously sat down, expecting the worst. No excuses. I put the domino in place for this mess. Yet, much to my surprise, he did not fire me. My boss, Sam, had met with the plant manager. They had discussed discipline as an option; however, they decided to use this as an investment in my learning.

To this day, I am grateful for their consideration. Lesson learned and I try to do the same for others.

How does this compare to conventional wisdom?

Be wary in setting a tone or example whereby mistakes equal failure or discipline. Public floggings may have dramatic employee relations and business ramifications.

Endnotes for Principle 8: The team with the most mistakes ... Wins!

Instill trust

Kambouris, A. (Date unknown). Your team will succeed only if they trust each other. *Entrepreneur.com.* Retrieved on December 6, 2018, from: https://www.entrepreneur.com/article/311725

Can a leader trust too much?

Gourguechon, P. (2018, February 20). Why inspiring trust and trusting others are essential leadership capacities (within bounds). *Forbes.com.* Retrieved on December 6, 2018, from: https://www.forbes.com/sites/prudygourguechon/2018/02/20/why-inspiring-trust-and-trusting-others-are-essential-leadership-capacities-within-bounds/#7229259c5359

Ways team members can develop trust

Price, H. (Date unknown). 12 practical ways to build trust at work. www.jostle.me. Retrieved on December 6, 2018, from: https://blog.jostle.me/blog/ways-to-build-trust-at-work

Fight fear

"Atychiphobia." (2014, October 30). Retrieved on December 20, 2018, from: https://www.healthline.com/health/atychiphobia

Davis, T. (Date unknown). Three ways to overcome fear of failure at work. *Berkeley.edu.* Retrieved on December 4, 2018, from: https://greatergood.berkeley.edu/article/item/three_ways_to_overcome_fear_of_failure_at_work

Learn from mistakes by keeping track of your most important decisions. (Date unknown). Decision innovation. Retrieved on September 24, 2020, from: https://www.decision-making-solutions.com/learning-from-mistakes.html

Loder, V. (2014, October 30). How to conquer the fear of failure—5 proven strategies. *Forbes.com.* Retrieved on December 4, 2018, from: https://www.forbes.com/sites/vanessaloder/2014/10/30/how-to-move-beyond-the-fear-of-failure-5-proven-strategies/#7895f24f1b78

Have fortitude

DiIonno, M. (2018, August 12). My top seven stories. *The Start Ledger,* p. A16.

Trust your instincts

Bennis, W.G., Brown, T., Champy, J., Crainer, S., Davis, S., Edwards, H., Goleman, D., Gottlieb, A., Heller, R., Larreche, J.C., Leyden, P., Meyer, C., Norton, B., & Rayport, J. (Advisory Board), (2002). *Business: The ultimate resource.* Cambridge, Massachusetts: Perseus Publishing, pp. 1120–1121.

Take a chance

Bennis, W.G., Brown, T., Champy, J., Crainer, S., Davis, S., Edwards, H., Goleman, D., Gottlieb, A., Heller, R., Larreche, J.C., Leyden, P., Meyer, C., Norton, B., & Rayport, J. (Advisory Board), (2002). *Business: The ultimate resource.* Cambridge, Massachusetts: Perseus Publishing, pp. 1110–1111.

Challenge the status quo

Gerstner, L.V. (2002). *Who says elephants can't dance?* New York: HarperCollins Publishers, Inc., p. 74, 75, 86, 131.

Persevere

Taube, A. (2014, September 9). What 11 extremely successful people learned from failure. *Businessinsider.com.* Retrieved on December 3, 2018, from: https://www.businessinsider.com/what-successful-people-learned-from-failure-2014-9#oprah-winfrey-learned-that-failure-is-only-an-illusion-after-her-cable-network-started-off-poorly-1

Be relentless

Steinberg, S. (2015, January 5). 5 spectacular examples of turning failure into success. Huffingtonpost.com. Retrieved on December 3, 2018. https://www.huffingtonpost.com/scott-steinberg/5-spectacular-examples-of_b_6477532.html

Fight back

Naseer, T. (Date unknown). What one successful leader learned about optimism from failure. Retrieved on October 3, 2018, from: https://www.tanveernaseer.com/power-of-optimism-in-leadership/

Your best guess may or may not be good enough

Roesler, P. (2015, April 20). 8 of the biggest mistakes in history. *Inc.com.* Retrieved on December 4, 2018, from: https://www.inc.com/peter-roesler/8-of-the-biggest-business-mistakes-in-history.html

Encourage appropriate risk-taking

Walton, B. (2000, March 2). Andy Hill notes. Private conversation.
Sinek, S. (2014). *Leaders eat last.* New York: Penguin Random House, p. 297.

A miscue by Coach

"John Wooden," Wikipedia. (Date unknown). Retrieved on December 21, 2018, from: https://en.wikipedia.org/wiki/John_Wooden
"Edgar Lacy," Wikipedia. (Date unknown). Retrieved on December 21. 2108, from: https://en.wikipedia.org/wiki/Edgar_Lacy

Rules are made to be followed, not broken

At the start of his 40-year career, Coach had several rules, but ended up with a few "suggestions."

Why?

As a high school coach, he threw two players off the team because they had attended a school dance and violated curfew (and lied about it). Coach also dismissed a player for smoking when it was not allowed. Later, Wooden realized these actions were too harsh for both the team and the young men involved, as those individuals subsequently lost their way.

Coach learned from these experiences. He ultimately recognized that a few substantive suggestions for behavior were far more effective than a litany of regimented rules.

In this vein, Coach relied upon his Midwestern values of punctuality, courtesy and mutual respect, no profanity, never speaking ill of a teammate, and proper grooming and dress—including keeping shirts tucked in during practice. These were non-negotiable. He also maintained that his players must accept responsibility for their actions and that grades and class attendances were not to slip. On the road, whether interacting with locker room staff or hotel personnel, players were reminded that they should act with appropriate decorum and dignity. Housekeeping also mattered. After all, they were representatives of the University of California at Los Angeles, and their behavior reflected upon the institution, as well as themselves and their coach.

As occasional discipline matters arose in later years, Coach came to understand that every situation should be reviewed for its own circumstance and merit. Generally, this meant private handling behind closed doors, although there were circumstances when disciplining a player in public was a needed message for all.

Your coaching imperative: Bring values to life

Be it General Motors, UPS, your local hardware store, or a boutique law firm, all organizations have values. The challenge is to find the "right" ones for your organization and team. Fortunately, there are ways to navigate this course. (Hint: A collaborative approach helps!)

Defining values

Dictionaries tell us that values—as a principle or ideal—are intrinsically desirable and of high personal use and importance. They are deeply rooted, long-lasting, and influence our behavior and attitudes. Values tell us how to behave when no one is looking.

DOI: 10.4324/9781003456902-15

In the corporate world, values are found as statements, credos, pledges, propositions, platforms, commitments, and pursuits. They are the underpinning for shared goals and beliefs. They provide purpose and direction. They identify the core operating principles by which the company conducts its business, supporting the vision and decision-making processes within the organization.

Why values matter

Individually, values define who we are and help guide and determine how we feel, think, and behave. They are critical to our core being as a person. They impact our religious outlook, our leadership style, our work ethic, and the way we process information (understand, memorize, evaluate). They help us determine right from wrong. They are personal.

According to Susan David, Psychologist at the Harvard Medical School and author of the best seller, *Emotional Agility,* "Having a clear understanding of your values is critical to finding change and fulfillment." She outlines seven characteristics of personal values:

1 They are freely chosen
2 They are on-going, not fixed
3 They guide, not restrain you
4 They are active and evolve over time
5 They foster self-acceptance
6 They bring freedom from social comparison
7 They bring you closer to the person you want to be

Organizational values are all encompassing

Organizationally, shared values define the norms of expected behavior, ways to interact, collective priorities, and decision-making processes. Values represent absolute standards of group expectations and behavior. They ultimately determine unwritten "rules" of interaction with others, as well as organization/governing structures and philosophies.

Organizational values are not intended to be sterile words behind decorative frames hanging in conference rooms. They intended to actively guide behavior and provide all organizational participants with a framework for decision-making. Thus, values should be the foundation and reference for all policy development, hiring, employment practices, corporate governance, and codes of conduct. They are core and purposeful to your organization. They should further the mission of your enterprise and be the bedrock of your culture.

Values enhance engagement

A global study by Right Management and Globoforce's Workforce Mood Tracker, cited by Dora Wang, indicated that personal commitment to an employer's core values is the top driver of employee engagement. The study also found that 88% of those surveyed who did know their organization's values reported being engaged and that 65% of workers who could name their organization's values said they had a strong grasp on company objectives. Further, research also indicates that values-driven companies achieve better brand recognition and business performance.

Creating values

Create your organizational values—macro level

Organizational, departmental, and team values should be created and aligned with a collective and inclusive dialog, as they will serve as the cultural underpinning for the entire organization. Thus, before embarking down this path, it makes sense to have a plan in mind.

• Determine what your organization does or for what it stands. List desired results and accountabilities.
• Perform research to determine and explore common insights, characteristics, and attributes of your team through individual interviews.
• Examine your findings from the above and synthesize common (shared) findings. You will be left with an extensive draft of possible values.
• Refine your findings by narrowing down the list of possible values using a participatory approach. Get your team involved. Values can distinguish your organization, perhaps leading to strategic and competitive advantage.
• Communicate your findings.

Recognize that leaders must "own" their organizational values. This is not an initiative to be delegated.

As a side note, given their all-encompassing impact, identifying values must be approached as a serious exercise. Case in point, I was once part of an executive committee discussion about creating our values scheme. Several characteristics were relatively easy to identify and define; however, there was a prolonged debate over the topic of "risk-taking." Specifically, we were trying to determine the degree to which our team members should take risk in the organization. After the better part of a couple hours, we identified the value as "prudent risk-taking" and later added the correlating description.

Yes, you read that right. We spent two hours on an adjective. Words matter!

Identify the specific behaviors that support your values

There is a fair amount of redundancy with the values listings and statements of companies within the *Fortune* 500. After all, what organization could possibly be against such noble aspirations as "trust," "community," "respect," and "integrity?" The separating factor among them is not the verbiage but the correlating actions. This begs the question of how best to *actively demonstrate* these intangible and idealistic qualities in the workplace.

An excellent early example of linking these seemingly intangible words to intentional action was found at the consulting firm Booz Allen (now Booz Allen Hamilton). Twenty years ago, they were one of the first companies to link values with behavioral descriptors. By illustration, the value of "integrity" was defined as:

Keeping commitments and promises; demonstrating courage to present and hear the truth in an appropriate manner; acting in the best interests of the client, the firm, and the team; displaying and reinforcing the highest ethical standards; and accurately representing (one's) own competencies.

The value of "professionalism" was defined as:

> Seeking out and listening to honest feedback from others; giving candid and constructive feedback to others; identifying and taking opportunities for maintaining or increasing skills; taking future organizational needs into account in planning own development; sharing own expertise and experience; and actively supporting, mentoring and coaching others.

If a more current example is preferred, an excellent sample can be found online with Procter & Gamble, where their integrated purpose, values, and principles, along with their supporting behaviors, are cited.

These descriptions allow employees to translate and readily understand how to bring values to life.

Your team can have values too—micro level

Much like your company's vision statement, you can also have a correlating set of values for your team—giving them more meaning, ownership, and individual connectivity. For example, if you work in a customer service or client-facing department, you might consider a model with a values/behavior proposition like this:

- We will be role models for the organization with our words, attitudes, and behaviors.
- We will add value through the lens of the business and our colleagues.
- We will respect one another as individuals and value our differences.
- We will operate to the highest standard of ethics.
- We will foster an environment of dignity and trust.
- We will embrace and demonstrate a "How can I help you?" approach.
- We will conduct our business politely and in a professional manner—with a "can do" attitude.
- We will proactively meet our commitments and act with a sense of urgency.
- We will act as a team—helping each other and crossing boundaries.
- We will strive for innovation and continuous improvement in all that we do.

Over the years, I have used a customized version of the above as a starting point for discussion with my HR teams. Our over-arching mantra has always been "easy to do business with."

Living your values

Whenever and wherever appropriate, you should seize every opportunity to publicize and advance your organization's values. This means developing and implementing programs to recognize and reinforce the desired behaviors.

Incorporate values into your performance management system

Values *and their correlating behaviors* should be a part of each employee's performance plan. You may also wish to consider related reward systems to keep this topic in front of people.

Let values guide your decision-making

Your employee manual or policy guides can only cover so much.

A high-profile public example of values framing organizational decision-making remains Johnson & Johnson's response to the cyanide poisoning of their product in 1982. J&J's handling of this matter is still considered to be the textbook recipe for values-driven crisis response. In this incident, seven people died from taking tampered Extra Strength Tylenol capsules in the Chicago area. The company immediately responded by recalling the product, running television commercials to spawn public awareness of the problem, setting up information hotlines, educating the medical community about recourse, and offering a reward for information leading to the arrest of the perpetrator.

The product recalls and related efforts to repackage and relaunch cost the company millions.

In later discussing the Tylenol tragedy, James E. Burke, then-Chairman and CEO of J&J, pointed to the company's embrace and guidance of its Credo—the company's statement of its values, responsibilities, and operating principles. He noted, "The guidance of our Credo (as it pertained to social responsibility) played the single most important role in our decision-making."

Teach your team

Companies use a variety of ways to continually communicate their values and to train their teams on their applicability and benefits. One such method involves a values workshop.

You may wish to consider getting help for such a forum—internally or externally, but if resources are not available and time is scarce, you can always create your own and tailor it to your needs. Be it in a small or large group setting, some fundamental exercises or thought-provoking discussion points can be planned around these types of questions:

- How do our values complement our business objectives?
- What core values do you bring to work and are they aligned with our team?
- What are the challenges of living our values?
- How do we spark enhanced knowledge, passion, and energy around our values?
- How do values influence our decision-making processes?
- If we had to add or delete a value, what might that be? Why?
- Are we passionately committed to our values? Why or why not?

You can also review available literature that challenges the team to consider the importance of compliance, diversity, or regulatory concerns.

Values come at a cost

If you believe that people are your most valued asset and deserve a certain type of treatment, how will you react when the bottom line becomes tight? Will layoffs ensue or can your company handle a few off-quarters in order to keep the team whole? Will you tolerate a "no questions asked" return policy from your customers at the risk of misrepresentation? Would you terminate a star employee who, after several warnings, continues to treat coworkers poorly? If you receive a tip that inventory is being smuggled out of your warehouse on the shift on a certain supervisor, how will you respond?

These are the types of decisions that may differentiate you and your organization.

Hold people accountable

No one enjoys discussions in the HR office involving the disciplinary options associated with inappropriate employee behaviors. Whether we are talking about questionable entertainment expenses, stretched lunch times, excessive vacation allowances, or inordinate Internet use, you must hold people accountable for their actions.

Most of the time, there will be a policy to assist or a precedent to compare; however, the employee manual only covers so much. You and your organization will be steered right by letting values be your guide.

Death, taxes, and ...

When you were recruiting candidates, you posed questions about character and how an individual might respond to certain hypothetical situations. You can now remove the word "hypothetical." Reality is here.

It is my experience that when people stray from their values, they can become isolated, feel victimized, possessed by self-doubt or insecurity, or live in fear of disappointment or failure. They may see chaos or threats around them and react poorly. Their heightened emotions and modified perspective may drive poor behavioral choices.

Like death and taxes, *your test of organizational values is coming.* It is only a matter of time.

- *Two coworkers squabbled over everything (window blind and thermostat adjustments, their respective wardrobe selections, work processes, who took more time at lunch, etc.). Any and all subjects were fair game for divisive debate and ridicule. They complained about each other to anyone within earshot. Did I mention that these two ladies sat next to each other?*

  One Monday, when all of the office staff came to work, they noticed an oversized Boston Bruins flag hanging from the ceiling. Coincidentally, the flag provided border between the two ladies.
- *In the course of having a reduction-in-force discussion, the separating employee indicated that he had been the subject of a hostile work environment by his supervisor and coworkers.*

  Claims like this usually do not have merit, as people try to deflect attention or deny blame for what is transpiring. However, in this case, the employee sounded quite credible, producing his own list of who did what and when. I awkwardly paused the RIF exercise, and an investigation was promptly started. It concluded that the employee's allegations were true. The harassing behavior and its related attitudes had become the norm in this individual's department. So "normal" in fact that no one thought to report it.
- *An anonymous report was received by our compliance officer that indicated that we had a prevalent drug problem in one of our facilities. The complaint mentioned a specific segment of the site's population. As a corporate management team, we had several options to investigate this claim, including having all or a select few take a drug screen. We opted to cast a wide net. The findings left us all dumbfounded.*

When it comes to values, your decision-making around how to handle these types of situations takes on an added public magnification. Therefore, when the fan does get hit, remember that you are not an island. Seek help. Your HR partner is an ally, as are other managers (assuming discretion).

If you must let someone go

The role of a boss is sometimes akin to that of a school principal, especially in disciplinary matters. Occasionally, you need to simply warn someone about their behavior and that is the end of it. Other times, matters become more serious and warrant termination.

When it comes to firing people for cause, I lose little sleep. That is not to say these discussions are easy; they are not. These conversations are carefully scripted and intended not to last more than five to ten minutes. However, I have always taken the view that people fire themselves. Egregious infractions warranting termination from your code of conduct or a values infraction come in all shapes and sizes and, after fair and objective assessment, cannot be tolerated. People make choices. The choices have consequences.

Be prepared for these discussions. An adverse reaction is always possible. Accordingly, have your talking points and information package ready, and have another member of management either in the office or nearby. Alert security of the pending action and take all appropriate precautions. *(Note: Assume, as you should with all sensitive employee relations matters, your comments are being recorded.)*

Remember, the impacted individual has their own version of reality. You may bump into denial, anger, finger-pointing, tears, and then some. They are likely only to hear and retain your first few words after you say "separation." Treat them with respect, and unless it is a grievous infraction, handle these matters with compassion and appropriate discretion.

In the best case, all goes well, and the individual takes counsel and moves on.

I have, unfortunately, led the termination discussions of many. Two interactions stand out.

Early in my career, I had to fire someone who was a Vietnam War veteran—an explosives specialist. He also had a mercurial personality. To say I was anxious would be an understatement. I did not know what to expect and had no experience to fall upon. I took all possible precautions. We had notified the local police ahead of time, had other supervision near my office at the time of the discussion, and I (already) had an emergency button linked to our receptionist under my desk. I led the conversation in my office with his manager present, quickly running through my script points.

Thankfully, the discussion went smoothly and he professionally separated from us. However, I did park my car elsewhere for many of the following weeks.

In another dismissal. I was letting go an IT professional for cause. He took the news in stride. At the time of our Friday morning meeting, I collected all of his company property or, at least what I thought was all of his company property.

Sometime early on Saturday, when our office was closed, he returned wearing a trench coat and hat. He gained entry by using an undisclosed access card that he had kept and proceeded to sabotage some of our IT systems. Fortunately, he left before too much damage was done. We were later able to identify him, despite his "disguise," through our video surveillance tapes. It got messy, and charges were pressed.

Stay beyond reproach

The road of corporate malfeasance is littered with recent scandals and those from days gone-by. Shameful headlines concerning Wells Fargo (mismanagement of client accounts),

BP (Deepwater Horizon), VW (false emissions reporting), Theranos (fraud), Lehman Brothers (hiding liabilities), and a long list of others can all be traced to individuals, namely, executives, behaving contrary to organizational values. Viewed then and now with public contempt, Enron's unforeseen collapse was the "poster child" of behavior-gone-awry in corporate America, when their leadership arrogantly failed to practice their stated values of respect, integrity, communications, and excellence. The executives were rightfully criticized and condemned for sending the company and its thousands of jobs to an unexpected graveyard. The correlating press coverage they received was not complimentary.

Organizational values and their associated behaviors apply to *all* parties. As a leader, the temptations of your position's power and authority are many; however, you must avoid even the appearance of any lack of congruity between your behavior and your organizational standards. You must set the tone at the top. All eyes are watching.

In a subsidiary company where I had HR oversight, there were whispers of unethical behavior by the CEO. We quietly proceeded with an investigation and determined, among other findings, that he had arranged for all of his employees' frequent flyer miles to be credited to himself. He also had the company make large political donations that influenced a family member's public standing. In addition, he had the company sponsor his son's baseball team in a tournament ... in the distant Caribbean. It was also found that several employees knew of these transgressions but were reluctant to raise them, fearing retaliation.

You must wonder why someone in his position would risk career and reputational carnage over such relatively inconsequential matters. Yet, it happens.

What if my personal values and organizational values don't match?

Perhaps management turned a blind eye to something, someone failed to keep a key commitment to you or your team, or the gap between "talk" and "walk" is too wide. You feel stifled and attempts to remedy have fallen short or are way above your pay grade. What do you do?

In my career, I have been involved in addressing multiple situations of ethical lapses. Rarely does it hit close to home, but it does happen. What do you do when it involves your boss?

I once worked for a CEO who seemed to be spending 24/7 time and company money with one particular employee. (Generally speaking, office romances, when reported, can be organizationally managed; misallocating company funds cannot.) As you might imagine, the rumor mill was rampant with buzz, and none of it was flattering. The CEO was obviously in a highly visible role, and he was doing little to conceal his attentions. His reputation was at risk, and his personal and professional credibility were quickly fading. It had reached the point where he was teetering on losing his team.

I certainly did not welcome hearing this news. I had been with the company only a few months, and these were rumors about the man that hired me. This was my dream job, and I certainly did not want to risk my paycheck by putting this topic into play.

But I did. Someone had to act. When you are the head of HR, that's what you do, even if it means lots of sleepless nights and weight loss. Lots.

In two private meeting, I challenged my boss about this topic. I was gentle with my wording the first time; more confrontational the second. His denials and defensiveness were on full display, but the evidence was indisputable. Our relationship spiraled. Ultimately, the board of directors became involved, and a formal probe was launched. This did not end well for the CEO. Months later, it did not end well for me.

I am not sure if I handled this the right way. I do know that I felt compelled to act. First, as noted, because of my position. Second, and of more importance, I felt a matter of personal responsibility to address what appeared to be the willful misconduct that contrasted with the organization's values in which I and other C-suite members believed.

There is no easy answer here. Dealing with values dissonance is a personal choice. In fact, it has been postulated that matching your belief system with your employer's is more important than matching your skill set. Said differently, when values do not agree, it is time for an exit strategy.

How does this compare to conventional wisdom?

Rules don't apply to organizational "superstars." Yet, nothing could be further from the truth.

Endnotes for Principle 9: Rules are made to be followed, not broken

Defining values

Kuczmarski, S.S., & Kuczmarski, T.D. (1995). Values-*based leadership: Rebuilding employee commitment, performance & productivity*. Englewood Cliffs, New Jersey: Prentice Hall, Inc., p. 25.

Blanchard, K., & O'Connor, M. (1997). *Managing by values*. San Francisco, California: Berrett-Koehler Publishers, Inc., p. 20.

Nichol. J. (Date unknown). A guide to defining your company values. CultureIQ.com. Retrieved on July 20, 2018, from: https://cultureiq.com/defining-company-values/

The origin of values

Kuczmarski, S.S., & Kuczmarski, T.D. (1995). *Values-based leadership: Rebuilding employee commitment, performance & productivity*. Englewood Cliffs, New Jersey: Prentice Hall, Inc., pp. 43–44.

Wooden, J.R. (2002, December 18). Private conversation.

Why values matter

David, S. (2021, February 6). "7 characteristics of personal values." LinkedIn post. Retrieved on February 6, 2021, from: https://www.linkedin.com/in/susanadavidphd/detail/recent-activity/shares/

Organizational values are all-encompassing

Satell, G. (2015, November 27). How to define your organization's values. *Forbes.com*. Retrieved on July 20, 2018, from: https://www.forbes.com/sites/gregsatell/2015/11/27/how-to-define-your-organizations-values/#78073db44054

5 exercises to help define your company's core values. (2013). Convercent: Ethics through insight. Convercent.com. Denver, Colorado. Retrieved on July 20, 2018, from: http://www.convercent.com/resource/convercent-ebook-5-exercises-to-help-define-your-companys-core-values.pdf

Values enhance engagement

Wang, D. (2016, October 20). 3 proven methods for bringing company values to life. Tinypulse. Retrieved on July 20, 2018, from: https://www.tinypulse.com/blog/methods-bringing-company-values-to-life

De Pape, C. (2017, June 15). Defining your company's core values: The complete guide (with templates). Recruiting Social. Retrieved on July 20, 2018, from: https://recruitingsocial.com/2017/06/core-values-guide/

Create your organizational values—macro level

De Pape, C. (2017, June 15). Defining your company's core values: The complete guide (with templates). Recruiting Social. Retrieved on July 20, 2018, from: https://recruitingsocial.com/2017/06/core-values-guide/

Lencioni, P.M. (July 2002). Make your values mean something. *Harvard Business Review*. HBR.org, Retrieved on July 20, 2018, from: https://hbr.org/2002/07/make-your-values-mean-something (strategic and competitive advantage)

Identify the specific behaviors that support your values

Seashore, C. (2003, April 2). Private conversation.

Procter & Gamble values. Retrieved on July 25, 2108, from: https://us.pg.com/who-we-are/our-approach/purpose-values-principles

Let values guide your decision-making

Greenberg, J., & Baron, R. (1995). *Behavior in organization* (Third edition). Englewood Cliffs, New Jersey: Prentice-Hall, Inc., pp. 546–547.

Leavitt, H.J., & Lipman-Blumen, J. (1995, July-August). Hot groups. *Harvard Business Review*, pp. 109–116.

Teach your team

Wang, D. (2016, October 20). 3 proven methods for bringing company values to life. Tinypulse. Retrieved on July 20, 2018, from: https://www.tinypulse.com/blog/methods-bringing-company-values-to-life

Values do not have an expiration date

Llopis, G. (2017, August26). Corporate values and mission statements are stifling innovation. Forbes.com. Retrieved on July 20, 2018, from: https://www.forbes.com/sites/glennllopis/2017/08/26/corporate-values-and-mission-statements-are-stifling-innovation/#38a3f39a34d8

Winicour, S. (Date unknown). Defining core values: How to create a successful company culture. Gibraltar Business Capital, SmartCEO.co. Retrieved on July 20, 2018, from: http://smartceo.com/gibraltar-defining-values-create-successful-company-culture/

Values come at a cost

Satell, G. (2015, November 27). How to define your organization's values. *Forbes.com*. Retrieved on July 20, 2018, from: https://www.forbes.com/sites/gregsatell/2015/11/27/how-to-define-your-organizations-values/#78073db44054

Hold people accountable

Samuel, M. (2000). *The accountability revolution: Achieve breakthrough results in half the time*. Printed in the United States of America: Impaq Publishing, p. 23.

Stay beyond reproach

Lencioni, P.M. (2002, July). Make your values mean something. *Harvard Business Review*, HBR.org, Retrieved on July 20, 2018, from: https://hbr.org/2002/07/make-your-values-mean-something

Hesselbein, F., Goldsmith, M., & Beckhard, R. (Eds.). (1996). *The leader of the future: New visions, strategies, and practices for the next era*. San Francisco, California: Jossey-Bass Publishers, pp. 266–267.

What if my personal values and organizational values don't match?

Smye, M. (1998). *Is it too late to run away and join the circus? A guide for your second life*. New York: Macmillan Publishing, p. 73.

Organizing and planning

The need for direction and focus

Coach was a firm believer in and practitioner of planning, *thorough planning*—and to say that he was almost "obsessive" in this regard is not a stretch of the truth. For this was a man who wasted no effort, and he was not about to waste any time—especially as it pertained to matters outside of his direct control.

Coach exemplified this philosophy through the following principles:

10 Keep it simple
11 Concentrate on your team, not the opposition
12 Adjust to your players—Don't expect them to adjust to you
13 Failing to prepare is preparing to fail
14 Practice doesn't make perfect; only perfect practice makes perfect

DOI: 10.4324/9781003456902-16

Keep it simple

Anyone who coached against a Wooden-led team knew what to expect. UCLA's plays were few in number and simple in design. Yet, despite this familiarity and routine with the opposition, UCLA's victories continued.

Coach knew what worked and what did not. He preferred to focus on doing a few things right, if not to perfection. He rarely changed from his man-to-man defensive scheme. He had one out-of-bounds play and his teams ran a simple high-post offense with multiple free-lance options for 34 of the 40 years he coached.

Coach instilled his system with crisp, clear, and simple communications. His players knew and understood the team's priorities, their respective roles, and their specific ac-countabilities. He repeated his mantra with intention, not randomness. His words were calculated and economical.

Your coaching imperative: Communicate, communicate, communicate

This principle touches many management practices; however, its core is communication.

As a leader, it is a very real and significant challenge to take what is often complex, incomplete, ambiguous, and imprecise information, interpret it, synthesize it, and break it into bite-size communication pieces that are easy to understand, relatable, and pave the way for accomplishment. Yet you are called upon to do this with *every* interaction, in real-time, in a way that provides appropriate simplicity underscored with appropriate accuracy.

Some communications refreshers

Communication is the process of creating a common meaning between two or more people.

Know what you are communicating

Whether information is fact, fiction, or opinion, be clear. You wish to convey the message in a way that minimizes the probability of distortion. Fewer words are better than more.

Know why you are communicating

Your message may be intended to inform, direct, influence, urge, or outline action, rec-ommend or take a decision, seek guidance, or instruct. Be clear in communicating your targeted outcome.

DOI: 10.4324/9781003456902-17

Know to whom you are communicating

- Who is your intended audience?
- Who else needs to know?
- Should you inform anyone else as a courtesy?
- Will anyone feel slighted if not included?

Know thy stuff (and thy sources)

One of the questions often posed to first-year Ph.D. students is, "How do you know what you know?" This inquiry will follow them throughout and beyond their advanced academic journey. Your information sources and references must also be reliable and valid (and cited). If they are the basis for your opinions and recommendations, they must pass scrutiny. Your credibility will be suspect otherwise.

Select the right channel

The medium of the message can affect accuracy and efficacy; therefore, choose the appropriate channel—e-mail, newsletters, message boards, bulletins, phone, text, managing-by-wandering-around, senior management "road shows," "fireside chats," lunches, formal staff meetings, social media, public relations, snail mail, employee/management question and answer forums, suggestion boxes, videoconferencing, webinars, posters, payroll stuffers, Zoom, Microsoft Teams, Skype, FaceTime, town halls, and more.

Have an intended outcome

According to Tubbs and Moss, communication is most effective when "… the stimulus, as it was initiated and intended by the sender, corresponds closely with the stimulus as it is perceived and responded to by the receiver." Worded differently, successful communication occurs when the "message sent equals the message received." Much easier said than done.

Communication challenges

Even the most skilled communicator needs to be aware that barriers, tangible and intangible, may cause messages to distort or entirely miss their mark.

- People absorb and interpret information differently. Factors such as the message's pace, complexity, and tempo may interfere with messaging effectiveness.
- Behavioral norms within the organization may dictate *who is allowed to interact with whom*. For example, "top-down" may be the only direction for communication. Senior managers might not engage with those on lower organizational rungs or might dismiss their input. Worse yet, lower-tiered employees might fear speaking-up. Also, these norms may restrict *the ways people communicate or interact*—where, for how long, its formality, and how the interaction may commence and come to an end.
- The physical layout of your workspace can have negative communication aspects. Lack of privacy, noise, and distractions are sources of interference.

- Office politics may impact communication. While we would like to think otherwise, selfish interests do exist. People do use or withhold information for their own career advancement.
- Our opinion of the source of the information may impact our impressions of the message's meaning or credibility.
- Geography plays a role in communications. Time zones come into play as managerial spans of control expand in global environments.
- Working remotely has its own communication challenges.
- Personal factors such as gender, age, predispositions, religion and ethnicity, language proficiency, etc., may distort message meaning.
- Culture has significant influence (e.g., the meaning of time).
- Other factors such as visual perception, technological restraints, comfort levels with ambiguity, trust levels, mood, etc., can pose significant communication challenges.

Mitigating misfires

You can reduce the impact of communication dissonance through your own active listening, clarifying, and checking for understanding and feedback. Some tips are worth noting when interacting with others:

- Speak slowly and distinctly.*
- Do not use acronyms and unfamiliar technical terms.
- Avoid hard-discerning references, acronyms, abbreviations, slang, or jargon.
- Be conscious of any physical constraints and personal space.
- Environmental factors can disrupt or distract from messaging intent.
- Prejudice can lead to false assumptions or stereotypes.
- Time can lead to selective attention tendencies.
- A parties' emotional state can influence how a message is sent or received.
- Personal values, beliefs, and attitudes can sidetrack mutual understanding.
- Cognitive abilities vary by individual.

*These instructions were part of Coach's phone message on his answering machine.

Becoming an effective communicator

Managers spend two-thirds of their day "communicating." In fact, an argument can be made that you are never not communicating.

Seize "face-to-face" opportunities

Face to face matters. It opens all communication channels and minimizes potential barriers. It adds a personal touch, builds relationships, and sends a very clear message that you value and care about the other party. Trust is an outcome. As opportunities present themselves for face-to-face communications, seize them. It is a valuable investment of your time and attention.

Be a critical listener

Leaders need to know when to speak and when to listen. These skills are equally important, and the latter should be your first move.

In one of the most bizarre meeting exchanges I have ever witnessed, one of my colleagues, with two dozen global participants around the conference table, decided to announce his decision to leave the company. He took the floor and spoke for 20 uninterrupted minutes. His heartfelt and sincere comments were full of passion and disappointment. He had joined the company a few years earlier with hope and promise but felt that his impact was now limited by corporate restraints and senior management inertia. His tone was sad. His energy had been drained. His professional spirit and his heart were broken. Almost everyone in the room had a tear in their eye. Emotions were bubbling over.

At the end of his comments, there was a long and very awkward pause. He needed a hug.

The meeting host (and most senior person in the room), perhaps not knowing what to do or say, seemed dumbfounded and confused. Maybe anyone would have been. However, his response caught everyone in the room by surprise. In not even acknowledging the prior dialog, he simply and succinctly stated that it was time for lunch and that we should reconvene around 1:15.

Wait … Did he really just say that? Our poor colleague just bared his soul. and all our host could come up with was "lunch time!" "Tone-deaf" were the first two words that crossed my mind before stronger terms.

Critical listening occurs when you are truly trying to understand the messaging of the other party AND you are subsequently evaluating the message as well. Be patient with the process. Its steps include focusing on the message, repeating key points or asking reflexive questions, and encouraging the speaker to elaborate further.

Exercise appropriate discretion

When someone walks into your office and asks if they may confide in you, stop. Before you say "yes," ask them if the matter involves safety, potential harassment or discrimination, gross misconduct, criminal activity, or the like. Tell them, if it does, you have an affirmative obligation to intervene or further report the matter.

As a leader, you have privilege to have confidential information. This applies to a wide range of topics ranging from your team members' personal lives to company "insider" information. Escalate what is appropriate; however, do not share information that should be protected. A misstep here will erode your followers' confidence and could even jeopardize your employment.

Timing counts

What happens when you are halfway to your destination on a cross-country flight and the meal you expected an hour ago is still nowhere to be found? You obviously assume the worst. The meals were not placed on the plane, the cooking equipment is broken, the flight crew is incompetent, or the chicken was found to have salmonella. If the flight attendant had simply announced earlier in the flight that the meal would be served at some later time or point, your mind would be at ease. Instead, your eagerness has now turned into anxiety, concerned that you will not find an open restaurant upon arrival.

To the extent possible, communicate information to your team in a timely manner. This will help set their expectations and heighten their trust in you.

Be wary of "load"

Where I once worked, a senior director shouted at his vice president, "F--- you!" and walked out of the conference room. This was at the end of yet another long finance meeting to discuss a seemingly endless set of demanding action items.

As director of HR at the time, my gut reaction was to immediately fire this individual. However, when I went to the company's Chief Administrative Officer, to whom I reported, and explained what happened, he suggested that before we pull the trigger, we should explore the comment's impetus. Perhaps among other possibilities, the senior director's words were a cry for help.

After several behind-closed-doors interviews and discussions with all involved parties and witnesses, we found that the senior director was publicly wilting under the growing pressures of his expanding job, as well as some life-changing events unfolding outside of work. We opted not to fire him. We were able to significantly repair his fractured relationship with his vice president and adjust some of the overwhelming demands of his position. Things did get into a better space for the individuals and the organization.

Admittedly, I learned a great deal from that experience.

Communication "overload" occurs when people are overwhelmed by the rate and complexity of the stimuli coming at them. It affects their judgment, decision-making, and potential actions. Often this happens when an organization is trying to take on too many initiatives or when a manager is pushing too many priorities.

Keep an eye open for this situation. Warning signs include omission—when people fail to handle their day-to-day responsibilities—or mistakes. Errors happen. Queuing and "pile-ups" result. Tempers may flair. One-time urgent demands are greeted with a yawn or shoulder shrug. Of real danger, beware when work standards become lower. You may also see people delegate or refuse assignments. These are indications that something is dramatically wrong.

Test for understanding

Behavior is the true test of understanding. If your team members understand and grasp your message, their behavior and attitude will reflect such. Absent such validation, it is time to regroup.

Stakeholder communications

Answering stakeholder interests is an important managerial task. You should plan for and be prepared for these likely encounters.

Multi-directions

In an upward direction, give regular, "heads-up," and "time-sensitive" updates to your manager in the form of executive summaries for key activities and projects. Show him or her what is changing and why. These informative updates are critical for sound decision-making and constructive feedback, as well as for enhancing and validating support and encouraging ideas and suggestions. *(Note: Some suggestions that have served me well: Be proactive with your communications; never surprise your boss; have the details ready to discuss; and always walk into his or her office with solutions.)*

To your peers, you should provide periodic updates. Keep them informed of the progress of key projects, and solicit feedback and suggestions to instill their vested stake. Such communications will assist with task coordination, problem solving, information sharing, and potential management of conflict before it has the chance to arise.

With your team, communication is one of the significant levers available that can heighten a feeling of organizational connectivity on behalf of the employees, as well as build a bridge of trust. Continual guidance, support, and feedback are required. This is in the form of providing direction, shaping behavior and attitudes, keeping a pulse on morale and engagement, reinforcing mission and values, further delineating role clarity, and setting and reviewing performance expectations.

One-on-one conversations

Author Stephen Covey in *Principle-Centered Leadership* suggests that effective communication on a personal basis starts with a positive personal attitude. He states that individuals, especially leaders, should demonstrate good faith, care, and openness. Covey further suggests that one's behavior is a fundamental underpinning of effective communication—beginning discussions with common points, demonstrating critical listening, and speaking in order to promote understanding by using reflexive phrases like, "I think I hear you saying..."

Be empathetic. Listen before speaking. Do not make the business dialog personal. Recognize that disagreement can be healthy on the path to win/win solutions.

Customer and supplier communication

These communications can be a bit dicey, often walking the fine line between staying positive with a negative message. This is especially true if you work in an environment where the customer is always right (even when he or she is wrong).

In this exchange, maintain a positive attitude. Show you care. Talk in an open manner, be empathetic, and respectful, and listen keenly. In terms of a solution, if possible, under-promise and over-deliver. When wrapping up the discussion, never underestimate the power of a smile and a "thank you."

Running effective meetings

There are several tips to help you run effective meetings.

First and foremost, do you even need to hold the meeting? Often, ad hoc communication may solve the inquiry at hand.

If you must hold the meeting, be sure that you are inviting the right and fewest number of parties. Nothing is worse than trudging off to a conference room or a video call only to find out that the meeting must be rescheduled because the sponsor forgot to include a key stakeholder or there was a schedule conflict. Also, if the meeting requires preassigned work, be sure to communicate it well in advance and assure its completion.

Communicate the meeting's intention and desired outcomes. This will also help people prepare and keep the meeting focused. If the topic is controversial, try to understand everyone's point of view ahead of time in order to prepare for the potential of divergent views.

Distribute an agenda ahead of time so expectations may be set. If needed, assign roles, preferably ahead of time or at the meeting's start. Who will be the facilitator? Who will take notes? Who might even play devil's advocate? Often, in small meetings, multiple hats are worn.

During the meeting, stay on topic. Be conscious of the time and progress. If discussions become muddled or go sideways, the facilitator should suggest taking them offline. Keep a running log of action items and recap accordingly. There is a growing trend to try to limit meetings to less than an hour.

If necessary, especially for larger projects and those with more organizational visibility, examine your meeting processes to determine where inefficiencies may be improved. Finally, follow up as needed.

Under brighter lights

Business writing and presentations are critical to your success. In these forums, you have the stage to yourself, or you may choose to share it with others. Either way, your work product, and reputation are being assessed.

Business writing

The "Five C's" apply to all aspects of meaningful and effective personal and organizational communications:

- Concise—Clarity and precision are paramount. Keep your messaging as simple and focused as possible. State your objective, supporting arguments, and recommendations in a concise manner. Less is more.
- Candid—It is incumbent for organizational leadership to portray any situation honestly and to outline the bias for action in a compelling manner that sets realistic expectations.
- Contextual—Communication does not happen in a vacuum. There is context. Context can be psychological, referring to the participants' needs, values, and desires, or it can be situational, taking into account the "place" of the communication. The physical environment—aspects such as noise, lighting, time of day, and similar factors—and culture also have influence.
- Constructive—Given the choice of using a positive or negative comment to reinforce the point that you are making, be constructive.
- Consistent—Do not waffle. Inconsistencies in messaging are the fodder for water cooler conversations.

If possible, have someone proofread and/or share feedback about your more important/ visible works.

Presentations

At face value, presentations are relatively straightforward. Some research, some organizing of notes, a few PowerPoint slides, dress the part, and you are on your way. However, these communication forums require more preparation beyond that which is cursory. There is actually a lot at stake here, and some degree of anxiety is always a part of the equation.

Know (and prepare for) thy audience

Known as the "great communicator," President Ronald Reagan was an outstanding public speaker. His oratory skills were honed from earlier career roles in broadcasting baseball games, acting in Hollywood movies, and appearing on various television shows.

Most of us do not and will not have access to that type of professional training. However, there are some lessons that we can glean from Reagan's ability to connect with his audience.

Reagan was a master at articulating his message with his eloquent voice, using terms that every man and woman could understand. He spoke to his audience, not at or above them. He used every day, relatable language. He used repetition as a tool, hoping his message would "sink into the collective consciousness." He could take complex topics, synthesize critical points, and make concise arguments and expressions. He referenced notable quotes and created "catch phrases" to emphasize or color his comments.

Have a hook

In every presentation, be sure to keep the attention by continually addressing two key questions (covered in the next principle): WIIFM (What's in it for me?) and WSIC (Why should I care?)

Practice

Whether you or a team member are preparing to make a sales pitch or facilitate a key presentation, conducting a key meeting, rolling out a new program, participating in a panel, tweaking your advertising campaign, or interviewing on either side of the table, practice in "game" conditions. This means making every moment of practice count. This is the time to catch those unwanted tendencies when you speak too fast, sheepishly lower your head or voice, or to overuse "um." Practice over and over.

Have congruence

We listen with our eyes.

In the 1960 U.S. presidential debate that was on both radio and television. During the debate, Richard Nixon sweated profusely under the bright stage lights while John F. Kennedy was cool, calm, and collected. Polls taken afterwards found that radio listeners gave the debate nod to Nixon. Television viewers viewed Kennedy as the winner.

Albert Mehrabian's Rule of Personal Communication suggests that our messaging is a combination of verbals, vocals, and non-verbals. To maximize the effectiveness of message delivery, his research concluded that only a small portion, 7%, of our words (verbals) hit their desired mark. Thirty-three percent of communications resonate through our vocal tone, volume, and emphasis, and the majority of our message is conveyed by our body language. This includes our posture, gestures, eye contact, physical behavior, physical expressions, the way we dress, and mannerisms.

Deliver!

A presentation is not about reading your slides; it is about bringing your script to life.

The best presentation materials will not save you if you stumble in your delivery. Easier said than done, try to stay calm. A little adrenaline is fine and to be expected, but find a way to bring on your confident demeanor. Deep breathing may help. Take solace in knowing that you have prepared and that your materials are in great shape. Get to the physical place of your presentation early and get comfortable in the environment. Visualize what you are going to do and how you are going to do it. Warm-up as needed. Have water handy. If you are prone to perspiration, wear a blazer or light sweater. *(Note: If needed or preferred, use notes or "cheat sheets" for presentations, hiding them in the room or above your laptop for a video call.)*

I do not mind confessing to you that even today, as I give more and more presentations, I still get a bit socially anxious before showtime. To fight this, I follow my own advice. In addition to all of the preparatory steps previously highlighted, I always play the theme song from the movie "Rocky" in my head ("Gonna Fly Now" by Bill Conti). Inspirational! Most importantly, it works for me.

When the lights are bright, bring energy with you and exude passion! Use concrete, illustrative, and easy-to-understand examples that appeal to the broadest number in your audience. Use anecdotes, tell stories, maintain eye contact at all times, and repeat key points for emphasis. Move your hands and walk about the room to engage the audience and demonstrate your enthusiasm. Ask rhetorical questions to provoke thought and ask open-ended questions to encourage participation. Lastly, be sure to close the deal.

There is an adage that summarizes the flow of presentations succinctly and accurately: Tell them what you are going to tell them; tell them; tell them what you told them.

Showmanship

Sometimes, a little dramatic flair helps.

When we were at a critical juncture of negotiating a major labor contract, the spokesperson for the union across the table emphatically exclaimed that I must have "a set of big, brass balls" to suggest the changes that the company wanted to make to the collective bargaining agreement. After he fired that verbal missive, he promptly got up from his chair and led his team out of the room, abruptly breaking off the session.

His words and actions were real attention-getters.

Later that evening, I saw him at the bar. I took out my "nothing personal" persona, and we had an impromptu meeting. He told me that he understood the company's position and could eventually work with me toward a compromise on some of our demands; however, for his own credibility and tone-setting, he needed to show the reactionary push back.

Unusual actions and props can surely assist in amplifying a point. A more illustrative example was Nikita Khrushchev's alleged shoe-banging at the United Nations in 1960.

Learn

Encourage feedback. Learn from the presentation experience.

Improving communications

Some reminders and tips to improve workplace communication:

- Think before you speak and gauge reactions.
- Check in with your team members on a regular basis; daily huddles.
- Make internal documents and standard operating procedures easily available.
- Publicize, reinforce, and reference your mission and values at every opportunity.
- Have an "open door" policy and mean it!
- Get out of your office!
- Organize team-building activities from time to time.
- Ask questions, and encourage others to do so.
- Show some love for your introverts respectfully drawing them out.

The most critical messages

Research tells us that people have defined communication needs for information in the workplace. Specifically, they want to know:

- Business strategy: How will we grow our business? How will we compete?
- Strategic focus: What are the obstacles to our growth, and what should we do about them?
- Performance focus: What is expected of me?
- Performance feedback and management: Who has an impact on my work? How well am I doing? How do I get specific, timely feedback on my work? (*Almost nine out of ten people want to know how their work contributes to the bottom line!*)
- Performance consequences: What happens to me if I do a great job? What will happen if I do not perform at the expected level?
- Outcomes: What if it all comes together? What if it doesn't?

Communicate these topics and themes regularly and often. This will assist with engagement.

How does this compare to conventional wisdom?

When it comes to communication, people can drink from a fire hose.

No, they can't. Your messaging requires keen attention and focus.

I worked in a matrixed organization where I reported to two bosses. We were making a significant organizational announcement, which had been approved by boss #1 and a team of lawyers. On Thursday evening, I had the announcement polished and ready to go out first thing in the morning.

When I came to work early on Friday, I found an e-mail from boss # 2 suggesting some minor changes. I made the seemingly minor edits and issued the announcement. What I did not catch was that boss #2 did not copy boss #1.

Mistake. Big mistake! They were not on the same page. I did not bridge the gap. The revised announcement had errors. When I realized the mistake, I was beyond words. Stunned would be the best description, given my perfectionist tendencies. When I had time to sort out what happened, I realized that my attention had shifted from the announcement to meetings with some of our employees who were to be impacted by a layoff that morning. Multi-tasking gone awry, and boss #1 was rightfully not happy.

Studies suggest that juggling too much is actually less efficient—especially for complicated or unfamiliar tasks. You can only focus on one task at a time. Multi-tasking is an illusion caused by quickly switching gears between activities. (Driving and texting come to mind.) It is not effective. It is not efficient. And then there are environmental and self-inflicted distractions that enter the equation.

Your attention span—and that of others—is short enough. Keep your messaging sharp, concentrate on its crafting, and give it appropriate priority.

Endnotes for Principle 10: Keep it simple

Basics

Tubbs, S., & Moss, S. (1977). *Human communication*. New York: Random House, p. 19.

Desired outcome

Tubbs, S., & Moss, S. (1977). *Human communication*. New York: Random House, p. 13.

Challenges

Barriers to effective communication. (Date unknown). Skillsyouneed.com. Retrieved on January 14, 2019, from: https://www.skillsyouneed.com/ips/barriers-communication.html

Norms

Farace, R.V., Monge, P.R., & Russell, H.M. (1977). *Communicating and organizing*. Reading, Massachusetts: Addison-Wesley, pp. 104–125, 134.

Pope, A. (Date unknown). 5 deadly communication barriers and how to solve them. Timedoctor.com. Retrieved on January 14, 2019, from: https://biz30.timedoctor.com/communication-barriers/

Grossman, D. (2016, September 12). 7 ways to fix poor communication in the workplace. Yourthoughtpartner.com. Retrieved on January 14, 2019, from: http://www.yourthoughtpartner.com/blog/7-ways-to-help-fix-poor-communication-in-the-workplace (commitment, metrics, and accountability)

Effective

Farace, R.V., Monge, P.R., & Russell, H.M. (1977). *Communicating and organizing*. Reading, Massachusetts: Addison-Wesley, p. 1.

Critical listening

Jay, J. (2005, January). On communicating well. *HR Magazine*, p. 89.

Pass, A. (2015, August 6). Three steps for critical listening. Apasseductaion.com. Retrieved on January 17, 2019, from: https://apasseducation.com/three-steps-for-critical-listening/

Load

Farace, R.V., Monge, P.R., & Russell, H.M. (1977). *Communicating and organizing.* Reading, Massachusetts: Addison-Wesley, p. 141.

Tubbs S., & Moss, S. (1977). *Human communication.* New York: Random House, p. 351.

Multi-directions

Tubbs S., & Moss, S. (1977). *Human communication.* New York: Random House, p. 354.

Tubbs S., & Moss, S. (1977). *Human communication.* New York: Random House, p. 358–359.

Harris, J. (1996). *Getting* employees to fall in love with your company, AMACOM, a division of the American Management Association, New York, New York, p. 37.

Townsend, P., & Gebhardt, J. (1997). *Five-star leadership: The art and strategy of creating leaders at every level.* New York: John Wiley & Sons, Inc., p. 57.

Covey, S.R. (1991). *Principle-centered leadership.* New York: Summit Books, p. 110.

Customer and supplier

Adubato, S. (2006). *Make the connection.* New Brunswick, New Jersey: Rivergate Books, pp. 147–149.

Business writing

Farace, R.V., Monge, P.R., & Russell, H.M. (1977). *Communicating and organizing.* Reading, Massachusetts: Addison-Wesley, pp. 104–125, 134.

Concise

Smye, M. (1998). *Is it too late to run away and join the circus? A guide for your second life.* New York: Macmillan Publishing, pp. 158–160.

Farace, R.V., Monge, P.R., & Russell, H.M. (1977). *Communicating and organizing.* Reading, Massachusetts: Addison-Wesley, pp. 117–125.

Contextual

King, D. (2000: copyright). Four principles of interpersonal communication. Retrieved on January 17, 2019, from: http://www.pstcc.edu/facstaff/dking/interpr.htm

Know thy audience

Edwards, L. (2018, February 5). What made Reagan a truly great communicator. Heritage.org. Retrieved on January 15, 2019, from: https://www.heritage.org/conservatism/commentary/what-made-reagan-truly-great-communicator

Congruence

Belludi, N. (2008, October 4). Albert Mehrabian's 7-38-55 rule of personal communication. RightAttitudes.com. Retrieved on January 14, 2019, from: http://www.rightattitudes.com/2008/10/04/7-38-55-rule-personal-communication/

Segal, J., Smith, M., Robinson, L., & Boose, G. (2018, October). Nonverbal communication: Reading body language and improving nonverbal skills. Retrieved on January 14, 2019, from: https://www.helpguide.org/articles/relationships-communication/nonverbal-communication.htm/ (Trust, clarity, and rapport)

Deliver!

Adubato, S. (2006). *Make the connection.* New Brunswick, New Jersey: Rivergate Books, pp. 33–35.

Improving

Lucas, A. (2018, November 27). The importance of verbal & non-verbal communication. Livestong.com, Retrieved on January 14, 2019, from: https://www.livestrong.com/article/156961-the-importance-of-verbal-non-verbal-communication/

Eisenhauer, T. (2014, July 20). 30 smart tips to improve workplace communications. Axerosolutions.com. Retrieved on January 15, 2019, from: https://axerosolutions.com/blogs/timeisenhauer/pulse/210/30-smart-tips-to-improve-workplace-communication

The most critical messages

Huselid, M., Becker, B., & Beatty, R. (2009). *The differentiated workforce.* Boston, Massachusetts: Harvard Business Press, p. 120.

How does this compare?

American Psychological Association. (2001, October). Multitasking undermines our efficiency, study suggests. Apa.org. Volume 32. No. 9. Print version: p. 13. Retrieved on January 15, 2019, from: https://www.apa.org/monitor/oct01/multitask.aspx

Concentrate on your team, not the opposition

If you are executing at the highest level with the right players on your team, the competition does not matter.

Coach did not spend endless hours reviewing film clips of upcoming opponents. In fact, he joked that if he spent too much time analyzing the competition, he might become awestruck or anxious, and lose his own internal focus. He kept abreast of his competition through the newspapers, some scouting reports, and other sources of information. As a team, they might walk through the opposition's plays or discuss their competition's strengths and weaknesses for the bigger games, but that was it.

His focus and his time were spent with an internal focus. And he did not waste a minute.

Coach believed that if his team was playing to its potential and playing within themselves, they would emerge as victors. He set a tone for this by the type of player he recruited. He wanted players from high schools with winning programs. He wanted hard-driving, highly-competitive, coachable players that knew how to win and had an endless thirst for it. He wanted players that would play harder for him than they had ever experienced. He wanted individual and collective desires to excel.

He also wanted players who were self-motivated and whom he felt he could further inspire for performance.

Coach built and instilled his system where, through refined and repetitive execution, the team expected to win the game every time they took to the court. Not that they wanted to win; not that they hoped to win; rather, that they *expected to win* every game!

Your coaching imperative: Motivate!

As noted, Coach hand-selected each of his team members year after year. However, as previously discussed, talent alone does not guarantee success. Talent needs to be developed, integrated, and motivated.

Motivational theory

Sonia Kukreja noted, "The role of motivation cannot be understated in an organization. It is a simple process that requires an understanding of the human mind and behavior. Such an understanding and proper action thereby stimulating the motives of an employee helps in initiating and maintaining action and helps extensively in satisfying organizational objectives." To this end, there are terms and conditions of employment that a manager can influence that motivate employee efforts toward desired outcomes (enhanced discretionary

DOI: 10.4324/9781003456902-18

effort, satisfaction, loyalty, and reduced turnover). In turn, these employee outcomes drive your strategic imperatives (greater productivity, heightened quality, innovation break-throughs) and financial performance (profit, return on assets).

Motivational carrots and sticks may sound almost psychologically sinister; they are not. They are basic managerial theories. You need to know this foundational framework.

Frederick Herzberg

In 1959, Frederick Herzberg, along with two research colleagues, published the book, *The Motivation to Work*. Based upon his studies of two hundred engineers and accountants, Herzberg found that we have two sets of needs that are derived from different factors in the workplace: one to avoid pain, and the other to grow psychologically.

The former needs ("hygiene factors") are such things as status, security, relationships with subordinates and peers, salary, working conditions, and company policy. These needs and their extrinsic rewards are important; however, once achieved, dissatisfaction results like a pill losing its efficacy.

The latter needs ("motivators") provide worker satisfaction. These needs include achievement, recognition, the work itself, advancement possibilities, and personal growth. It was Herzberg's conclusion that these intrinsic factors were truly the motivation, presumably helping the worker feel satisfied, engaged, and productive on a long-term basis.

Abraham Maslow

Abraham Maslow, one of humanistic psychology's early influences, developed the "Hierarchy of Needs," a five-tier pyramid, which suggested that lower tier needs must be satisfied before people can attend to higher-level needs.

- Physiological needs form the base of the pyramid. These include food, water, warmth, shelter, and rest.
- Safety needs are at second level. This includes the need for safety and security.
- The third level includes a person's psychological needs for love and belonging.
- Esteem needs are at fourth level. These include prestige and a feeling of accomplishment.
- At the apex of the pyramid is self-actualization. Though rarely achieved, this is where the painter paints and the poet writes. Here, individuals achieve self-fulfillment by realizing their full potential, including creative activities.

If Coach Wooden was not "self-actualized," then he was certainly on the doorstep.

Victor Vroom

Victor Vroom, along with Edward Lawler and Lyman Porter, suggested that employees are motivated if they believe that:

- There is a positive correlation between their efforts and performance.
- The favorable performance will result in a desirable reward.
- The reward will satisfy an important need.
- The desire to satisfy the need is strong enough to make the effort worthwhile.

This theory is predicated upon individual valence (emotional orientation), expectancy (people have different expectations and levels of confidence), and instrumentality (the perception of fulfilled promises) toward seeking pleasure and avoiding pain.

Edwin Locke

Researcher Edwin Locke found that individuals who set specific, difficult goals performed better than those who set general, easy goals. Locke proposed five basic principles of goal-setting: clarity, challenge, commitment, feedback, and task complexity.

This theory is a core element of performance planning.

David McClelland

American psychologist David McClelland identified four types of motivational needs: achievement, power, affiliation, and avoidance.

- Achievement is a derivative of striving for an average task complexity, responsibility for one's own performance, the need for feedback, and the use of innovation/creativity.
- Power is about control status, reputation, and recognition.
- Affiliation is about group belonging and a heightened need to be liked.
- Avoidance concerns staying away from the unpleasant.

Related to this theory, McClelland was also known for his iceberg model. Here, a person's skills, knowledge, and behaviors are "above the water line," i.e., visible, and motivational attributes such as values, beliefs, self-esteem, and predispositions are hidden.

J. Stacy Adams

According to Adams, we are motivated by the perception/reality that we are being treated fairly compared to others. For example, an employee doing comparable work (input) with a peer, but getting paid less (output), will likely be less satisfied or motivated.

This theory plays heavily into the discipline of employee relations.

Daniel Pink

Employee engagement studies suggest that people perform better when they are motivated. In his 2009 book, *Drive*, Daniel Pink argued that new models of motivation are required to address the needs of today's innovative and creative workplace. He identified three key drivers of employee motivation:

- Autonomy—The need to direct your own life and work. Motivation is a function of control. Autonomy releases an individual from conformity and spurs creative thinking. It loosens the policy handcuffs around employees.
- Mastery—Employees have the desire to experience and improve. They want to tap their potential. They desire to learn and grow in order to be subject matter masters.
- Purpose—Employees want to understand what they do, why they do it, and how it contributes to the bigger picture. They want purpose in their work.

Coach's recipe

The Coach knew how to get the most from his team with an approach grounded in strategy, as well as psychology. Using what Andy referred to as "Frustration Tolerance" theory, Coach spread praise, albeit rarely ("Atta-boys," pats on the back, compliments), along with constructive feedback (reprimands, bench time, and exclamations of "Goodness, Gracious, Sakes Alive!"), delivered in real-time, as well as randomly. This blend was intended to encourage his players to both excel in performance and to learn from any miscue. This technique instilled confidence and enhanced their ability to handle adversity along the way.

A few samples:

- Every minute of Coach's practices was built around physical conditioning and mental toughness.

  In a courtside television interview right after Marques Johnson held the game ball to secure the 1975 title against a tough Kentucky squad, Coach Wooden shared one of his motivational techniques when he was asked about the endurance and stamina of his team. "We are in good condition … . One of my theories is to get our players *to believe* that they are in better condition than any team against whom we will participate. Whether they are or not, if they believe that, it can help a lot."
- Coach used encouragement, sometimes with a bit of a curve. Yet, it was always effective.

  Steve Patterson played from 1969 to 1971, between the Lew Alcindor (later known as Kareem Abdul-Jabbar) and Bill Walton years. He was the starting center of the 1970 and 1971 championship teams, and later played for five years in the National Basketball Association. Every once in a while, Steve would be exhausted toward the end of a game. On one of these occasions, rather than berate Steve for being winded or shout a few words of desperate encouragement, Coach looked at him and said something to the effect of how all his hard work had more emphatically worn down the guy covering him. Motivation, indeed!
- Because Coach ran the same offense (over and over again), other teams would be familiar with UCLA's plays. This could have eroded his own team's confidence as the competition anticipated every move. However, the Bruins, even if they started out slowly, would inevitably continue steadfast in their execution, never panicking or breaking form, until the victory was secured.

The quest for the motivational workplace

Have you noticed a downturn in individual or collective morale or productivity? People working less and seemingly less committed? An increase in employee relations issues and complaints? Less hands raised for volunteering. You can't put a finger on it, but you sense others have updated their resumes.

If you are the manager of a less-than-optimal work environment, your team likely has retention risk.

The "motivational" workplace is in the eye of the beholder, but in general terms, it is a physical, emotional, and intellectual environment that appeals to both sides of the brain—logic and creativity. It is a place where an individual can be highly motivated, engaged, satisfied, and challenged.

It is a setting where Maslow's Pyramid is alive and well—as one's physiological, safety, emotional, and status needs are addressed on the way to self-actualization. It is a place where one is performing meaningful work for a meaningful purpose, toward a standard of excellence.

It is a place that causes you to race through a morning shower toward the most positive employee experience.

General motivational factors

To provoke some general topical thinking, Alexander Hiam, in his book, *Motivational Management*, outlines an "incentive profile." Administered using a scaled survey, it examines employee motivation by considering fifteen different motivational factors, including affiliation, self-expression, achievement, security, career growth, excitement, status, etc. Hiam suggests that managers should know and understand the primary motivational factors for their respective team members—either through survey, observation, experience, or discussions. However, bear in mind that your team members are capricious. What motivates them today might not do so tomorrow.

Drilling down: My six dimensions

My personal model for workplace utopia is fairly comprehensive. Many of its attributes are covered in far more detail in other Principles in this book (such as in Principle 4 regarding engagement). They are captured here as I have blended and borrowed applicable research with my experience and observations, in order to provide you with food for thought. These are some of the basic motivational levers available to you—each with its own customizable influence—to help drive individuals and your team toward heightened satisfaction and performance.

Where I want to work

It is almost impossible to walk by a newsstand or scroll the Internet and not see a glaring headline about some recently completed business survey citing the "best," the "most admired" the "most family-friendly" or the "most respected" places to work.

I suspect that most of us want to work in a place where all these attributes can be found.

- *Noble cause—Many people prefer to work for an organization that promotes the general well-being and quality of human life.*
- *Vision—Tell your team why they are here, where they are going, why it makes a difference, how they can help, and why they should trust you to get them there.*
- *The pursuit of excellence—Strive for world-class excellence, industry leadership, and set high expectations and standards for all aspects of performance, process, and delivery. Focus on quality improvements and emphasize urgency.*
- *Employee centric—Employees are the company's most valuable asset. Period.*
- *Customer centric—The relationships with your customers should be a partnership. You should be providing compelling and continuous reasons for your customers to do business with you—not only to satisfy their needs, but also to anticipate their needs around speed, price, quality, and innovation.*
- *Societal responsibility—Have a solid and unyielding commitment to society, equality, common good, and the environment.*

Environmental factors

The workplace needs to be safe and clean; however, there are other considerations:

- *The business casual workplace—"Be neat." "Dress for your day." "Individual discretion." If Goldman Sachs, GM, and PWC can do it, so can you.*
- *Location—You want the best of that talent. You need to find a way to reach them. Give due thought to your office location(s) and/or place(s) of community such as cluster groups.*
- *The physical space—Employees want to work in office settings and on shop floors with space that enhances productivity, innovation, comfort, and collaboration, balanced with an appropriate level of privacy.*
- *Remote working capabilities—Jump-started by the pandemic, the worlds of remote working, hybrid scheduling, and hyper-collaboration are here. With technical enablers, you and your team members should be able to work with anyone, anytime, anywhere.*

Cultural factors

As we have touched upon, culture is a combination of symbols, rites, practices, and traditions. It is a key differentiator when employees have choices in a tight labor market.

- *DEI—This is exceptionally good for business; it is good for everyone. No excuses.*
- *Openness—Establish a culture where individuals may freely express their ideas, suggestions, and opinions.*
- *Balance—Allow your team the schedule flexibility they need as they bring you results. Be sure that your policies and practices encourage work/life balance. Make it a priority.*
- *Open door—You need to be visible, accessible, and responsive to your team, sometimes after hours. They also need to be comfortable knocking.*
- *Social aspects—Create occasional opportunities for your team members to get to know each other by meeting and affiliating outside work.*
- *Traditions and practices—Town hall meetings, lunches, special recognition programs, employee service awards, significant milestone acknowledgments, and success celebrations—all of these events trigger opportunities for communication, bonding, and internal networking while building morale.*
- *Stability—To the extent possible, provide a stable and predictable work environment, which enhances psychological security.*
- *Compensation—Pay employees fairly and competitively for the value they bring to the organization.*
- *Benefits—Adequate and affordable healthcare coverage and savings plans are critically important.*
- *Ownership, if you can—One of the most significant benefits that you can extend to your team members in order to motivate them is equity. To this end, employers are wise to offer well-designed, strategic programs that allow for stock options, grants, discounted stock purchases, or 401k matches.*
- *Fun and stress relief—If you must have a ping pong table, its use should not be frowned upon nor seen as a pitstop for the bored. Ask before you install.*

The work itself

Design a job for each of your team members that is too good to leave.

- *Flexible Job descriptions—When extraordinary talent is at the doorstep, create the job around them, rather than trying to fit an individual into a prescribed role.*
- *Challenge and variety—Variety is the spice of life. It can also be professionally stimulating.*
- *A voice (if not a vote) in decision-making—Participative management is practiced.*
- *Job enlargement and enrichment—Employees may desire expanding their tasks across the organization or attaining new skills.*
- *Learning and career development—Provide an opportunity for team members to continuously learn. Give stretch assignments. Rotate jobs. Share and apply new knowledge. Assign mentors. Invest in those who warrant such consideration. Encourage people to invest in themselves.*
- *Leverage people's strengths—Give a gentle (or stronger) push to team members who excel in given areas to apply or enhance those skills.*
- *Autonomy—Allow self-expression. In the ideal world, work is a natural extension of our individuality. Give people the latitude to be creative.*

For whom to work

The best leaders treat everyone with respect and dignity, embrace collegiality, keep team members highly motivated and inspired, care, share, and continually strive for excellence. To this end, you must:

Lead—You must provide purpose, direction, and inspiration.

- *Live by values—Live by your organization's values proposition, ensuring that your organizational values are integrated into all aspects of your company, and by clearly defining the expected norms of behavior. You are the role model.*
- *Be trustworthy—Trust is the root of success and failure in all relationships. It must be earned. Do the right thing, tell the truth, be consistent with your words and actions, do what you say you will do, and show you care.*
- *Communicate constantly—Meet often with your team. Be n active listener. Give them your time, the information they need to do their jobs, and prompt feedback. Transparency and honesty are a must.*
- *Get the best and most competent talent on your team—For your team to perform as a team at the highest level and to derive synergy, you need the right blend of "A" players and good corporate soldiers. Let knowledge, skills, and abilities drive your staffing processes and decisions. Be sensitive to team chemistry.*
- *Embrace change—Challenge the status quo. Create some chaos. Seek the "better, faster, cheaper" solution.*
- *Take appropriate risks—Success may not happen on the first try. Share the learning from victories and defeats.*
- *Manage conflict—Team chemistry is important. Once you have it, do not let it slip away. Distinguish between people and positions. Face problems together. Make changes if needed in a timely manner.*

- *Be fair—Treat everyone fairly in all aspects of their employment relationship—individually and relatively. Pay people what they are worth.*
- *Get results—Have goals, action plans, involve all, and monitor metrics. Things that get measured and rewarded get done.*
- *Say thank you—As warranted, say thanks privately and publicly, and with sincere intent. This cannot be done often enough.*
- *Laugh—A sense of humor aids relationships and it can be an important organizational medicine. Of note, laugh at yourself before laughing with others.*

With whom to work

As a manager, you have direct responsibility for your team's productivity and morale. Co-workers, too, have such influence on each other. Make every attempt to create and monitor an environment with the following characteristics and relationship keystones:

- *Mutual respect and dignity—Differences in values, attitudes, experiences, skills, and beliefs are welcome. Exercise empathy and compassion when needed. Treat others as you wish to be treated.*
- *A sense of belonging and commitment—On our common organizational and life path, first prize is that we all get along; second is that we can at least find ways to harmoniously co-exist.*
- *Positive attitude—Cynicism, skepticism, pessimism, doubts, apathy, drama, and complacency are the enemy. Deal promptly and directly to address any of these concerns.*
- *Camaraderie—Nurture the positive attitude employees have toward each other and about your corporate culture.*
- *Maturity—Responsible behavior and self-accountability are welcomed.*

Sticking to basics

The field of research concerning employee motivation is quite wide and deep. The factors cited above as part of the six dimensions are an attempt to synthesize much of traditional and more recent findings. You should explore them with intent; however, at its core, human motivation at and outside work) often boils down to the two most important answers you must provide on an individual and team basis:

- "What's in it for me?" (WIIFM?)
- "Why should I care?" (WSIC?)

Answer these two questions and you will hold the attention of your audience, compelling them to take action. Absent such, you will likely be greeted with apathy.

Why they leave

Employee survey results from the U.S. marketplace generally indicate that the majority of employees are not happy, engaged, or satisfied with their current work experience. In fact, it seems that more than half of current workers would flee for greener pastures if the opportunity presented itself. Many would even take a cut in pay if it meant the ideal job awaited. The desire to move on is generally driven by a less-than-healthy relationship with their boss, a lack of recognition or appreciation, stalled career movement, burnout, or a toxic environment. Compensation is also a factor, and it rises closer to the top of this list during tougher economic times. Keep this on your radar.

What motivates you?

Intrinsic versus extrinsic.

As a leader, are you driven to make an impact in the lives of others and for your organization through embracing purpose, living your values, displaying passion and empathy, helping others grow and succeed, and furthering your own development? Or do you march ahead in pursuit of title, status, compensation, competitive conquests, and prerequisites?

In the next principle, we discuss servant leadership. This should help frame your answer if you have any doubts.

How does this compare to Conventional Wisdom?

You have heard the question, "What's your competition doing?" used as a motivator.

Part of this Principle does concern knowing your competition, but not obsessing over it. After all, you cannot control what your competition is doing, but you can control what you are doing.

--

In the spirit of open-mindedness, I offer an exception to this part of Coach Wooden's philosophy.

The late legendary New Jersey high school coach, Gary Kehler, led his Westfield teams to unparalleled winning records in three sports—coaching teams and individuals (football, golf, and wrestling). Kehler shared many of Coach Wooden's views and practices about repetitive execution, discipline, and individual accountability. There was, however, one area where Kehler had a divergent view. Kehler liked to know everything about his competition.

Stories in this regard ran from his staff's laborious studying of his competition's game tapes to in-game analysis from his assistants (and others) regarding the energy level of opposing players. For one particular football game, it was purported that Kehler's defense knew whether a running or pass play was coming as tipped by the number of fingers placed on the ground by one of the opponent's offensive lineman. (Respectfully, I will neither confirm nor deny Coach Kehler told me that.)

Competitive intelligence is not *the* key to success; however, it can be an asset. For example, in the airline industry (as with any product or service deemed to be a commodity), carriers would only ignore the advertised fares of their competitors on highly-traffic routes at the risk of their own peril.

Endnotes for Principle 11: Concentrate on your team, not the opposition

Motivational theory

Kukreja, S. (Date unknown)). The role of motivation in organizational behavior. Retrieved on August 24, 2023 from: https://www.managementstudyhq.com/role-of-motivation-in-organizational-behavior.html#goggle_vigntette

Frederick Hertzberg

Kuijk, A. (2018). Two factor theory by Frederick Herzberg. Retrieved on August 29, 2018 from: https://www.toolshero.com/psychology/theories-of-motivation/two-factor-theory-herzberg/

Abraham Maslow

McLeod, S. (2018). Maslow's hierarchy of needs. *Simply Psychology*. Retrieved on August 29, 2018 from: https://www.simplypsychology.org/maslow.html

Victor Vroom

Cambridge Institute for Manufacturing. (Date unknown). Vroom's expectancy theory. Retrieved on August 29, 2018 from: https://www.ifm.eng.cam.ac.uk/research/dstools/vrooms-expectancy-theory/

Edwin Locke

Castellano, William G. (2014). *Practices for engaging the 21st century workforce: challenges of talent management in a changing workplace.* Upper Saddle River, NJ: Pearson Education, Inc. ISBN 13:978-0-13-308637-9

David McClelland

Mulder, P. (2015). McClelland motivational theory. Retrieved on August 29, 2018 from: https://www.toolshero.com/psychology/theories-of-motivation/mcclelland-motivation-theory/
McClelland, D.C., & Burnham, D.H. (2003, January). Power is the great motivator. *Harvard Business Review*. Retrieved on August 29, 2018 from: https://hbr.org/2003/01/power-is-the-great-motivator

J. Stacy Adams

Castellano, William G. (2014). *Practices for engaging the 21st century workforce: challenges of talent management in a changing workplace.* Upper Saddle River, NJ: Pearson Education, Inc. ISBN 13:978-0-13-308637-9

Daniel Pink

Mind Tools Content Team. (Date unknown). Pink's autonomy, mastery, and purpose framework. Mind Tools Limited, 1996-2019. Retrieved on March 18, 2019 from: https://www.mindtools.com/pages/article/autonomy-mastery-purpose.htm

Coach's recipe

Tobias, K. (Date unknown). Reflections and frustration. The Albert Ellis Institute. Retrieved on November 7, 2018 from: http://albertellis.org/reflections-on-frustration/
Wooden, J.R. (2010, January 16). UCLA vs. Kentucky, NCAA Tournament post-game interview on March 31, 1975 with Jim Simpson. YouTube.com. Retrieved on November 13, 2018 from: https://www.youtube.com/watch?v=3qAfNQEJqX0

The quest for the motivational workplace

Hunter, J.C. (1998). *The servant*. New York: Crown Business. p. 69.

General motivational factors

Hiam, A. (2003). *Motivational management*. New York: American Management Association. pp. 188–208.

Kane, W.S. (2008). *The truth about thriving in change*. Upper Saddle River, NJ: Pearson Education, Inc., pp. 134–135.

Cultural factors

Pozin, I. (2015, November 17). 14 highly effective ways to motivate employees. *Inc.com*. Retrieved on October 30, 2018 from: https://www.inc.com/ilya-pozin/14-highly-effective-ways-to-motivate-employees.html

Economy, P. (2016, March 18). 9 super effective ways to motivate your team. *Inc.com*. Retrieved on October 30, 2018 from: https://www.inc.com/peter-economy/9-super-effective-ways-to-motivate-your-team.html

Castellano, W. (2018, October22). "Employee Ownership, Equity Compensation." Presented at the Rutgers University/ HR Advisory Meeting at the Wyndham Hotel, Parsippany, NJ.

The work itself

Surbhi, S. (2015, October 8). Differences between job enlargement and job enrichment. Retrieved on October 30, 2018 from: https://keydifferences.com/difference-between-job-enlargement-and-job-enrichment.html

O'Reilly, B.O. (1994, June 13). The new deal. *Fortune Magazine*, pp. 44–52.

Lobo, S. (2018, June 12). How can managers motivate their team to learn. Peoplematters.com. Retrieved on October 30, 2018 from: https://www.peoplematters.in/article/create-the-future/how-can-managers-motivate-their-team-to-learn-18516

Goler, L., Gale, J., Harrington, B., & Grant, A. (2018, January 11). Why people really quit their jobs. *Harvard Business Review*. Retrieved on October 19, 2018 from: https://hbr.org/2018/01/why-people-really-quit-their-jobs

Lipman, V. (2018, November 4). What motivates employees to go the extra mile? *Forbes.com*. Retrieved on August 29, 2018 from: https://www.forbes.com/sites/victorlipman/2014/11/04/what-motivates-employees-to-go-the-extra-mile-study-offers-surprising-answer/#2b0156e2a055

Weisbord, M.R. (1987). *Productive workplaces: organizing and managing for dignity, meaning, and community*. San Francisco, California: Jossey-Bass Inc., Publishers, pp. 167–168.

For whom to work

Covey, S.R. (1991). *Principle-centered leadership*. New York: Summit Books, p. 31.

Nelson, B., & Economy, P. (Date unknown). Ten ways for managers to motivate employees. A Wiley Brand, dummies.com. Retrieved on October 30, 2018 from: https://www.dummies.com/business/human-resources/employee-relations/ten-ways-for-managers-to-motivate-employees/

Economy, P. (2016, March 18). 9 super effective ways to motivate your team. *Inc.com*. Retrieved on October 30, 2018 from: https://www.inc.com/peter-economy/9-super-effective-ways-to-motivate-your-team.html

With whom to work

Lipman, V. (2018, November 4). What motivates employees to go the extra mile? *Forbes.com*. Retrieved on August 29, 2018 from: https://www.forbes.com/sites/victorlipman/2014/11/04/what-motivates-employees-to-go-the-extra-mile-study-offers-surprising-answer/#2b0156e2a055

Kane, W. (2005). Answering the alarm clock's call: A paradigm for my ideal workplace. Submitted to meet the academic requirements in Knowledge Area 8: Learning and Motivation. Fielding Graduate Institute. Prepared for Leonard Baca, Ed.D.

Why they leave

Schwantes, M. (Date unknown). Why do employees really quit their jobs? research says it comes down to these top 8 reasons. *Inc.com*. Retrieved on October 19, 2018 from: https://www.inc.com/why-do-employees-really-quit-their-jobs-research-says-it-comes-down-to-these-top-8-reasons.html

Fisher, A. (2018, October 13). This is the top reason people quit their jobs – it's not money. *Fortune*. Retrieved on October 19, 2018 from: http://fortune.com/2018/09/27/bored-at-work-why-people-quit-jobs/

How does this compare to the conventional wisdom?

Kehler, G. (2003, August 7). Private conversation.

Adjust to your players

Don't expect them to adjust to you

Coach was focused and intense; fiery and competitive. A man of few, but meaningful words, he earned and commanded his player's attention and respect through his own love of the game, mastery of its subject matter, and his personal stature.

Wooden's leadership style was relatively stable and consistent over time. However, he also knew that, given the annual turnover of his roster, the different maturation levels of his players, and the nature of the game itself, he would have to be somewhat flexible. Not full pendulum swings: rather, necessary adjustments tailored for the talent on his team.

In the best example of this, Coach, a student of the game, spent hours in the "off-season" studying and speaking to other basketball professionals and coaches about how to adjust his team's offensive scheme from high-post to low-post when he had a talented incoming freshman named Lewis Alcindor coming to campus.

Your coaching imperative: Flexibility

You read about it every day. A company in "turnaround mode" names a new CEO, who, in turn, quickly proceeds to throw out everyone associated with the old regime. A new executive team is installed, coincidentally comprised of the CEO's former cronies or folks they can hand-pick. Out with the old and in with the new; no reasons or feedback provided. It is done almost matter-of-factly.

This is hardly leadership. Anyone can walk-in and do that. It takes a leader to separate the wheat from the chaff, and, barring unique circumstance, this is not an overnight or few-day assessment.

A new general manager was hired to lead a major industrial company where I worked. The company had been financially bleeding; eight of the ten divisions were in the red. Not long after he started, the new general manager brought the top twenty-five executives of the company to the national headquarters on a religious holiday weekend and fired them all in one meeting.

I was appalled at this ruthless approach. My boss was one of those fired and we were one of the profitable divisions, having just gone through a significant turnaround effort. I could not believe that my boss would be painted with the same brush as the others. I was angry. I also knew this new general manager was no fan of human resources. He saw people as anonymous commodities to be used for his end game. And while he did have some short-term success with his unprecedented austerity measures, it was not, predictably, sustainable.

As you read this chapter, recognize that one of the most common reasons why leaders crash and burn is their inability or unwillingness to change or to be flexible with their leadership

DOI: 10.4324/9781003456902-19

style. It is not a factor of birth order, IQ, family wealth, family stability, education, ethnicity, and race or gender. Failure is rooted in a lack of adaptive capacity.

Leadership defined

At its roots, leadership is the process by which you guide and direct followers in order to transform your organization from its current state to one deemed more desirable.

Leadership responsibilities

Supervisors motivate. Managers plan, staff, organize, control, and coordinate. Leaders identify vision, enunciate and align strategy, inspire commitment and shared mindset, allocate resources, and deliver results.

Leadership demands

Peter Drucker said it best. Leaders …

> … require the capacity to analyze, to think, to weigh alternatives, and to harmonize dissent. But they also require the capacity for quick and decisive action, for boldness, and for intuitive courage. They require being at home with abstract ideas, concepts, calculations, and figures. They also require perception of people, a human awareness, empathy, and all together a lively interest in people and respect for them.

The foundation of leadership: Service

The latter part of the above Drucker quote focuses on the people aspect of leadership, predicated upon connectivity and respect. These attributes are key components of servant leadership.

The servant leader humbly places the needs and priorities of others as paramount, thus becoming a servant first. Fundamentally, this leader desires to help and empower others to grow, develop, and succeed—becoming healthier, wiser, and free. Nelson Mandela, Mother Teresa, and Mahatma Gandhi, all of whom the Coach admired, are examples of this paradigm.

To embrace servant leadership, one must possess and exemplify several authentic characteristics. These include "listening and understanding; acceptance and empathy; foresight; awareness and perception; persuasion; conceptualization; self-healing; and rebuilding community." In addition, servant leaders see the path toward an ideal future through a personal lens, perhaps in a visionary manner. They can uniquely communicate and provide direction. They make sacrifices to attain their ends.

One of the early scholars in this area, Robert Greenleaf, identified several key elements that distinguish servant leadership's philosophy, including:

- Moral compass—Servant leaders have personal morality and integrity. They are values-driven and have the highest ethical standards. They believe in doing the right thing, even if it may not be the popular choice.

- Concern—Servant leaders put subordinates and all stakeholders first. They hear the voices of and give volume to those less or least privileged. All players at the table are respected. They do not display arrogance or an air of superiority. Quite the opposite.
- Self-reflection—Servant leaders are lifelong learners. They take time to think. They seek their own self-fulfillment through the growth they personally experience and share through helping others.

Coach Wooden was the epitome of a servant leader.

Leadership steps

John Maxwell is a preeminent expert on the study of leadership. He has written over two dozen books on the topic, many of which are bestsellers. He lectures across the globe to organizations large and small. He developed a leadership paradigm worthy of due consideration, suggesting that leadership is not about one's placement on the organization chart; rather, it is about your ability to inspire and get things done through people. The model has five levels, each of which is foundational for the next.

1   Position: People follow you because they have to. This is an entry-level leadership position. Your ability to lead is based solely upon your title and organizational standing. There is little or no ability to influence. Rules and regulations are how people are controlled. Formal and limited authority is how things get done.
2   Permission: People follow you because they want to. Level 2 leadership is based on relationships. You want to get along with people and you treat them as valued colleagues. You want them to trust you and you wish to extend influence. Hopefully, everyone likes each other and it is a pleasant work environment.
3   Production: People follow because of what you have done for the organization. At this level, results happen! Influence and credibility are derived from previous accomplishments. Success and productivity increase. People feel more engaged as morale improves and goals are achieved. Level 3 leaders are change agents.
4   People Development: People follow you because of what you have done for them. This is about empowering others. At this level, leaders use their position, influence, and productivity to invest in their team members for their development. They keep doing so, to the extent possible, until they have reproduced themselves.
    Teamwork is at the core. Investment in people becomes deeper. With shared knowledge of each other's capabilities, everyone's performance improves.
5   Pinnacle: People follow you because of who you are and what you represent. This requires skill, effort, intention, and—toughest of all—talent. Level 5 leaders develop level 5 organizations. They create unique opportunities and have outstanding reputations that transcend their position, company, and perhaps their industry. They create legacy. Followers want to be associated with this type of leader.

Leadership styles

In the early days of organizational psychology, there were two identified theories or styles of management, "X" and "Y." The former was about command and control; the latter was more "hands-off" and empowering. *(Note: I was once, and I believe accurately described as a "Closet X" with my own style.)*

Management theory has come a long way since then. Today, there are as many as 12 styles.

In an effort to synthesize the research, I am showing a representative sample that should cover most of the situations you will encounter in an organizational setting. Please note that there are blurred lines between a few of these styles and that multiple labels may be used. For example, autocratic is often referred to as directive; democratic is often referred to as participative, etc. Of note, many textbooks do not distinguish between a "management style" and a "leadership style;" therefore, I will refer to all styles in the context of leadership.

As you read these descriptions, which single style or blend is consistent with your natural disposition? More importantly, which style(s) does your team need you to practice now in a way to lead them toward transformation and enhanced performance? How about tomorrow?

Autocratic

Think of the desk-pounding executive in the corner office. Forceful, manipulative, and ego-driven; it is all about control. By design, he/she holds all the cards.

In this style, management runs the organization with a top-down approach. They know best. It is highly regimented and structured. Employees are exploited. They do what they are told and generally act out of fear of the consequences. Their opinions are not generally welcomed and certainly not sought. Strict and detailed rules and policies govern behaviors. Everyone is on their toes and on notice for the next edict to filter down from the ivory tower. Intimidation is rampant. Threats are part of management's general vocabulary.

The upside of this style is that employees know what is expected of them. Everyone has a role and tasks to be completed. Decision-making is quick and generally in only a few people's hands. This style works well in a crisis. On the other hand, there is no empowerment. Only very few have a voice. Morale and enthusiasm likely run in the range of fair to not so great. As such, innovation is stifled and collaboration is hard to find. Feedback that might otherwise be critical for management goes unaddressed. Talented employees will resent being micro-managed.

Consultative

This style is also top-down, but it includes seeking employee input before virtually all decision-making. Thus, employees feel like their point of view has influence and impact.

Leaders using this style keep a real-time pulse on the workplace and have better relationships with their team members. They look out for employee needs and are generally responsive to such. They seek acceptance and influence through cooperation. Conflict is generally avoided. An open-door policy is an example of this style, as it encourages two-way communication regarding what is working and what is not.

On the downside, because this style seeks continual harmony, divergent views may be pacified instead of addressed. This may lead to less than optimal decision-making options and timing. It may also create a general resistance to change.

Expertise

Experts make terrific individual contributors. However, as you might surmise, your best or most senior accountant may not be your best CFO.

Expert leaders place all their credibility on their functional knowledge. They have been there, done that—or at least read or heard about that. In leading their teams, they do so with intellectual superiority of the given subject matter. They are not generally collaborative, and they are hardly team players. They are less in-synch with their team's needs. They rule with the mindset that their opinion is the only one that matters. Critical listening is not their forte. They share an autocrat's attitude of "my way or the highway."

Clearly, this style will dampen a team's enthusiasm over time, and it will likely lead to less effective and efficient decision-making.

Achiever

The achiever challenges and supports his/her team. They try to build a positive work environment within and across their organization. They strive for excellence, focus on the task at hand, and keep a strategic mindset. They get results.

Achievers can visualize the "big picture" and comprehend how the pieces fit together. They understand complexities and processes. They are open to and receptive to feedback and willing to act upon it accordingly. Achievers recognize the differing views of others and how that can yield strength. They tend to appropriately manage conflict. Achievers also tend to trust their subordinates and delegate as warranted.

The caution of this style is that these leaders sometimes inhibit thinking outside of the box and may hold people to unreachable standards. It can be exhausting for the followers.

Persuasive

In a style predicated by one-way, top-down communication, a leader attempts to persuade his/her constituents about why the path being selected is in everyone's best interests. This relies on the leader's charisma, ability to influence, track record, subject matter knowledge or experience, and overall goodwill with the employees. If the leader is fair and has credibility, they may get the respect and cooperation necessary to bring their vision to life. The key is convincing employees to follow. The leader provides feedback and recognition at each step of the transformation. Focus and direction are clear.

While this style can be efficient, its effectiveness may be questioned. Employees may feel like they are on the outside looking in, and they may even resent that their input is not welcomed. Given these yellow flags, leaders should use this approach sparingly.

Democratic

The democratic leader gives everyone a stake in decision-making. This participative style, best suited for a flat organizational structure, is based on collaboration. It allows employees to have a sense of ownership in their work. Decisions made in a majority's favor tend to be easier to implement and manage. There is a bond between management and employees, and open, two-way communications are generally the norm. Leaders embracing this style share information, tend to have a high degree of intellectual curiosity and are open to feedback. They welcome experimentation.

To the contrary, this style can be time-consuming. Multiple parties must be consulted. Edits and changes are made along the way; thus, feedback loops may be constantly changing, causing the need to recycle. Discussion often leads to debate. Compromise is often the result, which may impact efficiencies. If consensus and harmony are not achieved, groupthink or conflict may fester.

Laissez-faire

With this "hands-off" style, the manager assumes the roles of coach and mentor. He/she provides direction, guidance, and oversight without becoming too involved in the work. This distance allows team members to have a certain degree of freedom and latitude. Employees make level-appropriate decisions and enjoy relative independence.

This works well in situations where team members are more mature and also where the environment is one where innovation and creativity are required.

Chaotic

This is not so much of a style, as it is a game of chance. A chaotic style is practiced when managers leave teams to self-manage; stay out of the way. The hope is that the team will sort out its own leadership needs, develop its own voice, identify the challenges, and set out to tackle the remedies—shared or otherwise—needed to succeed.

This style has risk. It works best in two scenarios. First, when team members are highly capable and familiar with each other, they will have a high probability of success when tackling a project narrow in scope. Second, when a team has been somewhat dysfunctional, a manager might opt to get all team members in a room, challenge them to a specific task, and then leave them behind to figure out the best way forward. The intended outcome is team bonding and community building, assuming that they can get beyond their politics and differences. Managers may want to use a bit of a threat for motivational means as well as to provide a hard deadline to encourage urgency and importance.

If this style derails, confusion sets in and decision-making grinds to a halt. Inefficiencies and personality conflicts may quickly escalate. This will cause the need for you to promptly and strongly intervene or seek facilitation.

Bring your leadership to life

Here are some mindful tips to avoid leadership derailment.

Embrace self-discovery

You should welcome the opportunity for self-discovery. To this end, welcome regular feedback from your manager, peers, and subordinates. They know you best and are in a terrific position to comment upon your leadership strengths and developmental needs. If you wish for more structured feedback for self-assessment *(and I would recommend such)*, there are several psychometric tools available on the market.

Adjust as needed

Your ultimate success as a leader will likely depend upon your ability to quickly shift styles and "adjust to your players" (depending upon their developmental needs and experience levels) as you read the tea leaves in your business ecosystem—organizational changes, competitive pressures, industrial shifts, market changes, etc. Clearly, you need to be perceptive and well-rounded in your management skills. In executing your duties, you will likely gravitate to one more of the previously mentioned styles, but you need to be flexible to possibly transform again and again. Researchers Hersey and Blanchard coined the term "situational leadership" in 1969, and it still strongly resonates today. In this regard, leaders should continually assess their followers in terms of their *psychological maturity* (their self-confidence and ability and steadiness to accept the job) as well as *their job maturity* (their relevant skills and technical knowledge). These assessments allow you to adjust your level of individual or group support and guidance through the following activities:

- Delegating—turning over responsibility for decisions and actions to employees requiring the least amount of guidance.
- Participating—sharing ideas and facilitating decision-making.
- Selling—explaining decisions and providing opportunity for clarification.
- Telling—providing specific instructions and closely supervising performance.

MBWA

David Packard, co-founder of Hewlett-Packard, built a great business from humble origins. He did not do this while chained to his desk. From the company's onset in 1939 in a garage and all through the expansive years that followed, Packard spurred the executive trappings of his role and maintained a policy of openness and availability. In doing so, he practiced what was later referred to as "management by walking around" (MBWA*).

One can only imagine Packard walking around the factory floor, discussing the site's operations, finances, safety record, and the weather. He would have been constantly in motion, seeking out those who might otherwise be overlooked as well as those who needed a platform. His style was based upon sincere openness and genuine caring. He likely knew many of the site's employees on a first-name basis, viewing every individual as an important organizational asset and as their family's respective breadwinner. These "walkabouts" allowed Packard to not only deliver his messages, but to become a sponge about the employee's attitudes, motivation, and levels of job satisfaction. His visibility, accessibility, and responsiveness also likely endeared him to the employees by empowering them in their daily work.

*Also referred to as "management by *wandering* around."

Be friendly, but not friends

Coach was never a friend to any of his players while they were at UCLA. Certainly, Coach was courteous and respectful; however, if his players wanted a friend, they could seek out one of the assistants.

Why?

There is a fine line between leading people and being their friends. On the one hand, there should be commonalities such as wanting your team to experience altruism, loyalty, honesty, compassion, and trust. In fact, if we may be a bit bold here, there is nothing wrong with even loving what you do and with whom you do it. On the other hand, as a leader, you will be making decisions about your team members for hiring, promotion, performance reviews, and discipline.

Your ability to make people's decisions must be seen as unbiased, objective, and without prejudice. Emotions need to be detached and on the sideline. Difficult conversations may need to take place. There could even be pain involved such as decisions around facility closures or downsizing. Favoritism, or the appearance thereof, must be avoided.

A leader should not get too close to his or her followers. Some limited personal time or social interaction is fine, but remember that leadership is not a popularity contest. While it is nice to be liked, you will not always be liked. Therefore, it must be your leadership role first, friends second.

Humility helps

In a recent *Wall Street Journal* article, "The Best Bosses Are Humble Bosses," Sue Shellenbarger cites evidence that validates humility as one of the most important traits for a successful leader. In fact, more and more companies are taking humility into account for their senior staffing considerations.

This might seem counter to what we see in the headlines in today's world of business and politics.

Humble leaders have a natural intellectual curiosity. They are not afraid to ask questions or admit that they do not have all the answers. They are aware of their own assets and limitations and are eager to improve themselves. Their goals are beyond their self-interests. They listen, ask for help, and seek feedback. They are more collaborative and team-oriented. Chances are that they have learned from their mistakes. Of note, teams with humble leaders also perform better and have a higher quality work product, among other beneficial results.

Know that your decisions will be challenged

In Principle 9, I suggested that your values will be tested. I can also confidently state that your decision-making will face similar scrutiny.

To illustrate this point, Coach Wooden shared a story with Andy and me from his formative years with some disappointment about the way he handled a situation. It seems that early in tenth grade, young John, the soon-to-be all-state player, was not on the starting team. His coach decided to play others ahead of him. John was upset, angry, and in pain. He felt he was better than the others. Thus, at the end of one practice, he told his coach that he was quitting. He did not curse, scream, or throw a temper tantrum (although that may be subject to interpretation). There were no punches or elbows thrown. Unhappy and frustrated, John simply stripped off his jersey and shorts and marched into the locker room in his underwear. He was done.

If you were John's coach, certainly caught off-guard by this sudden unfolding, how would you have handled this? In this case, John's coach, when faced with the prospect of losing this rising talent, wisely revisited his decision about John's playing time.

To state the obvious, know that your decisions likewise have consequences. Think through and anticipate their ramifications.

Speak the language

Numbers are the language of business. To be credible with your colleagues and for your own development, you must have a working familiarity with financial terms, communication basics, technology literacy and use, and business analytics. If you are not comfortable with these topics at this point, an introductory course or refresher is in order.

Avoid these pitfalls

The world around us is changing at a revolutionary speed. You must be inspirational and compelling; convincing and motivating. Your goal is to align your resources around and toward the path to your shared destination and stay on top of course adjustments.

- Be the exemplar for attitude and behavior for your team. Your IQ, pedigree, track record, charm, and charisma will not matter one bit if you cannot exhibit complete integrity and honesty.
- You must adhere to the highest ethical standards.
- Never ask anyone to do anything that you would not or have not done. Be committed to the cause. Keep your performance at the highest level and live your company values.
- Be accountable. Leaders do not blame others. They are accountable for all of their success and failures. They are accountable to themselves and their team.

How does this compare to conventional wisdom?

What do you mean that "I" must adjust?

The common reaction to this Principle is that subordinates should adjust to their supervisors. While there is some give and take here, it is incumbent upon the supervisor to provide proper latitude. This will ultimately help team members further engage.

Endnotes for Principle 12: Adjust to your players—Don't expect them to adjust to you

Coach's embodiment

"John Wooden," Wikipedia. (Date unknown). Retrieved on October 10, 2018, from: https://en.wikipedia.org/wiki/John_Wooden

Hill, A., & Wooden, J.R. (2001). *Be quick but don't hurry*. New York: Simon & Schuster, p. 152.

Flexibility

Bennis, W.G., & Thomas, R.J. (2002). *Geek and geezers: How era, values, and defining moments shape leaders*. Boston, Massachusetts: Harvard Business School Press, p. 91, 92.

Sugarman, J., Scullard, M., & Wilhelm, E. (2001). *The 8 dimensions of leadership: DiSC strategies for becoming a better leader*. San Francisco, California: Berrett-Koehler Publishers, Inc., p. xi, xii.

Demands of leadership

Drucker, P.F. (1967). *The effective executive*. New York: HarperCollins Publishers, Inc., p. 58.

The foundation of leadership

Keith, K. (Date unknown). To serve first, the servant leadership journey. Retrieved on August 16, 2018, from: http://toservefirst.com/definition-of-servant-leadership.html

Steps of leadership

Maxwell, J.C. (2013). *How successful people lead.* New York: Hachette Book Group, Center Street, pp. 5–19.

Styles of leadership

Mulder, P. (2015). McGregor theory x and theory y. Retrieved on August 29, 2018, from ToolsHero: https://www.toolshero.com/leadership/mcgregor-theory/
The Executive Connection. (2015, June 24). 9 common leadership styles: Which type of leader are you? Retrieved on August 16, 2018, from: https://tec.com.au/resource/9-common-leadership-styles-which-type-of-leader-are-you/

Autocratic

Rhatigan, C. (2016, October 25). An in-depth look at six different management styles. *Tinypulse.* Retrieved on August 24, 2018, from: https://www.tinypulse.com/blog/six-management-styles
Anastasia. (2016, December 18). Management styles and when best to use them. *Cleverism.com.* Retrieved on August 16, 2018, from: https://www.cleverism.com/management-styles/

Consultative

Rhatigan, C. (2016, October 25). An in-depth look at six different management styles. *Tinypulse.* Retrieved on August 24, 2018, from: https://www.tinypulse.com/blog/six-management-styles

Expertise/Achiever

Rhatigan, C. (2016, October 25). An in-depth look at six different management styles. *Tinypulse.* Retrieved on August 24, 2018, from: https://www.tinypulse.com/blog/six-management-styles
Rooke, D., & Torbert, W.R. (2005, April). Seven transformations of leadership. *Harvard Business Review.* Retrieved on August 16, 2018, from: https://hbr.org/2005/04/seven-transformations-of-leadership

Persuasive

Rhatigan, C. (2016, October 25). An in-depth look at six different management styles. *Tinypulse.* Retrieved on August 24, 2018, from: https://www.tinypulse.com/blog/six-management-styles

Democratic

Rhatigan, C. (2016, October 25). An in-depth look at six different management styles. *Tinypulse.* Retrieved on August 24, 2018, from: https://www.tinypulse.com/blog/six-management-styles
Anastasia. (2016, December 18). Management styles and when best to use them. *Cleverism.com.* Retrieved on August 16, 2018, from: https://www.cleverism.com/management-styles/

McDermott, A. (2017, August 28). The top 7 management styles: Which ones are most effective? *Workzone.com*. Retrieved on August 16, 2018, from: https://www.workzone.com/blog/management-styles/

Laissez-faire/Chaotic

Rhatigan, C. (2016, October 25). An in-depth look at six different management styles. *Tinypulse*. Retrieved on August 24, 2018, from: https://www.tinypulse.com/blog/six-management-styles

Adjust as needed

Society for Human Resource Management. (2005). The SHRM learning system, Section 3: Human Resources Development. *Alexandria, Virginia*. pp. 153–156.

MBWA

Bennis, W., Brown, T., Champy, J., Crainer, S., Davis, S., Edwards, H., Goleman, D., Gottlieb, A., Heller, R., Larreche, J.C., Leyden, P., Meyer, C., Norton, B., & Rayport, J. (Advisory Board) (2002). *Business: The ultimate resource*. Cambridge, Massachusetts: Perseus Publishing, p. 1126, 1127.

Some basics

Myatt, M. (2012, October 18). 15 ways to identify bad leaders. *Forbes.com*. Retrieved on August 16, 2018, from: https://www.forbes.com/sites/mikemyatt/2012/10/18/15-ways-to-identify-bad-leaders/#3c2f1a3315da

Be friendly, not friends

Daskal, L. (Date unknown). The fine line between friendship and leadership. Retrieved on October 5, 2018, from: https://www.lollydaskal.com/leadership/the-fine-line-between-friendship-and-leadership/
Peterson, S. (2014, August 2). Separating friendship from leadership. W. P. Carey School of Business, Arizona State University. Retrieved on October 5, 2018, from: https://www.azcentral.com/story/money/business/career/2014/08/02/friendship-leadership-separation/13528001/

Humility helps

Shellenbarger, S. (2018, October 10). The best bosses are the humble bosses. *The Wall Street Journal*, p. A11.

Failing to prepare is preparing to fail

To be best prepared for the season, Coach spent his summers relentlessly researching and investigating all aspects of the game that pertained to his returning and in-coming talent. He would read books, speak to other coaches, and watch films. He would then meet with his assistants for countless hours in order to discuss the strategy and related action plans for the upcoming season. This detailed preparation and planning would ultimately guide and drive the team to perform at its highest level.

One of the more notable examples of the Coach's preparation involved his discussion of socks and sneakers. With no detail too small for attention, Coach would have a locker room talk with his players early in the season about how they should attend to their footwear. You may recall that Coach grew up in the pre-depression era. Sneakers were not readily available or affordable; therefore, a pair had to last. Thus, relaying his own experience, Coach gave a personal tutorial to his players on how to properly put their socks and sneakers on, mitigating the probability of any potential blisters. Yes, the players quietly scoffed, but no one could question his intention.

Another example of the Coach's preparation involved his practice sessions. Here, his attention to planning was on full display as the agenda for each of these practices was meticulously outlined on "3 × 5 × 5" cards.* Each minute was purposeful and precise, stressing skills development and conditioning. Each minute!

*Coach kept these detailed agendas in a notebook, dating back two years, listing all the drills from each practice as he did not want any redundancy for the veteran players.

Your coaching imperative: Plan the work and work the plan

Through the years, I have worked with several leading management consulting firms such as PWC, WTW, BCG, Kepnor-Tregoe, McKinsey, and A.T. Kearney. These firms and others offer a variety of services to assist organizations through change processes. They can also help you create and hasten the implementation of your business and operating plan.

Absent your ability to consult with these types of firms, there are several steps you can take to get started with the research and planning associated with your team's direction and ultimate success.

Survey the landscape

If you do not know where you are, you will never get to where you want to go. Find out where you are! To this end, you must cast a broad net and gather information from your key

DOI: 10.4324/9781003456902-20

stakeholders in the form of a SWOT analysis (strengths, weaknesses, opportunities, and threats). Representative questions you may wish to consider are as follows:

Strengths

- What advantages does your organization have?
- What do you do better than anyone else?
- What is the unique value-proposition of your product or service?
- What is the unique low-cost resource you can draw upon?

Weaknesses

- Where are you vulnerable?
- What can you improve?
- What can you avoid?
- What can you do differently?
- If you were starting with a blank slate, what would you change?
- If you suddenly had a burning platform, what would you change tomorrow?

Opportunities

- What product or service opportunities are on the horizon?
- What are the trends in your industry?
- Are there ideas to consider outside of your industry?
- Is there synergy to be gained with any strategic partnerships?
- How might technology help you leap ahead?

Threats

- What could inhibit your progress?
- What are your competitors doing?
- Is technology a threat or disruptive force of concern?
- Will you have the talent necessary to compete?
- Do you have needed financial resources for the future?
- How do we stay focused?

Imagine your future state

With your SWOT analysis complete, it is time to determine if a change is warranted in direction. This takes a fair amount of cerebral energy. Involve others. Take a fresh and objective look at your earlier research. Make an initial problem diagnosis, identify critical challenges and concerns, and list the pros and cons of all viable alternatives with associated risks.

Once a path is chosen, get the appropriate management support.

Develop your mission statement*

A mission statement is forward-looking. It provides purpose and direction. It brings your desired future state to life and answers the question, "Why are we here?"

When crafting this statement, bear in mind that the words should engage followers in a way that solicits voluntary commitment. It should appeal to the individual to become part of an exciting and invigorating roadmap toward tomorrow. Accordingly, a mission statement should be aligned with your desired future state, as well as compelling and plausible, inspiring, and appealing to both intellectual and emotional appetites. It should have focus, be unique, be relatable, and be easy to communicate and understand.

Some examples of statements related to corporate purpose found in annual reports or on company websites include:

- Google: "To organize the world's information and make it universally accessible and useful."
- Nike: "To bring inspiration and innovation to every athlete in the world."
- Pfizer: "To be the premier, innovative biopharmaceutical company."
- American Express: "We work hard every day to make American Express the world's most respected service brand."
- Smithsonian: "The increase and diffusion of knowledge."
- Microsoft: "Empower every person and every organization on the planet to achieve more."

Do not be misled into thinking that mission statements are only for multinational corporations. If you are in a group, division, country, unit, sub-unit, department, or smaller team, you should also have inspirational words to commence action. Whether is it "Quality is our priority," "Zero-defects," or the common HR mantra of "Right person, right place, right time," such statements will drive your common purpose.

Once your mission statement is identified, be sure to communicate it throughout your organization. This will foster an internal dialog and examination of activities, i.e., if the work that is being performed does not support the organization's mission, why is it being done? Engaged followers will generally experience greater job satisfaction, motivation, commitment, and loyalty around this.

* Vision statements tend to be "big picture" oriented, aspirational, and long-term in nature. Mission statements are more pragmatic and near-term in nature. I am using them somewhat interchangeably.

Identify your strategic objectives

Strategy is not hope and prayer. It is not about trying to be all things to all people. It is not about blindly managing your business with year-over-year metrics without considering environmental changes. As Tregoe, Zimmerman, Smith, and Tobia (1989) state, strategy is "the framework which guides those choices that determine the nature and direction of an organization." It brings your mission to life and drives people toward an identifiable end. It should articulate your basis for sustainable competitive advantage.

At their foundation, strategic objectives direct employees' actions as they help secure commitment, are goal-oriented, are clear and concise, and address identifiable outcomes. They can be crafted for corporate, business, functional, and operating levels.

Strategic objectives generally have a 24–36-month outlook and are in a SMART format (specific, measurable, achievable, relevant, and time bound) format. They will be crafted in a manner that likely allows for categorization such as markets and customers, products and services, technologies, people, facilities, and business processes. They must answer the question, "What key activities must be accomplished in order to realize our mission?" Ted Jackson, in his excellent article, "56 Strategic Objective Examples for Your Company to Copy," cites numerous business factors for your consideration. By example:

- Grow shareholder value: The top goal of your organization may be to increase the value of your organization for your shareholders, stakeholders, or owners.
- Increase revenue: Revenue represents growth in your organization, so increasing revenue is a sign of company health. You can make this more specific by defining revenue from a key area in your organization.
- Reliable products/services: If your organization takes pride in the reliability of your product or service, this objective—which reflects that you are targeting customers that also value this reliability—may be right for you. This could indicate the on-time reliability of an airline or the dependable reliability of a printer that generates high-quality output.
- Best service: This strategy indicates you want your customers to consider your organization easy to deal with. Customers may choose to work with you even if you have a product similar to your competitors simply because your service is better.
- Improve customer satisfaction: If customer satisfaction is critical in your company, this may be a good objective to home in on. Because it is generic, the definition for your organization needs to be more focused around particular areas of satisfaction you place focus on.

Align your tactics

Tactics are the detailed, short-term action steps, generally comprised with a 12-month forward-looking horizon, required to execute the business plan. The tactics are identified by *management and employees* and address "how" the organization, at various levels, will implement its strategy.

Tactics should be developed in a collaborative manner, through a cascading process. This will allow each of the organization's functions, teams, and individuals to sequentially articulate and align goals and action plans that are in concert with and in support of the organization's overall strategic goals. For example:

- If your strategic objectives delineate offering a product of superior *quality*, then functional tactics might include specific performance targets for introducing defect-free manufacturing processes, attaining certain quality certifications, standardizing work processes, providing related training and education, achieving better internal audit scores, partnering with suppliers, benchmarking, reducing service call rates, implementing continuous improvement initiatives, etc.
- If your strategic objectives identify a specific *cost reduction* target in a manufacturing area, then tactics might include increasing productivity, reducing scrap, reducing material handling, cross-training staff, reducing manpower or reallocating skills, reducing energy costs, redefining facility layout, upgrading equipment, reducing raw materials and finished inventory, etc.
- If talent *acquisition* by becoming the "employer of choice" in your neighborhood is critical, tactics might include broadening your recruiting sources, improving the selection process, refining your orientation process, increasing community exposure, creating programs around work/family balance, remote working, enhancing healthcare benefits programs, adjusting compensation scales, etc.

To the extent possible, functional, team, and individual tactics should also be in the SMART format as drivers of individual and collective performance. They should be formulated by consensus, with a high degree of participation, and identify the party or individual of primary responsibility. They become, in effect, the scorecard of your progress.

Have a fluid organizational structure

With clarity around your mission, strategy, and tactics, you next focus on your people. What is the best way to organize your people in order to make the vision a reality, and to execute the strategy and tactics? Start from scratch.

Design based on needs

Adapting to change is never easy; however, redesigning an organization's structure, if done properly, can invigorate all involved. In this vein—and using a bit of an old-fashioned approach—get all stakeholders in a conference room that has a whiteboard (or the like). Shut the door. Begin by asking questions about the desired end-state of the organization, Focus on what structure will optimize your results. Bring several packages of different colored "sticky notes" to represent functions and their needed job titles (noted below). Memorialize what you need to with each step.

At the corporate or business level, the design of your organization will be predicated upon which structure works best to accomplish the strategy of the organization. Consider best practices. Do your research. Among colleagues, you will likely discuss the priorities and economics around what you make, the services, you provide, the markets you serve, technological capabilities, capital requirements, market trends and forecasts, and the geographies in which you operate or target. Your findings will likely cause you to have a flat, hierarchical, or matrixed organizational structure.

At the functional, local, or operating level, organizational factors may include the effectiveness and efficiency of work processes, tasks, and the division of labor; possible centralization of common functions for synergy and responsiveness; the need to balance local and global requirements; and the number of organizational layers, spans of control, and line/staff support ratios. Some starting questions are as follows:

- How do we divide up the work?
- What functions complement each other?
- How many direct reports should a supervisor have?
- At what level of the organization should decisions be made?
- How do we enable communication among people in different departments and at different levels?
- How many levels are needed for optimal governance and control?
- Does the structure support the intended culture?
- Does this structure allow us to attract, select, develop, and retain the best talent?

As part of this exercise, you must also determine what resources or talent may be bought, sold, leased, or outsourced.

Design for empowerment

Do not underestimate the need for leadership debate and consensus regarding the amount of trust and latitude to be given to employees when it comes to organizational design, as you attempt to balance decision-making and authority with organizational discipline.

Empowerment is a term that has come to take on a broad and not always positive meaning. In this context, I am referring to the freedom employees have to act independently on behalf of the organization. Too little freedom and people feel suffocated; too much and you can have chaos. The litmus test is—and this will vary for every organization as a form of risk management—when your organizational design finds the "sweet spot" where employees feel like "owners" of their work, while recognizing appropriate boundaries and limitations. It is the optimal blend of individual freedom and responsibility. Decisions and authority are at the "right" level. Employees have the right information and capabilities to advance execute your strategy.

Design for agility

Speed and the ability to change direction count.

For years, corporations have tried to walk that fine line of organizing their people resources in the most effective, efficient, and financially responsible manner possible in order to accomplish their goals. In years gone by, the word "lean" was often associated with these efforts.

The fast pace of our dynamic business world dictates that lean is still good; agile is even better. Agile teams started in Information Technology as a way of developing software, but the approach is spreading. Agile teams are small and have members from various disciplines. As noted in a recent *Harvard Business Review* article by Rigby, Sutherland, and Noble, agile teams are designed to be

> … confronted with a large, complex problem, they break into modules, develop solutions to each component through rapid prototyping and tight feedback loops, and integrate the solutions into a coherent whole. They place more value on adapting to change than on sticking to a plan, and they hold themselves accountable for the outcomes (such as growth, profitability, and customer loyalty), not outputs (such as lines of code or number of new products.)

These teams are quick, focused, continuously learning, and empowered to make decisions.

Agile teams are not right for every function or challenge. They require amplified empowerment, support, resource allocation, and specific focus. However, this approach is certainly worthy of your consideration where speed, creativity, and innovation are requirements.

Identify roles and accountabilities

One of Coach's strengths as a leader was his ability to define roles and accountabilities. Everyone knew their respective role and its expectations. Everyone knew each other's roles. Everyone understood dependencies.

With your organization structure coming into place, it is time to sort out *who does what*. Now is the time when you can put names on those sticky notes. This can be particularly messy if politics creeps into the discussion (as it inevitably does); however, all attempts should be made to objectively focus on what each role needs to accomplish and the potential match of the existing or possible talent pool available. Do not compromise!

At the start of this exercise, the only sticky note with a name is the CEO (or equivalent). From there, it is a "sticky note by sticky note" discussion. Discretion may wish to be exercised as to whom participates and when in these discussions.

Communicate

As we have touched upon, communication is critical in every leader's role, particularly when setting new sights. When you have the new vision, strategy, and structure in place (or getting close), it needs to be communicated. There are three ways to introduce change: force, such as a "burning platform;" charm and persuasion; and education through shared knowledge. If time permits, the latter method is the most effective and efficient for driving organizational transformation.

In terms of communication specifics, you will be emphasizing a new cause and direction. Ideally, your script should focus on the strategic elements of where you are going, why it is important to go there, and the path ahead. Let everyone know how and why their role in critical and what the new expectations are. Compel them to act! Stress the team over the individual. If applicable, be sure to focus some of your discussion on what is familiar and what will not be changing. This will help quell the fears of some who might be otherwise resistant.

And if you must downsize ...

If your new organizational structure indicates that have too many employees, you have some options. Namely, you should consider furloughs, early retirement or voluntary leave incentive packages, hiring freezes, not-too-deep budget cuts, eliminating temporary workers, reduced hours, a salary freeze and/or some salary cutbacks, stepped-up job sharing, and retrained or reallocated staff.

If all of the above has been exhausted and the financial bleeding continues, it is now time to consider a layoff. Ugh!

In my career, I have been in the room when decisions were made to terminate anywhere from a handful to hundreds of people because of business downturns, operational/technological upgrades, or outsourced efficiencies. These decisions are gut-wrenching. Careers, families, and communities are all impacted. I can attest that significant sleep is lost as these matters are debated and ultimately executed. The worst part is identifying the reduction-in-force candidates and the "package" preparation that goes on behind closed doors. Augh!

When the day arrives, the individual separation discussions are downright painful. The impacted employees are personally and professionally wounded as they exit; those remaining must deal with their own significant emotional reactions. Everyone needs care. Respect should be shown to everyone at all times.

As a leader, if you must go down this path, treat everyone with respect and dignity. Do not mail this in! And if you ever bump into me, ask about the time that a company put security guards on horseback in their parking lot during a staff reduction or when employees were directed to one of two conference rooms upon their arrival at work ("keepers" versus "layoffs"). Both true stories!

How does this compare to Conventional Wisdom?

"Winging it" can only take one—and one's organization—so far. Every business leader needs his or her equivalent of "3 × 5 × 5" cards.

Endnotes for Principle 13: Failing to prepare is preparing to fail

SWOT

Mindtools. (Date unknown). SWOT analysis, discover new opportunities, manage and eliminate threats. Retrieved on May 14, 2018, from https://www.mindtools.com/pages/article/newTMC_05. htm SWOT questions)

Mission

Bennis, W.G., & Townsend, R. (1995). *Reinventing leadership: Strategies to empower the organization.* New York: William Morrow Company, p. 37.

Hamel, G., & Prahalad, C.K. (1994). *Competing for the future: breakthrough strategies for seizing control of your industry and creating the markets for tomorrow.* Boston, Massachusetts: Harvard Business School Press, p. 129.

Covey, S.R. (1991). *Principle-centered leadership.* New York: Summit Books, pp. 244–249.

Kouzes, J.M., & Posner, B.Z. (1995). *The leadership challenge: How to get extraordinary things done in organizations.* San Francisco, California: Jossey-Bass Inc., Publishers, pp. 95, 97, 124–126.

Kotter, J. P. (1996). *Leading change.* Boston, Massachusetts: Harvard Business School, pp. 68–69, 72.

Strategy

Repper, D. (2020, June 15). Private conversation.

Tregoe, B., Zimmerman, J.W., Smith, R.A., & Tobia, P. (1989). *Vision in action: Putting a winning strategy to work.* New York: Simon & Schuster, pp. 33, 38.

Mercer Delta Consulting, LLC. (1998). "The Congruence Model: A Roadmap for Understanding Organizational Performance." *Mercer Delta Insights.* New York: Mercer Delta Consulting, LLC. p. 6.

The Price Waterhouse Change Integration Team (1995). *Better change: Best Practices for transforming your organization.* New York: Irwin Professional Publishing. pp. 171–181.

Jackson, T. (2017, April 3). 56 strategic objective examples for your company to copy. Retrieved on May 8, 2018, from: https://www.clearpointstrategy.com/56-strategic-objective-examples-for-your-company-to-copy/

Tactics

The Price Waterhouse Change Integration Team (1995). *Better change: Best practices for transforming your organization.* New York: Irwin Professional Publishing. pp. 171–181.

Design for success

Tregoe, B., Zimmerman, J.W., Smith, R.A., & Tobia, P. (1989). *Vision in action: Putting a winning strategy to work.* New York: Simon & Schuster, p. 79.

Gladwell, M. (2002, July 22). The talent myth – Are smart people overrated? *The New Yorker,* pp. 28–33.

Design for empowerment

Gulati, R. (2018, May–June). Structure that's not stifling. *Harvard Business Review*, p. 70.

Design based upon needs

Academic Insight: 6 Questions Guiding the Basics of Organizational Structure | Fargo INC! Magazine: www.https://fargoinc.com/academic-insight-6-questions-guiding-the-basics-of-organizational-structure

Design for agility

Rigby, D.K., Sutherland, J., & Noble, A., (2018, May-June). Agile scale. *Harvard Business Review*, pp. 90–91, 94.

Practice doesn't make perfect

Only perfect practice makes perfect

You play like you practice.

> Coach taught me how to practice. He planned and executed his practice sessions whereby drills were run stressing increased tempo and fitness; skills were developed and sharpened until confidence emerged; contingencies were rehearsed until flaws were minimized, if not eliminated; and plays were repeated under game conditions to increase poise and effectiveness. (Bill Walton)

Coach loved practice. In fact, he loved practice more than the games. It was his favorite part of coaching. Watch video from back in the day and you will see Coach actively engaged with and participating in every practice, often out on the court for the full session. He is in shorts, leading the drills, and demonstrating (over and over again) the fundamentals.

Practice sessions were Wooden's opportunity to experiment. The gym was his classroom; it was his laboratory. He was always looking for incremental and continuous improvement, keeping drills fast-paced, competitive, intense, and physically demanding. In his minute-by-minute choreography (as noted in the previous principle), he relentlessly pushed his players to pivot sharper, sprint quicker, change direction faster, and pick-up the pace better than they had the day before. Each blown whistle was a command. Less than full effort was not acceptable. His ultimate quest was that you always had more to give and could perform better. A high level of competitive practice performance and related confidence would yield greater game results.

Your coaching imperative: Strive for excellence

It was reported that Ernest Hemingway rewrote the ending to *A Farewell to Arms* over 30 times to get each word right.

Brian Wilson of the Beach Boys labored for over six months to produce the 1966 classic "Good Vibrations." In that same vein, the classic album of "Pet Sounds" (my personal favorite) was recorded in four different studios to take advantage of particular site sound dynamics.

It has been said that Bruce Springsteen will start with a rough draft of a song and revise it 100 times.

Not many will quarrel with their finished products.

DOI: 10.4324/9781003456902-21

Embrace continuous improvement

As boss, you must challenge people to come up with a new, innovative, out-of-the-box purpose or process. Push them to consider your current situation or a combination of existing or possible ideas differently. Get creative!

Continuous improvement is the constant and on-going effort to enhance products, services, and processes within your organization. Incremental or innovative breakthrough, these improvements help increase productivity, upturn quality, decrease costs, or streamline logistics. As by-products, if management uses a participative approach, employee satisfaction, and morale may increase.

There are several tools for continuous improvement. You should have a working familiarity with these and other techniques as they promote overall efficiency and effectiveness.

Kanban

Kanban helps you "visualize" outcomes through workflow analysis. It uses sticky notes on a whiteboard as participants document workflows for analysis. It has four major ideas: visualize your process; limit work in process; focus on flow; and continually improve.

A3

A3 (derived from a standard large European paper size) is a structured approach to project planning. It entails problem-solving where planning, decisions, and learning are documented; structure is provided; and communications are facilitated. Ideal for working in cross-functional teams, problem elements such as background, current and future conditions, cause analysis, and recommendations are examined.

PDCA

Plan-do-check-act (PDCA) cycle identifies and tests hypotheses through their various stages: plan (identify the preferred state and what needs to change); do (make it happen on a small scale); check (has the intended outcome occurred?); and act. (If the ideal solution worked, then broaden the approach. If not, begin the process again.)

Gemba Walks

Gemba Walks are when leaders informally solicit ideas and suggestions from employees by increased site access and visibility. This is a version of managing by walking around, with specific intention. It aids a manager's understanding of what and how things are evolving in the workplace in real time.

Five why's

"The five whys" begin with a problem statement and keeps asking "why" until you get to the root cause.

Refinement

Your competition is with yourself. You want to perform at your highest level. Here are some ways that you and your team can sharpen skills in practice environments.

Role-playing

Think of the last time you had a challenging presentation or an emotionally charged discussion. What worked? What did not? If you could repeat it, what would you have done differently? Could practice have helped?

In anticipation of that next like-interaction, perhaps advanced role-playing can help.

Role-playing, as a training technique, has its roots in psychology and education, but it clearly has implications for the corporate world. As a practice vehicle, it prepares you for those unique situations and difficult discussions that stoke anxiety or social unease by allowing you to assume a role or persona and rehearse for the various scenarios that may confront you.

Once participants are gathered, the following steps will help take you to practice success:

- Brief participants. Identify the situation and its relevant problems and issues. Add details to the scenario.
- Make the setting as "real" as possible.
- Assign roles. These tend to be both supportive and confrontational. Remind participants to stay "on script."
- Start with open-ended questions. Bring emotion and negativity into the discussion.
- Let the discussion evolve in a natural way. Embrace flexibility, as things rarely go as planned.
- Try to visualize, gain experience, build confidence, and understand your audience.
- Learn how to appropriately act and react to potential outcomes. Try to maintain your poise.
- Stay positive and professional. Be relaxed, natural, and confident.
- Experiment. Add some intensity. Test and practice.
- Bring the session to closure with a recap.
- What is the learning? Discuss the key takeaways and share observations.
- Repeat the exercise as needed.

The real benefit of role-playing is self-insight.

Mirroring

By definition, mirroring is when one person subconsciously imitates another. This certainly has merit for worthwhile pursuits and characteristics.

By extension and with some literary license, I also interpret mirroring to mean self-discovery—i.e., role playing in front of a mirror to learn more about yourself. To this end, I recall working with an outplacement firm several years ago when I was "in transition." They suggested recording my mock interviews.

My narrative was fine, but I had a habit of tilting my head to the left when I responded to questions. I had no idea that I was doing this. I was appalled! This may have given the mistaken impression that I was nonchalant about the interaction, perhaps even bored, and my energy level was flat. Clearly, my verbals and non-verbals were not congruent!

Needless to say, I am now far more conscientious about posture. Try it yourself and see.

Improv

You may recall that I cited improvisation in Principle 2 when discussing conflict management. However, its applications are much broader.

Improvisation, as an art and discipline, is the intersection of reacting, adapting, and communication in real time. It involves sending and receiving messages clearly with minimum chance for misunderstanding. Detailed listening (words and sounds) and observation (facial expressions, body language, and gestures) are at its fundamental core. It is an essential leadership competency in environments characterized by uncertainty and chaos.

Improvisation has three steps:

- Reacting involves being in the moment and remaining focused. It is about appropriate openness and transparency.
- Adaptation is about awareness of the changes around you while bearing in mind what you are trying to achieve.
- Communication brings all improvisational elements together, bringing forth productive engagement between and among all parties.

Whether preparing for or participating in critical conversations, these skills are important to develop and master.

Simulations

Simulation provides a virtual environment where participants enter a space that mimics real-life conditions. The environment is often digitally created, employing multiple media.

Simulations are a highly effective training methodology as participants gain firsthand knowledge and experience with tools, programs, and devices. They also learn related protocols, processes, and procedures.

The instructional method is iterative in that trainers continually test innovations and change conditions to improve and round-out the training experience. Progress is easy to measure and evaluation is highly structured.

Simulation practice is most widely associated with flight training, medical procedures, driving a car, air traffic control, and military exercises.

As with any training, the design of the course curriculum should consider the objective, the number of participants, their general backgrounds and experience, the structure and timetable, content and exercises, instructor alignment, and evaluation methods.

The benefits of simulation are many. There is immediate feedback, the environment is risk free, knowledge retention is higher, and outcomes are quantifiable.

If your organization offers simulation training as a form of practice for your position, or for any of your team members, you should take advantage.

Focus groups

A focus group is a small group of selected individuals whose reactions and feedback are sought after in a test environment. As a form of qualitative research, focus groups have their roots in the military propaganda of World War II, but are more widely used today for political and market analysis.

During a focus group session, a scripted facilitator will prompt participants to share their thoughts, ideas, attitudes, and responses to presented ideas. You may be touching upon your next early-stage product or service idea, advertising campaign, brand launch, health-care benefit offering, or organization design prototype. Discussion freely evolves, meeting notes are recorded, and analysis is performed to determine the best way forward.

There are several variations to conducting a focus group discussion. As a general rule, it is a terrific option to explore this type of forum and dialog before spending an inordinate amount of time and money on formal market research. The feedback received will likely steer you in a better direction.

Business case studies

Case studies are detailed accounts and scholarly explanations of the subject matter and its environment. They are used as a "practice" vehicle in that they provide significant, relevant, and applicable learning opportunities. They may also be used as open-ended exercises to solicit participant input on how they might proceed with handling certain business challenges; thus, allowing for feedback.

Written and produced in highly structured format, they appear in formal research and business journals. Case studies are often presented in conferences and their content may be featured in periodicals or books. They are also a popular graduate school teaching tool.

Typically, the "case" being studied is an individual, organization, or a business quandary, relationship, experiment, or process. The contextual study is defined over a specific period and may be interdisciplinary. The research methodology may vary (i.e., qualitative, quantitative, or a mix). It generally starts with a question of investigative inquiry.

The findings of case studies allow study participants to learn from the facts and information. This shared knowledge, combined with pragmatic experience, should result in wisdom for the benefit of all.

Develop a continuous improvement mindset

There is some truth to the joke about how to get to Carnegie Hall ... practice, practice, practice.

Repetition

Repetition of an improper technique or further perpetuation of a lackadaisical attitude is worse than no practice at all. This is not about "practice makes perfect." Nor is it about more practice somehow giving you more or greater skills. You can shoot hundreds of foul shots in your backyard each day, but you will only improve if you can simulate game conditions and fine-tune your nuances. Otherwise, you are simply gaining some exercise.

Do not confuse the intention or verbiage of this principle. This is about *learning from repetition* by making the necessary adjustments, striving for improvement, and building confidence!

Raise the bar

Know best practices. Speak to thought leaders and market experts. Touch base with the academic community. Stay current in your field. Take courses. Take a consultant to lunch. Move forward with some market research.

Anticipate obstacles

Companies must have operational, financial, and staffing contingencies, as well as business continuity and emergency response plans (i.e., data retention, disaster recovery, crisis communication, business impact forecasting and analytics, customer assistance plans, etc.).

You need a similar outlook. Prepare for contingencies. The adage "if it can go wrong, it likely will," comes to mind.

A Fortune 500 company where I worked was implementing a new software system to help manage its sizable manufacturing processes. The system impacted every logistical movement on the factory floor and it was to be implemented over a three-day weekend.

Unfortunately, like many companies taking on a significant change initiative, we were not fully prepared for the task. The implementation floundered (to be kind). Deadlines slipped, costs escalated, and expectations eventually fell short. The factory's operations soon came to an abrupt halt.

What was the root cause of the problem? Simply, in our haste to move forward, we had not fully anticipated the holistic impact of this change. Not only was there a new technology at the doorstep, but the majority of job descriptions were also changing. As later realized, absent the upfront investment of broad-reaching and proper communications, handholding, and training, it was a very bumpy and inefficient ride.

Reduce complexities to understandable and attainable parts

Anyone with a firsthand familiarity of the pharmaceutical industry has a genuine appreciation for the complexity and number of activities that must be coordinated and completed in order to submit a new drug application to the U.S. Food and Drug Administration in the United States. It will drive a project manager to hair pulling. A related Gantt chart looks something like spilled spaghetti. Yet things must get done.

Do not become so immersed in or overwhelmed with trying to serve multiple parties and tasks. Rather, take every opportunity to touch upon realizable short-term goals as they relate to the intended longer-term objective (i.e., quality improvements, increased market share, cost reductions, etc.). Do this in individualized terms, explaining why everyone's efforts help. Remember, you eat an elephant one bite at a time.

Apply systems thinking

If you push on one side of a balloon, what happens to the rest of it? Pressure causes the shape to shift. If you squeeze too hard, it pops or springs a leak. Systems thinking is a holistic way to view your organization. It considers how making a change in one area might affect another within the same environment by examining and understanding the relationship of a system's related components and linkages, and how they integrate and interact over time.

As you strive to improve your performance in one area, is there a potential ripple effect somewhere else?

Build confidence

Building your team member's confidence is a repeated phrase throughout this book. Of note, your team will not win many games without it as it is an important mental stimuli. However, confidence is not a strong predictor of performance or an indicator of talent. It is attitudinal—simply what you believe or think.

Your goal, as manager, is to develop and sharpen their focus and execution habits; thus, in day-to-day or when the pressure is heightened, they have the optimal chance of performing.

How does this compare to Conventional Wisdom?

In *The Leadership Challenge,* Kouzes and Posner suggest, "Trying to do well and to beat others are two different things."

This principle is about practicing for the former. Do it well and the latter will likely result.

Endnotes for Principle 14: Practice doesn't make perfect; only perfect practice makes perfect

Coach's embodiment

Hill, A. (2000) *Interview notes.* 1–2, pp. 13–14.

Your coaching imperative: Strive for excellence

Cutler, J. (2019, March 17). 'Stories' breaks down The Boss, song by song. *The Star Ledger.* p. E3.
Kane, R. (2020, October 20). Private conversation.

Embrace continuous improvement

Leankit. (2018: copyright). Continuous improvement tools and techniques. Retrieved on December 31, 2018 from: https://leankit.com/learn/kanban/6-continuous-improvement-tools-and-techniques/

Role-playing

Assessmentcentrehq. (Date unknown). Role-Plays: The 7 steps to role-play interview success. Retrieved on December 18, 2018 from: https://www.assessmentcentrehq.com/assessment-centre-exercises/role-plays-the-ultimate-guide/
Dombeck, M. (1995–2018: copyright). Social kills: Role playing. *CenterSite.net.* Retrieved on December 18, 2018 from: https://www.centersite.net/poc/view_doc.php?type=doc&id=9774&cn=353

Mindtool Content Team. (Date unknown). Role-playing: Preparing for difficult conversations and situations. Mindtools.com. Retrieved on December 18, 2018 form: https://www.mindtools.com/CommSkll/RolePlaying.htm

Zwolinski, R., & Zwolinski, C.R. (2011, February 3). Therapy tools: Role playing. *Psych Central.* Retrieved on December 18, 2018 from: https://blogs.psychcentral.com/therapy-soup/2011/01/therapy-tools-role-playing/

Improv

Kulhan, B., & Chrisafullu, C. (2017). *Getting to "yes and," the art of business improv.* Stanford, California: Stanford Business Books, Stanford University Press. pp. 6, 8, 9.

Simulations

Lindenberger, J. (2017, November 9). 8 top benefits of training simulations in the workplace. *Lindenberger Group.* Retrieved on December 18, 2018 from: https://www.lindenbergergroup.com/8-top-benefits-training-simulations-workplace/

The National Academies of Sciences, Engineering, and Medicine. (2018: copyright). Effective training with simulation: the instructional design process. Retrieved on December 18, 2018 from: https://www.nap.edu/read/5065/chapter/5#74, pp. 2, 3, 8, and 14 of 48.

Focus groups

Focus Groups. *Wikipedia.* (Date unknown). Retrieved on January 3, 2019 from: https://en.wikipedia.org/wiki/Focus_group

Business case studies

Wikipedia. (Date unknown). Case Study. Retrieved on January 4, 2019 from: https://en.wikipedia.org/wiki/Case_study.

Conventional Wisdom

Kouzes, J.M., & Posner, B.Z. (1995). *The leadership challenge: How to get extraordinary things done in organizations.* San Francisco, California: Jossey-Bass Inc., Publishers, p. 152.

Reinforcing desirable behavior

Managing performance

A fierce competitor reaching back to his schoolboy days, Coach had an appreciation for those who exemplified maximum effort and hard work. He often cited from memory this Grantland Rice poem, "How to be a Champion," as his representative view on this subject:

> You wonder how they do it,
> You look to see the knack,
> You watch the foot in action,
> Or the shoulder of the back.
>
> But when you spot the answer
> Where the higher glamours lurk,
> You'll find in moving higher
> Up the laurel-covered spire,
> That most of it is practice,
> And the rest of it is work.

The philosophy of this poem was embedded in the way the Coach managed the performance of his players, as depicted in the following principles:

15 Focus on effort, not winning
16 Seek consistency—avoid peaks and valleys
17 Great leaders give credit to others, but accept the blame themselves

DOI: 10.4324/9781003456902-22

Focus on effort, not winning

Coach rarely spoke of winning. In fact, the only time he mentioned "winning" was at the beginning of the season in reference to the conference championship. Back then, winning your conference was the only way to get into the NCAA tournament.

Coach, however, did have a laser focus on effort. He believed that gains in effort, rooted in learning, would lead to enhanced individual and team performance and synergy—and that the scoreboard would take care of itself. To this end, he stressed fundamentals, pushed for incremental improvement, and fostered healthy competitiveness.

Coach recognized and respected that each player had assets and limitations and, therefore, required individualized coaching. Broadening his own point of view, he even went as far as having the players rate each other.

All games were "managed" one at a time, half by half, minute by minute. Course adjustments were made as needed.

Your coaching imperative: Manage performance

From my perspective, the performance management system of an organization reveals—more so than any other area of employee interface—how serious the organization's leadership is about achieving its vision *through targeted effort*, as well as the regard it has for its employees.

The business case

An effective performance management system is the key to aligning mission and strategic execution toward the achievement of your goals. Studies have illustrated that those companies with performance-enhancing cultures significantly outperform those without. It is paramount to the organization's overall success.

Identifying the best-suited performance management system for your organization is a complex challenge. It starts with defining the system's organizational purpose, business needs, culture, and talent priorities. As its design is a significant investment in time and people, be clear about what you want to achieve. An effective performance management system should be easy-to-use, easy-to-understand, fair, consistent, and reliable. It is to be supported by all levels of management and fortified with employee and manager training. The system should seek to maximize employee participation, contribution, and performance.

According to the Society of Human Resource Management, an effective performance management system should also clarify roles and expectations, enhance individual and

DOI: 10.4324/9781003456902-23

group productivity, develop employee capabilities, drive desired behavior, provide a basis for making decisions about talent placement, and improve communications. That's a lot to ask.

(Note: If you are on a path to re-engineer your performance management system, do not "over-engineer" it. Simple is better than complex. More communication is better than less. Also, legacy performance management systems were designed to be top-down and primarily focused on human resources utilization. Today, systems are being fashioned for both employee and managerial use.)

Planning

Most companies use a Management by Objective process ("MBO") for performance management.

At the beginning of the performance cycle, each individual, in collaboration with their manager (and, in the ideal case, their manager's manager), to identify four to six critical objectives to be completed during the performance cycle. These four to six objectives are where the employee's contribution will have impact. Objectives are goal-oriented; they state what needs to be accomplished and assert the means and behaviors toward those ends.

These objectives should be in the SMART format covered below.

Theory

MBO is grounded in Edwin Locke's *Goal-Setting Theory*. It has stood the test of time since the 1960s. It suggests that having specific goals, along with correlating feedback, will contribute toward higher and better task performance. It specifies, among other findings, that more challenging goals are greater motivators. Accordingly, goals must be specific and clearly understood, goals must be realistic and challenging, feedback will direct behavior and contribute toward higher performance, and, of most importance, employee participation in goal setting makes the goals more acceptable and leads to a heightened sense of ownership.

Breadth of goals

While performance planning should include bottom-line indicators, there is more. *In my opinion, broader planning considers three different targeted performance categories for any performance cycle*:

- *WHAT needs to be accomplished? Business/operational performance objectives highlight what must be accomplished during the performance period in a manner that leads, supports, or contributes toward the overall viability of the team or organization. These objectives are directly tied to the organization's strategy and business plan.*
- *HOW should things be accomplished? These performance objectives focus upon values and behaviors—how things are done in your organization.*
- *WHERE do you want to go? These objectives target your team member's professional growth and development needs, in conjunction with their career-related aspirations. They outline the path toward where they want to go as the next step in their career.*

Goal characteristics

Expanding a bit on Locke's theory, as you create individual performance goals, remember the SMART acronym:

- Specific, clear, and understandable
- Measurable, verifiable, and results-oriented; "That which gets measured gets done."
- Attainable, yet appropriately challenging
- Relevant to the mission of the department and/or greater organization
- Time-bound with a schedule and specific milestones

In addition:

- Goals should be organizationally aligned. Identify the "big picture" goals and then "cascade" them through the organization.
- As noted, goals should be "stretch" in nature. Setting goal expectations too low will leave your team members bored and stifled. Set them too lofty and employees will either crash and burn trying to attain them, or withdraw their efforts in despair. Find the fulcrum.
- Goals should be collaborative. Open and honest communication is critical for success.
- Goals should support career desires. Be sure to emphasize how success impacts the options and potential for other career opportunities. This will help enhance career development and motivation.
- Goals should be easy to communicate and be understandable.
- Your organization's values should be a fundamental part of the process and be inculcated, as applicable, into an individual's objectives. This pertains specifically to "how" ends will be accomplished.

A well-written and thorough job description outlines the needs and expectations of the role for the incumbent—individually and through others—in order to advance the organization's agenda. Performance goals should tie into the job description.

The Internet can provide you with countless examples of individual SMART goals by job title and function.

Connect the dots

Your performance management system is an important tool in your organization's overall talent management scheme. It should be linked to strategic planning, succession planning*, career development, reward and recognition systems, and other organizational programs.

*Note: As business is constantly changing, do not underestimate the need to have a succession plan, at least for leadership and critical positions. Performance management and related training are great tools to get the next generation of talent ready.

Execute

Successful organizations recognize that people want personal and professional fulfillment from their work, as it contributes toward their short- and long-term motivation, satisfaction, and retention. It causes us to exhibit pride. However, deriving meaning from work is also difficult to define, as it is highly personal and individualized.

What is meaningful work?

Work's meaning is often found in its purpose. It is the extension of ourselves, perhaps in quest of a noble cause. It also results from colleague relationships that form bonds, build community, and provide human connectivity. In taking a deeper look at this subject, Bailey and Madden's recent research has uncovered five common qualities of meaningful work, based on interviews conducted across a broad array of occupations. As a leader, you should be mindful of these as you can influence these factors, both positively and negatively. These include:

- Self-transcendent—People view work to be more meaningful when it has impact and relevance for others than just themselves.
- Poignant—People often find their work to be meaningful when they come through difficult situations, cope with challenging conditions, solve complex problems, and/or help others.
- Episodic—While generally not sustainable, people experience a heightened sense of meaning in their work at times of peak performance.
- Reflective—Meaning is derived from retrospect when people are able to see the connection between their efforts and achievements.
- Personal—Work that has broader context beyond one's professional scope can provide meaning, as well as satisfaction and appreciation.

Your performance management system plays a role in these factors.

How you can make work more meaningful

Research has shown that people experiencing meaningful work report better health, well-being, teamwork, and engagement. They view mistakes as learning opportunities and bounce back faster from disappointments. They grow and prosper.

To address employee matters about the significance of their work and contribution, the best managers keep an open door *and* get out of their office. They have and encourage dialog with and between team members. They work on and manage their relationships, trying to keep them in a productive place. They are candid, helpful, open, and transparent. Specifically, they manage performance and interact with their team in the following ways:

- Show them that their work matters—Discuss purpose. Do it daily. Show and tell how their work helps others and the organization fulfill its goals. Be intentional about making individuals feel of value and demonstrative about how their work matters.
- Be curious and inquisitive—Ask questions. Explore. Discover. Listen. Help employees by finding new or different ways to approach their work. Provide some variety of thought or action.
- Challenge limits—Fight inertia and the status quo. Push for more. Set higher ceilings. Give those around you a sense of progress, creation, or growth.

- Keep values at the forefront—Values are a vehicle through which we see the world and derive meaning. Pay attention to individual values. Seek congruity. Hire people who promote teamwork and collaboration. Stress community.
- Trust—Lose the "control and command" style and empower those around you. To the extent possible, allow some latitude for employees to tailor their roles and take ownership. Give people a voice and room to experiment.

At the other end of the spectrum, be sure to avoid taking your employees for granted, treating people unfairly, or overriding people's better judgment. These actions will erode meaning, causing your team to psychologically disconnect and disengage.

Provide ongoing feedback

Feedback is a gift. It is also a managerial obligation. A good feedback or coaching session is like a routine maintenance check; one needs to know where some touch-up work is required.

Observe to provide feedback

Actions speak louder than words. Make opportunities to get with your team in their element. Listen at the call center. Accompany them on sales calls. Get in the trenches. Join in at the retail counter, on the assembly line, or at the next presentation. Find a way to be by their side.

Watching gives you the chance to hear what is said, what is done, and how your team is handling the choices put in front of them in actual work situations. It minimizes bias, as your input is direct. Careful listening will also provide insight into the team's attitudes and opinions.

Feedback to coach

As a practical matter, feedback means providing constructive direction, guidance, counsel, and support in order to help the individual grow, as well as to attain organizational goals.

Your employees presumably want to do better. They need you to tell them how and in a format from which they can learn. In fact, 57% of recent survey respondents indicated that they prefer "corrective" instead of "positive" feedback. Your team will think more highly of you for providing this.

When it comes to providing this feedback, promptly address concerns and issues related to performance. Start with questions of self-discovery. Build the relationship. Help your team explore their capabilities and to push boundaries as an inquisitive tutor.

Here are some tips that will help you with coaching feedback:

- Frame your feedback around specific behaviors and use metrics
- Focus on improving one or two areas at a time
- Tie feedback into professional growth opportunities
- Give assurance as new skills are undertaken and discuss any potential barriers
- Provide required training and resources
- Allow time for processing
- Collaboratively plan next steps
- Follow-up with acknowledgment of any changes

The hoped-for outcome is that individuals will further engage and become increasingly motivated by their incremental learning on a path toward self-management.

Feedback to remediate

If coaching does not get traction, you must be more progressive in tone and directive. This type of feedback has more of a "telling" approach. It is direct, firm, and instructive. It is used to correct subpar performance before it sidetracks by providing specific detail and instruction about the task.

You might start the discussion by saying, "Here is what I am seeing." This serves as an icebreaker, as well as an invitation to gain the person's perspective. In the course of this discussion, you must make it clear what needs to be improved, as well as the consequences of any future missteps.

It is best to check with your HR professional before going down this path, especially if discipline is a probable outcome.

Feedback now

This is important. Make feedback a habit. In the ideal world, feedback is in real-time, continuous, and dynamic. If real-time is not possible, at least have regularly scheduled two-way "check-in" sessions. No one likes surprises.

- *The general counsel in a company where I worked did not get along with one of his direct reports. Their relationship seemed strained from the start and, despite HR intervention attempts, never got on sound footing. It reached the point where he (the general counsel) and his direct report (a female attorney) hardly spoke, much less exchanged performance updates. Behind the scenes, he excluded her from key meetings and decisions. ... Yes. I did say general counsel!*

  As you might imagine, the year-end performance review was a battleground of "Got-Cha's," emotional finger-points, and animated rebuttals. Each had their own note-filled file. When the smoke cleared, there was a distinct winner and a loser. It was not pretty, nor cheap to reconcile.

- *I have been in the CEO's office on two separate occasions when C-suite executives have been terminated with no prior feedback. No warning, no clues, total surprise.*

  The reactions of these two impacted leaders was confusion, which quickly turned to disbelief and anger. Tempers flared. The language was not pretty. What should have been a ten-minute dialog had there been regular feedback sessions, turned into respective marathon sessions.

  Cleaning up these two messes was ugly, drawn-out, and expensive. It did not have to be that way.

No excuses

You see this all the time. Managers will sometimes sugarcoat feedback because they want to avoid possible confrontation, have a high need to be liked, or set low or fluid performance standards. In addition, they may hide or soften their feedback behind organizational "excuses" such as budget constraints, upper management edicts, resource pressures, or flawed company policy.

Any of these avoidant behaviors or blemished rationales will likely only exasperate what is an already difficult situation, as the following first-hand scenarios illustrate:

- *One of the key people in a corporate merger was told that the company was going in "another direction," and she no longer had a job. This was after many promises were made to the contrary. She sought and obtained a legal remedy.*
- *A supervisor failed to give a merit increase to an employee at the time of annual review due to what he considered to be less than standard performance. In avoiding the discussion about performance, the supervisor provided some lame (and untrue) explanations about budget woes. The employee eventually quit the organization, but not before trashing the company's name in the marketplace and compromising some of the company's proprietary information.*
- *A manager was passed over for a promotion. Upon inquiry, she was advised that she did not have the "right" experience. In response, she wallowed away, became disengaged, and her performance and attitude soon started suffering. She remains in place today as a performance and cultural liability, potential never to be realized.*

You are in the role of manager for a reason. Your responsibility includes providing honest performance feedback. No excuses, no matter how difficult the message may be to deliver.

Seek broad input

To the extent possible, it is best to seek various stakeholder inputs for gathering information about your team members at various points during the performance cycle, and in anticipation of a more formal mid or year-end review, especially if it involves scoring.

Encourage self-assessment

Most performance systems have a self-assessment element component. This is where individuals rate themselves against and provide a narrative about the previously identified goals. This gives employees a degree of input and a voice in the overall performance management review.

Self-assessment may not be necessary if you are holding regular feedback and coaching sessions, yet I would not dismiss it. it is still a useful tool. It allows you to discover any notable gaps between the individual's perceptions of outcomes and yours. If the disparity is significant, it suggests that something is dramatically wrong and that you need to prepare accordingly for the review discussion.

Use multiple sources

To minimize your own possible subjectivity and to gain as holistic a view as possible, evaluate your team members using appropriate and broad sources. Crowdsourcing, by definition, is the practice of gathering information about a given topic by throwing a wide net. This approach works if discretion is maintained. In fact, many organizations have institutionalized review processes wherein each individual's review receives multiple stakeholder input.

In whatever manner is most effective and expedient, solicit performance input about your team members from peers, subordinates, and other managers with whom the individual has worked, as well as other relevant internal and external stakeholders. As a word of caution, be especially mindful of peer assessments as some people may have hidden agendas.

Use a 90-degree view for managers

If someone has team members reporting to them, feedback in the form of confidential comments and observations from their direct reports will help you understand how the manager is performing, as well as validate or contrast your own opinions. This feedback can be attained based upon a predetermined competency model (or enhanced job description), wherein you want to know about the manager's creativity, innovation, responsiveness, credibility, communications skills, cultural adherence, service mindset, values adherence, professionalism, etc. This feedback can be highly effective as it gathers direct perspective, has credibility, clarifies critical performance variables, and supports a climate of continuous improvement. Its drawbacks include the required time investment and potential participant bias. The manager may also feel intimidated by the wide stroke of feedback, as well as his or her inability to refute the findings since comments are anonymous.

Calibrate

Before finalizing performance reviews, it is important to objectively calibrate, to the extent possible, your evaluation of your team members across the broader organization. This is especially true if ratings are involved. This calibration takes place in three steps:

- Human Resources has a holistic view of the organization and can advise performance managers on any initial outliers and provide guidance on qualitative matters.
- Many organizations conduct a cross-organizational managerial meeting, coordinated by human resources, in order to compare notes. This addresses enterprise-wide consistency and fairness, while minimizing managerial bias.
- The highest-ranking official at the site/operation should conduct a review of the process and its potential outcomes to understand all salient matters.

These three review steps demonstrate to the organization that this subject matter is taken seriously and that each individual's review has received multiple views; thus, giving more confidence, uniformity, and reliability to the process.

I have implemented all of these steps in various organizations, always with favorable results. (Note: While there should be minimal surprises, an employee may still not like their rating, but this multiple-input process ensures a fair process.)

Conduct the review

Be honest

Honesty counts. A lot. Often in the corporate world, performance ratings are linked to compensation systems. Be wary of any tendency to skew an individual's performance evaluation by being more generous or lenient in an effort to get them greater rewards. This can come back to haunt you, especially if you ever need to downsize or there is a related employee relations matter.

Have an agenda

Formal face-to-face performance review meetings are generally held at the middle and/or the end of the performance cycle. In this session, summarize the work accomplished and the challenges faced. Start with positives by discussing accomplishments and then approach any shortfalls. Have documentation and illustrative examples as required. The goals of performance evaluation are to provide proper feedback to each employee about his or her performance, to share recommendations with each person regarding ways that they can more effectively perform their duties and enhance their contribution, and to provide managers with information for determining future job assignments.

Remember, this is personal. A private discussion setting is preferred. Keep your dialog professional. If desired, practice the anticipated dialog with a colleague or your human resources professional, especially if bumps are anticipated.

Know that there are not enough trophies

For players at UCLA, playing time was the ultimate trophy. That time was earned, not given.

Managing performance is tough. In some systems, much like compensation planning, it often involves a zero-sum result. In these cases, if you wish to rate one employee higher, it may be at the cost of another. These decisions are never easy. Regardless of what system your organization uses, remember that your obligation is not to please everyone, despite temptation. Rather, it is to be fair and consistent.

Critique, do not criticize

There is a fine line between constructive feedback (critique) and criticism. Criticism is personal.

Citing one of the people Coach most admired, in 1863 President Abraham Lincoln had the unenviable task of communicating some unflattering feedback to General "Fighting Joe" Hooker, head of the Union Army of the Potomac during the Civil War. Seems Lincoln needed to reign in this rambunctious general, who was apparently placing his personal zeal and ambition ahead of the collective good of the army. In crafting a thoughtful and balanced letter, the president provided timely and constructive feedback, while not demotivating his powerful field commander. Specifically, Lincoln praised General Hooker with heartfelt enthusiasm, and then he cited his specific concerns over his aggressive ambitions—ultimately pledging his support for the general. By taking this tack, Lincoln successfully utilized a conservative and diplomatic manner while relaying the needed message for a change in course.

This letter is a perfect example of constructive feedback. Lincoln, like all good coaches and managers, knew this type of response was a trigger for learning.

If expectations are not met

There will be times when team members fall short. This leaves you with a few options. Consider this an opportunity to readjust your sights to something more attainable, possibly requiring remediation, training, reassignment, or a performance improvement plan. If too far off course, an exit strategy should be considered.

If you must terminate someone for performance

Not easy to do when a team member has tried to perform and just cannot get there. If termination is being considered, you should consult with your HR professional or employment attorney for guidance and an assessment of any risk or potential liability concerns. Treat them with respect. Handle the matter with discretion. Assuming that you have been providing ongoing feedback and documenting such, there should be no surprises.

Appeals

Differences of opinion occur, even in the best performance management systems. When this happens, be sure that your performance management system has the option of an appeal step for the employee who wants further review or recourse. This might include an appeal step to an impartial executive, HR, or a peer-review board. This party can act as the employee advocate and potential arbitrator.

Take performance to the next level.

How does this compare to Conventional Wisdom?

I am too busy to be bothered with providing feedback. Once a year is enough. My team knows what to do and how they will be evaluated.

Wrong.

--

A bit more on this topic follows …

Performance management miscellaneous

Take performance focus to the next level

It does not matter which form, formula, or evaluation scale you use. It does not matter if you are using ink or a keyboard to capture and memorialize reviews. It does not matter if you are using a phone, a laptop, or face-to-face when giving feedback (though, in-person is preferred).

What matters is the commitment behind managing everyone's performance.

General Electric may not be the shining industrial star it once was; however, for years, they were the model of corporate growth. During that time, their performance system was intense, rigorous, and metric-driven. Managers were accountable for their operating results, balanced with forward-thinking, and prioritized talent management practices. Metrics such as developing future talent, regrettable talent losses, and degree of bench strength were the basis for managerial reward or penalty. Accordingly, managers would have candid dialog with their team members about their ongoing contribution, values adherence, strengths, and developmental needs.

This was not taken lightly. As an interactive quality check, the next level of management was also involved to ensure congruence of opinion or exposed points of attention. Their correlating business outcomes at that time were the envy of all.

The power of their system was in giving people the time, attention, honest feedback, and coaching required to move ahead or out.

A word about performance incentives

You want your team to not only meet their objectives, but also smash through them!

Certainly, this has been the long-standing basis for incentive programs. Build, ship, sell, or deliver more—and do it as efficiently and effectively as possible—as monitored by related metrics, and employees may reap the rewards. Pay for performance epitomized. Focus on scorecard issues. More and better output equals more compensation. Simple, straightforward, motherhood and apple pie!

Incentives come in all shapes and sizes as variable pay components. Profit-sharing plans give employees a sense of ownership of the company. Gain-sharing plans are generally designed to improve productivity and involve payouts based upon predetermined targets. Executives are often driven by goals related to earnings, returns, and market share. There are also sales commissions, group incentives, spot awards, and combinations of the above.

All these programs should be aligned with the organization's goals, and be appropriate for your team and its culture, while rewarding and recognizing desired behaviors and their outcomes. They must be easy to broadly communicate and be understandable.

Two cautionary concerns. First, do not fall into the trap of taking last year's results and simply applying a multiplier as the new target for the upcoming business cycle. This is like driving your car by looking in the rearview mirror. To this point, establish each performance target, to the extent possible, by considering all environmental factors—what is known, what is trending, as well as what is anticipated. Second, I mentioned Daniel Pink's research about motivation in Principle 11. His analysis has implications for performance incentives. In sum, incentives work well when the nature of the task is mechanical or routine (e.g., assembly line work). However, he raises a red flag when applying these types of incentives to creative work, suggesting that narrowly focused incentive programs can choke intrinsic motivation, confine thought, and stifle needed right-brain ingenuity. In his theory, which is evidence-based, one's autonomy, mastery, and purpose erode.

Pink's work should give pause to what you measure and reward when your quest is innovation.

To be fair

Some companies are questioning if it is all worth it. A recent *Harvard Business Review* article cited that 65% of all employees believe that the evaluation process is unfair and not relevant to their jobs! Other statistics share similar sentiments. A 2023 *HR Magazine* article highlighted survey results that expressed significant employee concerns about fair evaluation, managerial assessment capabilities, and a lack of alignment between their performance management system and career development support.

No doubt that performance management systems can be viewed as a "necessary evil." Planning, check-ins, and reviews take time—lots and lots of it; they can be an endless paper chase or periodic clog in an online queue. Deadlines slip; management support ebbs. There can be inconsistent administration and potential rater bias. Training is a huge expense and time-eater. The review ritual can suffer from routine fatigue. When the process is improperly executed, you can almost see the motivation seeping from the building.

But reports of the death of performance management systems are premature.

In taking a fresh look at this topic, some companies are making a purposeful philosophical shift—from systems for performance management to systems for *performance motivation* or *performance development*. These same companies are also re-engineering the related support processes.

I believe that these are shifts worth considering.

Microsoft is using their performance management system in new and creative ways, with a broader focus. Their system includes more frequent feedback, a scale that recognizes impact, objectives around learning, and goals for helping others and for being helped. This is an intentional transition to instill individual and collective learning into their cultural fabric. Likewise, companies like PricewaterhouseCoopers have embraced technology and utilize an app-based program to give colleagues feedback in real time. Successfully finish a client project during the day and you will likely have feedback that evening.

For out-of-the-box thinkers *(and I really like this, although I have yet to use it)*, consider the approach to performance management utilized by the Chinese telecom company, Huawei. They do not compare employees to each other. They compare employees to themselves. Much along the lines of one of Coach's more popular quotes, "Don't measure yourself by what you have accomplished, but by what you should have accomplished with your ability," this company evaluates each employee using their past performance as a reference point. Called temporal comparison, employees receive feedback on their individual growth and development as they have progressed over time and presumably, against expanded organizational needs. Fairness and individual treatment personified.

At a minimum, if you are discussing how to revitalize your organization's performance management system, consider applying the business principles of agile project management—being leaner, innovative, and more flexible—to their performance management systems. These trends include:

- Annual reviews are giving way to ongoing feedback models with brief and less formal summaries.
- Multiple sources for evaluative input are becoming the norm.
- Ratings and labels are disappearing and being replaced with descriptive individual feedback about impact and contribution.
- Performance feedback is now solicited and given via an app, with or without attribution.
- Teams are getting as much evaluative weight as individuals; peer reviews are becoming vogue.
- Performance management is starting to parallel project management.
- Learning goals related to upskilling, developing and applying new knowledge areas, and enhancing one's regenerative capacities are getting more weight in our global, automatized, and digital world.

Endnotes for reinforcing desirable behavior: Managing performance (introduction)

Wooden, J.R. (2002, August 22). Private conversation. (Grantland Rice poem)

Endnotes for Principle 15: Focus on effort, not winning

Your coaching imperative

The Society for Human Resource Management. (2015, September 17). Managing employee performance. *HR Knowledge Center*. Retrieved on August 15, 2018, from: https://www.shrm.org/resourcesandtools/tools-and-samples/toolkits/pages/managingemployeeperformance.aspx

The business case

Pulakos, E. (2004). The Society for Human Resource Management. Performance management: A roadmap for developing, implementing and evaluating performance management systems. *The SHRM Foundation. Alexandria, Virginia*. Retrieved on March 19, 2019, from: https://www.shrm.org/hr-today/trends-and-forecasting/special-reports-and-expert-views/Documents/Performance-Management.pdf. p.1,3,4.

HR-Survey, LLC. (Date unknown). Performance management systems: What is a performance management system? Retrieved on August 20, 2018, from: https://www.hr-survey.com/PerformanceManagement.htm

Walia, V. (2019, April 25). Private conversation.

Theory

Juneja, P. (2019: copyright). Goal setting theory of motivation. *Management Study Guide*. Retrieved on March 19, 2019, from: https://www.managementstudyguide.com/goal-setting-theory-motivation.htm

Breadth of goals

Pulakos, E. (2004). Performance Management: A roadmap for developing, implementing, and evaluating performance management systems. *The Society for Human Resource Management, The SHRM Foundation. Alexandria, Virginia*. Retrieved on March 19, 2019, from: https://www.shrm.org/hr-today/trends-and-forecasting/special-reports-and-expert-views/Documents/Performance-Management.pdf. p. 4,5.

Goals should be SMART

The Society for Human Resource Management. (2015, September 17). Managing Employee Performance. *The HR Knowledge Center*. Retrieved on August 15, 2018, from: https://www.shrm.org/resourcesandtools/tools-and-samples/toolkits/pages/managingemployeeperformance.aspx

Clear Company. (Date unknown). 5 noteworthy tips for successful employee goal setting. Retrieved on August 20, 2018, from https://blog.clearcompany.com/5-noteworthy-tips-for-successful-employee-goal-setting

Paychex. (2018, July 9). 7 tips for effective employee goal-setting to boost engagement and productivity. Retrieved on August 20, 2018, from: https://www.paychex.com/articles/human-resources/7-tips-for-effective-employee-goal-setting

Connect the dots

The Society for Human Resource Management. (2015, September 17). Managing Employee Performance. *The HR Knowledge Center*. Retrieved on August 15, 2018, from: https://www.shrm.org/resourcesandtools/tools-and-samples/toolkits/pages/managingemployeeperformance.aspx

Execute

Haigh, W.T. (1996). Effective Retention Strategies. Overview presented at the annual conference for the International Association of Corporate and Professional Recruitment. Philadelphia, Pennsylvania.

.

What is meaningful work?

Mautz, S. (Date unknown). 7 ways to make work more meaningful. *Lead Change Group*. Retrieved on August 15, 2018, from: https://leadchangegroup.com/7-ways-to-make-work-more-meaningful/

Weisbord, M.R. (1987). *Productive workplaces: organizing and managing for dignity, meaning, and community*. San Francisco, California: Jossey-Bass Inc., Publishers, p. 311.

Bailey, C., & Madden, A. (2016). What makes work meaningful – or meaningless. *MIT Sloan Management Review*, Summer edition. Retrieved on August 15, 2018, from: https://sloanreview.mit.edu/article/what-makes-work-meaningful-or-meaningless/

What you can do

DePree, M. (1989). *Leadership is an art*. New York: Bantam Doubleday Dell Publishing Group, Inc., pp. 122–123.

Quinn, R.E., & Thakor, A. V. (2018 July–August). Creating a purpose-driven organization. *Harvard Business Review*, pp. 78–85.

Garrad, L., & Chamorro-Premuzic, T. (2017, August 9). How to make work more meaningful for your team. *Harvard Business Review*. Retrieved on August 15, 2018, from: https://hbr.org/2017/08/how-to-make-work-more-meaningful-for-your-team

Mautz, S. (Date unknown). 7 ways to make work more meaningful. *Lead Change Group*. Retrieved on August 15, 2018, from: https://leadchangegroup.com/7-ways-to-make-work-more-meaningful/

Bailey, C., & Madden, A. (2016). What makes work meaningful – or meaningless. *MIT Sloan Management Review*, Summer edition. Retrieved on August 15, 2018, from: https://sloanreview.mit.edu/article/what-makes-work-meaningful-or-meaningless/

Feedback to coach

Impraise, Inc. (Date unknown). Giving constructive feedback. *San Francisco, CA*. Retrieved on August 15, 2018, from: http://www.feedback.tips/give-constructive-feedback-to-employees-team-members/

Encourage self-assessment

Community Foundations of Canada. (Date unknown). Keeping the right people. *HR Council*. Retrieved on August 15, 2018, from: http://hrcouncil.ca/hr-toolkit/keeping-people-performance-management.cfm

Use a 90-degree view for managers

Community Foundations of Canada. (Date unknown). Keeping the right people. *HR Council*. Retrieved on August 15, 2018, from: http://hrcouncil.ca/hr-toolkit/keeping-people-performance-management.cfm

Critique, do not criticize

Impraise, Inc. (Date unknown). Giving constructive feedback. *San Francisco, Ca*. Retrieved on August 15, 2018, from: http://www.feedback.tips/give-constructive-feedback-to-employees-team-members/

Carnegie, D. (1981). *How to win friends and influence people*. (Second ed.). New York: Pocket Books, pp. 207–208.

Basler, R.P, et al., (editor). (Date unknown). Collected works of Abraham Lincoln. Retrieved on August 16, 2018, from: http://www.abrahamlincolnon-line.org/lincoln/speeches/hooker.htm

If expectations are not met

Paychex. (2018, July 9). 7 tips for effective employee goal-setting to boost engagement and productivity. Retrieved on August 20, 2018, from: https://www.paychex.com/articles/human-resources/7-tips-for-effective-employee-goal-setting

Appeals

Community Foundations of Canada. (Date unknown). Keeping the right people. *HR Council.* Retrieved on August 15, 2018, from: http://hrcouncil.ca/hr-toolkit/keeping-people-performance-management.cfm

Take performance focus to the next level

Krishnamoorthy, R. (2014, April 17). The secret ingredient in GE's talent-review system. *Harvard Business Review*. Retrieved on May 14, 2018, from: https://hbr.org/2014/04/the-secret-ingredient-in-ges-talent-review-system

A word about performance incentives

McGuinness, M. (2009). Dan Pink on why rewards don't work. *Lateral Action*. Retrieved on September 16, 2019, from: https://lateralaction.com/articles/dan-pink-rewards/

To be fair

Silverman, R.E. (2016, June 8). GE tries to reinvent the employee review, encouraging risks. *Wall Street Journal*. pp. B1–B6.

Weber, L., & Silverman, R.E. (2015, August 26). Workers get new tools for airing their gripes. *Wall Street Journal*, pp. B1–B4.

Chun, J., Brockner, J., & De Cremer, D. (2018, March 22). People don't want to be compared with others in performance reviews. They want to be compared with themselves. *Harvard Business Review*. Retrieved on January 2, 2020, from: https://hbr.org/2018/03/people-dont-want-to-be-compared-with-others-in-performance-reviews-they-want-to-be-compared-with-themselves?utm_source=linkedin&utm_campaign=hbr&utm_medium=social

Middleton, Y. (2016, February 28). 100 unforgettable John Wooden quotes. Retrieved on January 2, 2020, from: https://addicted2success.com/quotes/100-unforgettable-john-wooden-quotes/

Agovino, T. (2023, Spring). Performance reviews are broken. *HR Magazine*, p. 33. (Citing WTW 2022 Performance Reset Survey of 837 organizations worldwide, including 150 North American employers.)

Seek consistency

Avoid peaks and valleys

In the locker room, Coach's game preparation and demeanor were calm and focused. He did not believe in "pep" talks or artificial motivation, fearing that if his team got too "high," there might be a subsequent letdown.

On the sideline, in sharp comparison to the antics portrayed by some of today's coaches, Coach Wooden rarely left his courtside seat. He knew that incessant screaming at officials, gesturing, throwing towels or nearby furniture in fits of rage, embarrassing players, or belittling the media were not the proper means to an end. He never resorted to emotionalism.

He believed that the only pressure was that which you put upon yourself, which you can control. He rarely called the game's first timeout,* but he usually did before a big win to remind the players to maintain their composure in victory and to leave the hysteria of celebration to the alumni.

*In a recent LinkedIn interview, Swen Nater, a former Bruin and NBA All-star, could not recall Coach calling one timeout during his three years playing career.

Your coaching imperative: An even keel

In their outstanding book, *Performing under Pressure*, Hendrie Weisinger and J.P. Pawliw-Fry discuss the science behind "doing your best when it matters most." Citing 22 strategies, the authors offer ways to make the best of "pressure" situations. Of note, they dispel the sports myth that certain individuals "rise to the occasion." In contrast, they suggest that "clutch" performers have figured out best how to manage the increased systemic stimuli and its potential disruption around our physical self (i.e., handling arousal overload), our mental state (i.e., the need for clear thinking), and our behavior (i.e., proper execution).

Do not get caught-up in the pressures or emotions of the moment. Attend to and prioritize your mental health. Maintain your objectivity and long-term perspective. Exemplify your organization's values. Most importantly, take care of yourself and each other.

Manage your energy, not just your time

For years, students in corporate training classrooms were taught to manage their time more effectively and efficiently. However, something was missing.

In 2007, Tony Schwartz and Catherine McCarthy co-authored an article featured in the *Harvard Business Review* that focused upon managing personal energy, not time. Their advice is not dated. Their basic premise was that time is a finite resource; energy is not. They hypothesized that energy could be systemically expanded and renewed through the adaption

DOI: 10.4324/9781003456902-24

of specific and intentional behaviors, and that this expansion and renewal could lead to enhanced productivity. Through this lens, they suggested that our capacity to do work comes from four sources, all of which may be rechargeable: the body, emotions, mind, and spirit.

Their findings were striking. By controlling these four variables in a study group at Wachovia Bank, research participants significantly outperformed their control group counterparts on many financial metrics. They also reported striking improvements in customer relationships, engagement, performance, and personal satisfaction.

Let's consider their multi-dimensional model.

Your body

This is about physical energy.

We all, at some point and perhaps more, have worked too many hours, skipped too many meals, and paid little or no mind to hitting the gym. Common sense tells us that these aberrations are wrong. The trick is to make sure that any are temporary.

As a first step, by taking an inventory of your physical habits, you can determine potential improvement areas. Sleep should be at the top of the list. Is it regular and routine? Is it long enough? Is it uninterrupted or disturbed?

How, when, and what you eat is a close second concern. Are your eating habits and times routine? Does intake match your physical energy burn? What does your nutritional profile look like? Do you eat a few large meals over the course of a day or several smaller ones? How much snack food is nearby? Is alcohol an occasional "social" habit or otherwise? Any vices of note?

Exercise is the third consideration. Do you do any? Do you do enough? Do you participate in cardiovascular and strength training? Are your weight and other physical and medical metrics where you want them to be? Do you feel good about your physical self?

The last physical variable is renewal. Do you take regular qualitative breaks? What do you do to recharge your body? How do you keep your focus? Do you yawn through and drain away your energy reservoir? Maybe take a walk every once in a while or as routine?

Facing the above questions is a start toward getting into a better place. Your answers may not look pretty at first, but at least you have established a baseline from which to work. Independently, or by consulting with a professional, you can now ratchet up your attention and related efforts toward making corrections, even if with baby steps. You will likely feel the difference.

Your emotions

Keep your emotions under control before they take control (and rob you of your energy!).

To what degree are you self-aware? Do you get your emotional vibes from others or from within? Does self-inflicted drama influence situational responses? Are you irritable with others? Do you spend enough time with your family? Do you have outside interests? Do you savor and celebrate accomplishments or plow ahead? Do you have a best friend or confidante to whom you can turn?

Most people perform best when they are feeling good about themselves. This translates into positive get-up-and-go. However, sustaining this vigor is challenging, particularly when we are continually bombarded with endless demands and lofty expectations. One minute we are riding the crest of an endorphin high; the next we are frustrated over the insensitivity of a boss. This emotional roller coaster ride in the workplace runs all day, every day.

Emotions are not mutually exclusive. They are not easily defined. They are not stagnant. When the negative vibes take over, be wary of the related side effects: irritability, impatience, insecurity, and anxiety. These reactions cloud your thinking and perspective. They drain your energy and cause sub-optimal concentration and performance. They could also damage relationships.

There are several strategies you might adopt in order to recover from these setbacks before they become consuming. Take a walk, take five for a cup of coffee, find a friend, or temporarily disengage. Any and all of these tactics (and some previously noted) should slow down or stop your negative derailment.

You are not a victim. Stop blaming others or your circumstances, take control, and be accountable. To the extent possible, try to let go of people or things that rob you of your vitality.

You have choices.

Your mind

The ability to concentrate fully on the task at hand is particularly challenging. People want your attention. Technology beckons. Deadlines loom on other matters. Then there is that personal matter that you just cannot get off your mind. Inevitably, distractions are everywhere and they take us down many rabbit holes!

To maximize your mind's energy, know your priorities and plan your time accordingly. To this end:

* Know what must be accomplished—Track your goals. Keep them in front of you at all times. If you are not working on these matters, why not?
* Know the time constraints and deadlines of your goals—What is most important? What is time sensitive? What can wait or has lesser impact? These answers will help you determine what to work on next.
* Say "no"—Easier said than done, but consider the big picture.
* Put out your clothes the night before—At the end of each day, look ahead to tomorrow. Lay out your schedule, tools, and project files.
* Delegate more—If you have hired and surrounded yourself with the right talent, they can surely lend a hand.
* Keep score—We all have the same 24 hours available to us each day, 168 hours in a week. Take an inventory. Accounting for and assessing how, where, and when you spend your time may reveal some opportunities for correction.
* Do not forget yourself—Find some downtime each day, perhaps in small increments, to decompress. As needed, put the cell phone down and walk away from the e-mails. The texts messages can also wait. Take a few minutes (or whatever time you need) to temporarily recharge and regain your traction. Your psychological well-being deserves purposeful attention.

Your spirit

Spiritual energy is described differently by various cultures and religions. Broadly speaking, it is considered the universal life force that exists in all living matter. We are discussing a subset of this topic here.

In the workplace, spiritual energy is derived, in part, from work with both personal meaning and purpose. Presumably, when you experience this type of connectivity, you feel positive energy. Spiritual energy drives you, gives you hope for the future, and creates value for stakeholders. What you do matters.

While realizing spiritual energy may sound like an elusive, utopian state, it is within reach. However, getting to this destination requires a pragmatic assessment. First, are you doing what you do best, what you enjoy the most, what you find personally and professionally fulfilling, and does it provide you with a path or ends toward your desired means—financial or otherwise? Second, are you allocating your time and efforts to the things in your life of most importance? Third, are you living your personal values at work? Last, what is your desired legacy?

Your answers to these questions will likely differentiate your work experience from being invigorating, immersing, passionate, and engaging or the opposite. They will spell the difference between your work as a natural extension of your being versus having just a "job." They will tell you if you are in the right place, on the right path, or in need of a course correction.

The more you can gravitate toward spending your time on what you value, the more spiritual energy you will realize.

Manage stress

Stress is defined as mental tension or a state of worry. It can be episodic, acute, or chronic. According to the American Psychological Society, 60% of people in the United States consider their job to be a major source of stress in their lives. Similar surveys yield similar results, with some indicating that this may be a conservative estimate.

Stress is a normal part of life. It is not all necessarily bad or bad for you. It can motivate you in the short term and give you purpose. Stress can sharpen your senses, boost your adrenaline, and raise your situational awareness.

On the other hand, stress can have serious health consequences.

Everyone interprets workplace stress and handles it differently. At work, low morale, excessive work demands, crazy hours, a jerk for a boss, career concerns, organizational changes, constant deadlines, or co-worker friction can bring it on. Some people brush problems away with hardly any notice. Others become expended or bottle the stress inside and fall into a downward spiral.

When stress is knocking, it can take on several forms and costs, most notably in one's health. An upset stomach, lost sleep, and headaches tend to be the early and most noticeable physical manifestations. Beyond these factors, high blood pressure, irritability, and loss of appetite may occur. More visibly, procrastination, inability to maintain focus, absenteeism and tardiness, and decreased productivity are also possible.

Longer-term negative effects include, but are not limited to, cardiovascular disease, psychological disorders, and musculoskeletal concerns.

To help combat organizational and individual stress, consider these practices:

- Ensure workload is appropriately distributed among your team members.
- Clearly define roles and responsibilities. Be sure that people are aligned against such to succeed.
- Provide opportunities for professional growth and advancement.

- Provide your employees with (or refer them to) an Employee Assistance Program.
- Encourage socialization and bond-building activities.
- Establish work schedules that enhance work/life balance.

And, if possible, embrace hybrid schedules, remote working, flextime, job-sharing, etc.

Manage anxiety

Anxiety, like stress, causes headaches, muscle tension, chest pain, and fatigue. It can impact your mood and focus. It can increase your restlessness and make you feel overwhelmed. It can cause undesirable responsive behaviors. Left unattended, individuals and their teams can unravel.

My friend Dr. Nick Molinaro is a psychologist and performance specialist who has worked with professional and Olympic athletes, select branches of the U.S. military, and corporate executives. His subject matter expertise lies in helping people work through stress and anxiety in order to perform at the highest level. (You may have caught Dr. Nick on the Golf Channel.)

Dr. Nick defines anxiety as the profuse feeling of disequilibrium. It is brought about by feeling uncertain about the future or by having a disproportionate fear that something is going to go wrong (i.e., escalating your trepidation about things that will likely never come to pass). We can all plead guilty to this.

Dr. Nick suggests that in order to perform at your peak, you must minimize your anxiety (i.e., not thinking about the future, fearing worst outcomes, or playing "what if" games), while maximizing your real-time psychological level of arousal (i.e., being in the here and now, blocking out distractions, and elevating your focus on the task at hand). Be specific with your intention and correlating attention through self-discipline and awareness. I can bear witness to the difference this psychological approach makes.

Mitigate anxiety

It happens. Apprehension. Stress. Fright. Panic. Anxiety on steroids! All leading to suboptimal performance, if not shutdown.

When things become overwhelming, they must be addressed as soon as possible.

The next time you are facing psychologocal overload, stop. Pause. Yank the reins back! Cool, calm, and collected may still be within reach—if you are willing to experiment.

- Deep breaths—Fill your lungs slowly and deeply several times, exhaling in a manner that figuratively takes your anxiety away.
- Loosen your grip—Have a clenched jaw, rounded shoulders, or a defensive posture? Let the physical tension go.
- Let your imagination run—Take a few minutes and picture yourself in a place that brings you comfort such as the beach or a hiking trail.
- Let it go—Sometimes you cannot control process or project outcomes. Best not to dwell otherwise.
- Focus on the positive—Easier said than done, but relish and magnify your blessings.
- Enjoy the journey—Establish milestones and celebrate the baby steps.
- See the big picture—Determine what needs to happen next and stop fretting over other challenges.

- Forget your perfectionist tendencies—Sometimes, not always, good enough is good enough.
- Plan, to the extent possible—It may not help you avoid a crisis from happening, but at least you will be prepared with contingencies. It can get scary when events overtake you.
- Hang out with other positive people—Cynicism, pessimism, and apathy are not part of your world. Folks with these attributes drain energy from all around them. Ditto for the gossipmongers and drama queens whose selfish motives attempt to discredit others in an attempt to make themselves look better.
- Practice patience—Losing your temper will most likely not improve the situation.
- Curse to yourself if it helps.
- Learn to love (or dislike less) your enemy—Not everyone will like you. Find a way to get along with those who do not. Try to think of them in a caring manner.
- Accept criticism—Release the reflexive hurt and anger. Do so without malice and grow from it.

Avoid burnout

Beyond the typical blahs and routine, you might think that most employees would arrive at work on Monday morning feeling energized and refreshed. After all, they had the weekend to relax and rest.

While many do, some do not. In fact, several among the latter seem constantly tired, detached, unmotivated, and exasperated. These could be signs of burnout.

Burnout is excessive exhaustion derived from demanding emotional strain and drain. It affects a person's physical, emotional, and mental states, leading to fatigue and frustration. Unlike stress, it happens over a longer period. It has deeper psychological roots that abut depression and feelings of lost control, meaninglessness, and isolation.

Burnout can sneak up on you, as people may deny what is transpiring around them, not recognizing or rationalizing otherwise about the downward spiral in which they are trapped. It can also choke you over time as you become perpetually exhausted.

While rest is part of the solution, it only addresses the physical aspects of burnout. It does not remediate symptoms such as cynicism, negativity, feelings of disillusionment, loneliness and emptiness, lack of interest, dread of another day, or colleague irritation.

Burnout's root causes vary. Lack of autonomy, values dissonance, a real or perceived lack of support, workload demands, lack of appreciation, and team dysfunction are among the usual suspects. If not careful, career burnout can carry over into your personal life and significantly affect your health.

To fend-off burnout, improve your self-care activities. As mentioned, do what you can to get proper sleep. Work with purpose, socialize and actively engage with others, and manage your time and energy—which may mean learning to say "no." Exercise, use laughter for therapy, and practice relaxation techniques.

If you or someone on your team shows signs of burnout, seek or appropriately suggest professional guidance sooner than later. Provide whatever management support is necessary to extend a helping hand.

When things seem (or are) out of control

In the classic comedy movie *Animal House*, the rambunctious fraternity boys of the Delta House have taken over the town parade and pandemonium abounds. Chip Diller, the

Omega pledge and ROTC cadet played by Kevin Bacon, attempts to return peace and order to the streets by screaming to anyone and everyone within earshot, "Remain calm. All is well! … All is well!"

Chip's efforts prove fruitless as the raging crowd promptly stampedes him onto the sidewalk. His harried actions got him a little too close to the chaos. Do not let this happen to you.

When the dam breaks

To the extent possible, you always want to control the conditions, circumstances, and narrative—until such point when you cannot. You just need to be as prepared as possible for all contingencies. Case in point, the first wave of the pandemic.

In December of 2019, my company began to notice delays and interruptions with our supply chain from China. The problem became so acute that we formed a multi-functional task force to oversee the situation and explore all contingencies. In no uncertain terms, our operational viability was being threatened.

Little did we realize that the missed parts shipments were only a symptom of a much bigger challenge lurking around the corner.

When COVID-19 hit the shores of the U.S. shortly thereafter, it became a "24/7" challenge for management (and everyone). As many of you know, it felt like a marathon with no end. Seemingly overnight, business decisions had to be made about how to handle confirmed and suspected cases of team members, related protocols, travel restrictions, customer touch-points, new ways of working, internal and stakeholder communications, discretionary spending, hiring freezes, furloughs, layoffs, salary and wage considerations, community relations, corporate social responsibility, healthcare provisions, site cleaning and sanitation, employee health checks, personal protective equipment, site reconfiguration, etc.

It was an unrelenting pace, with sprints inside the marathon. The list of real-time issues grew each day and correlating governmental guidance ranged from directive to confusing.

There will be many books written about the detailed corporate responses to the pandemic. At the time of this writing, it is less of a global, national, or local headline. But it's still "out there." Suffice it to say that dealing with this adversity was demanding and exhausting. The pandemic stretched our individual and team boundaries.

At my workplace, as part of the senior management team, working through the pandemic brought us closer and caused us to perform at a higher level and in ways not previously imagined. Strong and steady leadership (and a fortunately-timed pre-pandemic team-building exercise) made all of the difference. We trusted each other; we empowered each other; we did what we had to do to get through the crisis. Yes, there were bumps, but we were and became more agile along the way, steering our company and our employees toward a relatively safe harbor.

How does this compare to Conventional Wisdom?

Keep a cool head when those around you are losing theirs.

Endnotes for Principle 16: Seek consistency—avoid peaks and valleys

Nater, S. (2021, August 18). Timeout with leaders. Interview posted on LinkedIn by Tyler White and Kevin Rustici, episode 15, "Let's see how good we can get."

Your coaching imperative: An even keel

Weisinger, H., & Pawliw-Fry, J. P. (2015). *Performing under pressure: The science of doing your best when it matters most.* New York: Crown Publishing. p. 58.

Manage your energy, not just your time

Polevoi, L. (Date unknown). 8 tips for effective time management. *Intuit Quick Books Resource Center.* Retrieved on February 14, 2019 from: https://quickbooks.intuit.com/r/employees/8-tips-for-effective-time-management/ (time management)

Schwartz, T., & McCarthy, C. (2007, October). Manage your energy, not your time. *Harvard Business Review.* Retrieved on January 22, 2019 from: https://hbr.org/2007/10/manage-your-energy-not-your-time

Manage stress

Examinaetics.com. (Date unknown). Identifying and mitigating work-induced stress. Retrieved on January 22, 2019 from: https://www.examinetics.com/work-induced-stress/

Hussung, T. (2015, September 4). Understanding work stress: causes, symptoms and solutions. *Csp.edu.* Retrieved on January 22, 2019 from: https://on-line.csp.edu/blog/business/understanding-work-stress

Neuronup.com. (2018, October 9). Work-related stress: Definition, causes and consequences for health. Retrieved on January 22, 2019 from: https://blog.neuronup.com/en/work-related-stress/

Sherwood, J. (Date unknown). Work stress: Research-based causes and consequences. *Successfactors.com.* Retrieved on January 22, 2019 from: https://www.successfactors.com/content/ssf-site/en/resources/knowledge-hub/work-stress-research-based-causes-and-consequences.html

Manage anxiety

Molinaro, N. (2021, March 2). Private conversation.

Mitigate anxiety

Manzano, P. (2018: copyright). How to stay calm in frustrating situations (even if you have zero patience. *Tiny Buddha, LLC.* Retrieved on January 22, 2019 from: https://tinybuddha.com/blog/how-to-stay-calm-in-frustrating-situations-even-if-you-have-zero-patience/

Wallen, D. (Date unknown). How to stay calm and cool when you are extremely stressful. *Lifehack.org.* Retrieved on January 22, 2019 from: https://www.lifehack.org/articles/lifestyle/8-ways-stay-calm-and-cool-how-more-patient-and-less-stressed.html

Avoid burnout

Great-West Centre for Mental Health in the Workplace. (Date unknown). Workplace strategies for mental health: burnout response. *Workplacestrategiesformentalhealth.com.* Retrieved on January 22, 2019 from: https://www.workplacestrategiesformentalhealth.com/managing-workplace-issues/burnout-response

Stahl, A. (2018, July 26). 5 ways to avoid burnout at work. *Forbes.com.* Retrieved on January 22, 2019 from: https://www.forbes.com/sites/ashleystahl/2018/07/26/5-ways-to-avoid-burnout-at-work/#66c9fe7490a8

The Mind Tools Content Team. (Date unknown). Avoiding burnout: Maintaining a healthy, successful career. *Mindtools.com.* Retrieved on January 22, 2019 from: https://www.mindtools.com/pages/article/avoiding-burnout.htm

Great leaders give credit to others, but accept the blame themselves

Coach believed players, and only the players, won games. Losing was on him. He thought that he could have or should have done something differently to change the result if they came up short.

Wooden also believed that the spotlight belonged to those in uniform, often singling out players to the media who contributed in a way other than scoring. His overall intention was to make each player feel important through some type of public recognition or at least with an as-needed "pat on the back."

Your coaching imperative: Recognition

Employee recognition is a timely acknowledgment and a showing of gratitude for a job well done. Its goal is to reinforce desirable behavior, attitudes, efforts, and accomplishments that create better business results.

Why recognition matters

Recognition and reward systems are not the only organizational determinants for motivation, job satisfaction, engagement, or employee retention, yet they should not be underestimated. Surveys suggest that their absence may significantly contribute toward an employee's decision to leave an organization.

The thirst for appreciation

Companies that consistently recognize their employees' outstanding work and value are frequently cited as "great places to work." Recognition sets a tone for your culture, your relationships, and your ability to lead a team. Recognition also satisfies our individual craving for feedback and positive affirmation.

From the laboratory

It may seem to be a head-scratcher, but the complexities of our human behavior are explained, in part, by the observations of hungry rats from a century ago. That was when operant conditioning was used in a laboratory setting, and terms like "behavioral shaping and modification," "response rates," and "extinction intervals" came to life.

DOI: 10.4324/9781003456902-25

With operant conditioning, a positive event, outcome, or reward follows an intended behavior; thus, reinforcing that the behavior will be repeated. In considering choices, people will select the actions and behaviors likely associated with pleasure, not pain or punishment. Reward, as a welcomed consequence, becomes encouragement and incentive. This is the philosophical basis of all employee recognition plans.

Drilling down

Kim Harrison has been helping business leaders with their communication and business management skills for years. He has written about the topic of employee recognition, citing its research-based pros and cons. Of note, benefits include lower turnover, increased trust and productivity, greater employee satisfaction, higher retention, and less absenteeism. Conversely, the most significant costs include financial impact, and time in program design and administration.

This is a rather one-sided argument. Recognition can boost someone's morale and esteem, create loyalty, and show your organization's values in action.

The chicken and the egg

When employees are recognized, they generally feel happy. Happy employees are 12% on average more productive than those with less smiles. They feel respected.

Appropriate and timely recognition ➡ increased employee satisfaction and engagement ➡ greater employee productivity ➡ optimal employee performance ➡ increased organizational value

In looking at related research, studies have also found that employee happiness and satisfaction may be derived from the pride employees have in being more productive.

Are your team members happy *and then* productive or vice versa? Regardless of which camp you fall into, you should recognize there is a correlation between the two. Most importantly, if you have the choice (and you do), focus on helping people be productive!

Trends in employee recognition

In days gone by, employee recognition was commonly in the form of a watch at retirement, an "employee-of-the-month" parking spot, a Thanksgiving turkey, and the possibility of a performance bonus. Not anymore.

Employee recognition has evolved and changed in parallel with other employee engagement efforts. Today there are significant trends of note:

- It is ongoing and in real-time.
- It comes from multiple sources. Beyond bosses, it may come from peers, as well as customers.
- It is inclusive. While your top performers may get the top awards, you can also recognize the support team around them. Team recognition vehicles such as parties and events are more common.

- It stretches work boundaries. Rewards may also be given to employees who exercise, eat healthily, or quit smoking as ways and examples of role-modeling behavior for others.
- It includes contingent employees, as award pools are being expanded.
- It is contribution-based. The days of being recognized for just showing up for work are over.
- It is becoming socially responsible. Employees are donating their time and financial rewards to community service causes.
- Management plays an active role.

Some considerations

Employees want to know where they stand, and that their manager and their organization value them.

Differentiate who

Recognition is an individual matter. Some people crave it; others appreciate it in smaller, less frequent, and even less-visible bites. Your goal as a manager is to determine the person's appetite and satisfy it (assuming you choose to do so). Make it personal.

Generally speaking, recognition programs are geared to recognize differentiated performance. In this regard:

- "A" players have significant impact on your team's current and future growth. They add higher value to the organization based upon their unique or highly proficient skill set and knowledge. They are your top performers. They are your building blocks for the future. Covet them. Retain them. Invest in them. Put handcuffs on them.
- "B" players add high value, are solid performers, and are good corporate soldiers. They comprise the middle of your bell curve for performance. Develop and nurture them.
- "C" players add marginal contribution. Monitor them. Lead them. Reassign or replace them as needed.

Your "A" players should receive maximum consideration for recognition, as well as compensation. Reserve the average and below-average rewards for your "B" and "C" players, respectively.

Differentiate what

Today, recognition for continued high-level contribution, employee milestones, micro-moments such as birthdays, work anniversaries, and "above and beyond" performance, is more common and more individualized. Be sure you seek out appropriate opportunities.

Differentiate when

With so many related psychological benefits, it would seem foolish not to fully utilize employee recognition systems and methodologies. After all, it takes so little time and effort to say, "thank you." (And it costs nothing!) Yet, there is a sizable chasm between theory and practice.

The Gallup polling organization found that only one in three US workers strongly agree that they have received a genuine and warranted compliment in the past seven days. Further, Sirota Consulting found, based on a global sample of 2.5 million participants, that only 51% of workers were satisfied with the recognition they received after the completion of a satisfactory task.

Ouch!

Gallup consultants suggest that managers, for optimal results, should recognize their workers weekly, assuming it is deserved, as a way to reinforce the employee's engagement and connectivity to the organization's goals. If times are turbulent, do it more often. It matters.

Differentiate where

Is it best to recognize someone for their performance in a private office setting or in a staff meeting? Both situations have pros and cons. Take your guidance from balancing individual sensitivities (for the recognized individual, as well as any peers), and your desired outcome. (All things being equal, public recognition carries more weight.)

Differentiate the reward

Recognition should be at the right level or scale. Bigger rewards for larger contributions. With this as a backdrop, to the extent possible, customize the employee's preferences and choices. Know what people value, and usually, it is more than just money. For example, most employees would feel proud to take a promotion with a modest increase over a more generous merit increase and handshake. Likewise, a day off might carry more value than a gift certificate.

Perspective

No one has ever come home from work complaining about receiving too much recognition. Here, perspective may be given to this topic by thinking about our front-line healthcare providers and first responders who sacrificed so much during the recent pandemic. How are they best recognized?

Celebrate success

In the corporate world, we are generally off to our next challenge while the dust is settling on the last. In a sense, we have grown accustomed to moving forward without acknowledging key contributions or milestones. Stress, time, competitive pressure, and "What have you done for me lately?" are all easy excuses to keep the course. This is a mistake. A timely pause should be taken.

Individually, when you celebrate, your physiology changes. Endorphins release and you feel better and more energized. These are important feelings that reinforce your success and help prepare you for your next undertaking.

Collective celebration is also a form of team building. Celebrating with your colleagues is a bonding exercise. It may even expand your circle of colleagues and business partners. The good feeling of shared achievement is contagious. Positivity and momentum are forged.

One of the nicest examples for me of this type of celebration occurred at the conclusion of a major cost-saving project. My boss invited all of the team members, along with a guest, to a very fancy restaurant for a group dinner. It was a terrific night that I fondly recall. It marked the occasion and allowed us to truly build a sense of camaraderie over some fine wine. I have no idea what the meal cost, but its benefits were exponential and long-lasting.

Start today

Recognition should be part of your everyday culture. At their core, recognition programs acknowledge contribution, build community, AND establish emotional connectivity. Your role is critical in making these programs successful.

- Do not mail it in. Do it with meaning. Convey recognition personally and in an authentic manner.
- Be specific. When recognizing someone's efforts, cite the value created.
- Make it habit. If appropriate, walk the shop floor and interacting with colleagues on a daily basis—with compliments—goes a long way in relationship building.
- Spread the attention. Those who played for Coach Wooden will tell you that he was not one for patronization; in fact, his compliments were rare. However, when used, they were powerful and motivating. He made it a point to compliment those who did the little things right that contributed to the bigger picture.
- Consider expiration dates. Some rewards are quick, one-time hits and their efficacy fades quickly. Others have extended lives. Consider what matters,
- Keep it simple: easy to understand and administer.

Recognition potpourri

As a motivational tool, recognition is essential. For designing a program, you need to weigh several factors (budget, scope, scale, frequency, fairness, nomination sources, individual or group, cultural readiness and impact, training, communications, goals and metrics, periodic evaluations, understood and tax consequences) to determine what will work best for your organization.

This field is constantly changing as supportive technology improves.

Recognition typically falls into one of three categories: length of service, exemplary one-time performance, and performance over time. "Quick hits" also have merit. For the large and small appreciation demonstrations, Ashley Bell suggests some common methodologies and ideas with nominal associated costs:

- "On-the-spot" bonuses such as cash, merchandise, or local retailing discounts, gadgets, or gift certificates.
- Have a public celebration calendar in your department that marks birthdays and work anniversaries. Celebrate accordingly.
- Devote a portion of your regular staff meeting to acknowledge someone's contribution.
- Consider a program or a type of game where employees may give redeemable points or badges to each other for demonstrating care, teamwork, professionalism, above-and-beyond effort, collaboration, or other company values.
- Supplement your use of employee recognition by using social media.

- Put employee stories on your company homepage.
- Post employee pictures and caricatures to memorialize significant events or achievements.
- Perhaps there is an individual or group fitness or wellness goal worthy of recognition.
- An "employee of the month" program can commemorate special accomplishments.
- Recognize your team members' "outside of work" talent. Perhaps you can display employees' art, photography, or other tangible interests.
- Picnics, breakfasts or lunches, holiday parties, theater outings, ballgames, sightseeing, and charitable and social causes are terrific vehicles.
- Suggestion box. It is back to the future, but still effective.
- Philanthropy. Support employee causes.
- Publicize promotions to show opportunities for upward mobility within the organization.
- Traditional service awards. Make the awarding fun! Have the more senior folks reminisce and share tales from their early days.
- Start a prize drawing and put employees' names in the hat who have hit certain productivity (or the like) marks.

For example, in a company where we were introducing a new, online human capital management system, employees were allowed and encouraged to give recognition (for teamwork, extra effort, appreciation, and the like) to co-workers in the form of related icons or "badges." This would be displayed on the employee's public profile and viewed by others.

I was highly skeptical at first that anyone would pay attention to this, much less take it seriously. However, to my surprise, there was a high adaption rate and employees began to crave the recognition.

How does this compare to Conventional Wisdom?

If I give you credit, what do I get?

Everyone should share in the team's success. Conversely, sincerely, and genuinely accepting blame gives you stature in your subordinates' eyes. It promotes loyalty and team building.

Endnotes for Principle 17: Great leaders give credit to others, but accept the blame themselves

Your coaching imperative

Andriotis, N. (2018 May). Employee recognition in the workplace: the why and how. *eFrontLearning*. Retrieved on December 4, 2018, from: https://www.efrontlearning.com/blog/2018/04/employee-recognition-workplace-benefits-ways.html

What is employee recognition?

Greenberg, J., & Baron, R. (1995). *Behavior in organization* (Third edition). Englewood Cliffs, New Jersey: Prentice-Hall, Inc., p. 177.
Heathfield, S. (2018, November 6). Top 10 reasons why employees quit their jobs: a checklist for the retention of your talented employees. Retrieved on January 6, 2019, from: https://www.thebalancecareers.com/top-reasons-why-employees-quit-their-job-1918985 (Surveys)

The thirst for appreciation

The Society for Human Resource Management. (2018). Managing employee recognition programs. Retrieved on December 4, 2018, from: https://www.shrm.org/resourcesandtools/tools-and-samples/toolkits/pages/employeerecognitionprograms.aspx

Biro, M. (2013, January 13). 5 ways leaders rock employee recognition. *Forbes.com*. Retrieved on December 4, 2018, from: https://www.forbes.com/sites/meghanbiro/2013/01/13/5-ways-leaders-rock-employee-recognition/#2c1941af47ca

From the laboratory

Cherry, K. (2018, July 17). Positive reinforcement and operant conditioning. *Verywellmind.com*. Retrieved on January 9, 2019, from: https://www.verywellmind.com/what-is-positive-reinforcement-2795412

Drilling down

Harrison, K. (Date unknown). Why employee recognition is so important – and how you can start doing it. *Cutting Edge*. Retrieved on December 4, 2018, from: https://cuttingedgepr.com/free-articles/employee-recognition-important/

Cubukcu, C. (2017, November 4). The importance of recognizing your employees. *Entreprenuer.com*. Retrieved on December 4, 2018, from: https://www.entrepreneur.com/article/304183

The chicken and the egg

Craig, W. (2017, July 17). 3 reasons why employee recognition will always matter. *Forbes.com*. Retrieved on December 4, 2018, from: https://www.forbes.com/sites/williamcraig/2017/07/17/3-reasons-why-employee-recognition-will-always-matter/#24fda8763c93

Andriotis, N. (2018 May). Employee recognition in the workplace: the why and how. *eFrontLearning*. Retrieved on December 4, 2018, from: https://www.efrontlearning.com/blog/2018/04/employee-recognition-workplace-benefits-ways.html

Robbins, S. (2003). *The truth about managing people ... and nothing but the truth*. New York: Pearson Education, pp. 39, 40.

Harrison, K. (Date unknown). Why employee recognition is so important – and how you can start doing it. *Cutting Edge*. Retrieved on December 4, 2018, from: https://cuttingedgepr.com/free-articles/employee-recognition-important/

Trends

Nelson, B. (Date unknown). 10 trends in employee recognition. *Dummies.com*. Retrieved on October 30, 2018, from: https://www.dummies.com/business/human-resources/employee-relations/ten-ways-for-managers-to-motivate-employees/

Differentiate who

Haigh, W.T. (1996). Effective retention strategies. Overview presented at the Annual Conference for the International Association of Corporate and Professional Recruitment. Philadelphia, Pennsylvania.

Nelson, B. (Date unknown). 10 trends in employee recognition. *Dummies.com*. Retrieved on October 30, 2018, from: https://www.dummies.com/business/human-resources/employee-relations/ten-ways-for-managers-to-motivate-employees/

Biro, M. (2013, January 13). 5 ways leaders rock employee recognition. *Forbes.com*. Retrieved on December 4, 2018, from: https://www.forbes.com/sites/meghanbiro/2013/01/13/5-ways-leaders-rock-employee-recognition/#2c1941af47ca

Differentiate when

Harrison, K. (Date unknown). Why employee recognition is so important – and how you can start doing it. *Cutting Edge*. Retrieved on December 4, 2018, from: https://cuttingedgepr.com/free-articles/employee-recognition-important/

Celebrate success

Carmody, B. (2015, August 12). 3 reasons celebrating your many accomplishments is critical to your success. *Trepoint*. Retrieved on January 9, 2019, from: https://www.inc.com/bill-carmody/3-reasons-celebrating-your-many-accomplishments-is-critical-to-your-success.html

Start today

Bell, A. (2018, November 2). 39 thoughtful employee recognition & appreciation ideas for 2019. *Wordpress*. Retrieved on December 4, 2018, from: https://www.snacknation.com/blog/employee-recognition-ideas/

Harrison, K. (Date unknown). Why employee recognition is so important – and how you can start doing it. *Cutting Edge*. Retrieved on December 4, 2018, from: https://cuttingedgepr.com/free-articles/employee-recognition-important/

Potpourri

Heryati, R. (2018: copyright). 7 awesome methods for employee recognition. *The 6Q Blog*. Retrieved on December 4, 2018, from: https://inside.6q.io/7-awesome-methods-for-employee-recognition/

The Society for Human Resource Management. (2018). Managing employee recognition programs. Retrieved on December 4, 2018, from: https://www.shrm.org/resourcesandtools/tools-and-samples/toolkits/pages/employeerecognitionprograms.aspx

Bell, A. (2018, November 2). 39 thoughtful employee recognition & appreciation ideas for 2019. *Wordpress*. Retrieved on December 4, 2018, from: https://www.snacknation.com/blog/employee-recognition-ideas/

Engaging your team

A leader's role and responsibility

Coach would tell you, among many competencies, that a true organizational leader:

- Has followers gained through earned trust and respect
- Considers followers as partners in work and shares rewards; helps and encourages those under him/her to grow; has faith in people, believes in them, and draws the best out in them
- Has no ego
- Is a good listener
- Is a role model—whether he or she wishes to be one
- Has a responsibility to conduct himself or herself for the betterment of society as a whole
- Is a self-starter, creates plans, and sets them in motion
- Laughs and can laugh at himself or herself
- Is interested in finding the best way, not in having his or her own way
- Understands his or her strengths and devote energy to improving weaknesses

Coach demonstrated much of this through the following principles:

18 A good leader is first, and foremost, a teacher
19 A great leader cannot worry about being liked
20 Be honest, direct, and willing to risk it all for your beliefs
21 Game time is when the coach's job is almost over

DOI: 10.4324/9781003456902-26

A good leader is first, and foremost, a teacher

True to his sentiment about learning and about teaching, Coach had a plaque over his desk that read: "It's what you learn after you know it all that counts."

Coach began his career as a high school English teacher and most would agree that he never stopped his love or practice of this vocation, *inspiring* people to change—not by forcing them to do so—but by enabling them to do so. He saw his role as a "facilitator" in terms of impacting and unlocking an individual's potential and learning.

He always said that it was an honor and privilege for him to work closely in molding the young men under his guidance.

Coach had a lifelong relationship with many of his players—almost all of whom graduated and, in their own right, went on to perform meaningful work as scholars, lawyers, physicians, dentists, teachers, and ministers. This speaks volumes to the lessons taught and learned on the hardwood in the Coach's classroom, as Bill Walton so aptly summarized:

> Coach Wooden did not teach me to be a basketball player. He taught me to be a person. He taught me how to be part of a team. He taught me how to deal with other people. He taught me how to live life. He taught me to prepare for any eventuality.

Your coaching imperative: The best teachers push the hardest and demand the most

Remember your toughest teacher in high school? You likely resisted and complained about it at the time because of the heightened classroom demands, never-ending homework, the stockpile of readings, and the killer tests that required knowledge application. This teacher made you think critically, and not simply regurgitate answers from books. You were randomly or intentionally called upon in class. There were times when you wanted to be invisible.

Yet, with hindsight, not only were you mastering the subject (not that you had a choice), but you reluctantly learned about preparedness, planning, self-discipline, and time management. In your organizational capacity, you need to be that teacher.

Why invest in your team?

There is an often-repeated, quintessential maxim in Human Resources circles that captures the essence and relevance of training and its related expenditures:

DOI: 10.4324/9781003456902-27

CFO: What happens if we invest in all of our people and they leave?

CEO: What happens if we don't and they stay?

The CEO's response is the correct one.

Know the playing field

Learning is derived from one of four "E" sources: experience, education, exposure, or the environment. Training leads to learning that causes a change in behavior.

It is not what it used to be

Individual training and education programs come in a variety of shapes and sizes. However, one trend is clear: the days of going to seminars and sitting in facilitator-led classrooms for extended periods of time are becoming few and far between. Today's accelerated pace of business just about mandates that training be delivered in "real-time." It must be user-friendly, continuous, informal, mobile readily available, and delivered in "bite-size" pieces.

All resources should be considered for content, including those which are open-source. Studies show that often users may need the information once. For example, if you need to install a ceiling fan this weekend and you are not the handy type, it would be advantageous to check out "how to" videos on the Internet for some guidance. Likewise, if you need some help managing conflict in the office, online solutions must be available at your fingertips.

(Note: Today, in our globally competitive knowledge economy where talent sovereignty is paramount, the business skills and mindset expansion that create and enhance new or improved ideas for processes, products, and services are more critical than ever. To advance this agenda, we must do a better job of preparing and educating our current and future workforce regarding required skills and core competencies. Accordingly, there needs to be a fresh look taken at what and how technology-enabled content is developed and delivered in the world of training and education in both academic and corporate settings. A seismic change is coming and you will want to be a fast follower, if not the pioneer.)

Determine what training is needed

Training assessment is a process undertaken, usually in the form of observation or a survey, which helps determine the current "gaps" in skills that may be impeding individual or organizational progress. Its ultimate goal is to take required corrective measures to be sure that business objectives are met or exceeded.

Typically, this evaluative process considers any one of three areas:

- Organizational assessment looks at the macro-level of the entity to determine what skills, knowledge, and abilities are required.
- Occupational assessment that examines the skills, knowledge, and abilities at a group or departmental level.
- Individual assessment that analyzes employee performance and capacity to do different or new work.

Training assessments may be conducted by managers, usually with the help of HR professionals. Findings from these assessments may include learning voids for technical, systemic, business knowledge, leadership, and strategic planning or execution in any of the three areas.

My focus here is on individual training and education.

Types of individual or group training and education programs

While the landscape of program offerings and course titles can be rather daunting, basic training and education programs are generally organized into the following (or like) categories:

- Orientation—providing employees with the information required to familiarize themselves with the organization and to assimilate/onboard quickly.
- Compliance—providing employees with information about behavioral expectations, legal requirements, ethics, company values, case studies, incident reporting, etc.
- DEI—providing employees with information about DEI efforts in the company.
- Core business skills—establishing a common skills platform aligned with your business imperatives (i.e., identification of prioritized business topics and related course offerings for all employees. Courses may differ in complexity across job bands).
- General business skills—offering structured courses to develop an employee's skills in areas like critical thinking, problem-solving, communications, project management, etc.
- Industrial knowledge—understanding the company's relationship with the market, suppliers, customers, and competitors.
- Professional development—offering opportunities for enhanced skills development for employees within their respective fields.
- Self-development—offering a variety of development programs or assignments, which may be customized by individual needs (e.g., committee experience, action learning projects, classroom experience, white papers, job rotations, job enlargement, etc.).
- Technical/Digital transformation—providing employees with the needed information and training for them to perform the technical aspects of their position.
- Organizational foundations—Sharing information across functions such that individuals may gain a working familiarity with other disciplines—their responsibilities, processes, systems, protocols, and dependencies.
- High-potential—offering structured programs aimed at developing tomorrow's leaders and top performers in an accelerated manner.
- Leadership—offering structured programs to develop future leaders, often focusing upon topics such as strategic thinking, operations, financial acumen, management capabilities, building trust, high-performing cultures, team-building, etc.

If the opportunity presents itself, you should personally take advantage of these offerings.

Early in my career, I was selected to participate in a leadership development program for global appliance concern. I was one of six global participants. Our primary "action learning" objective was to redesign, as applicable, the organizational structure of the company. At the time (mid-1990s), the company had $16 billion in revenue with over 100,000 employees in 60 countries and 500 product lines.

For the better part of a year, while keeping our day jobs, we individually and collectively conducted extensive subject matter research. For my part, I visited about fifteen multinational companies with their headquarters in the US, learning why these entities were organized the way they were. It was a terrific study and an amazing learning opportunity. We also worked with a team of outside consultants who helped steer our journey and organize our findings. In the end, we made numerous recommendations around "One Company." The heavy lifting included a plan for consolidating operations, eliminating silos and duplication, expanding spans of control, and centralizing common functions. Cost savings were projected to be nine figures.

The pace of the project was unyielding. The demands and deadlines were brutal. Juggling everything was non-stop. And yet, this was also one of the most impactful experiences of my career! I was grateful for the opportunity and proud to have participated.

Tailor your approach

Unfortunately, some managers take individual development for granted, with a mindset that comes naturally from on-the-job training or practical work experience. Worse yet, many managers do not view the provision of training opportunities as part of their job. This is unacceptable.

While you will need to make some tough decisions around your training resources and available budget, individual development is crucial. Not only are you helping to shape an individual's professional proficiency, but you are also developing team members who will be brand ambassadors, cultural carriers, and succession candidates. To this end, recognize that there are different ways people learn and different methods for training content to be delivered. Your goal is to be sure that all of your team members are at the right skill and knowledge level, and that their individual preferred learning preference is being met, to the extent possible, in order to ensure the best chance for training success.

Appeal to the adult learner

In our early school years, for most of us, learning was fairly homogeneous, with common textbooks, homework, and lectures. We were sponges with the intent to soak up at least enough of the subject matter to successfully represent our learning on the next test.

Adults, however, are not blank tablets. A different level of engagement is required.

Research in this area is broad, extensive, and trending; however, it generally tells us:

- Adult learning is internally motivated.
- Adult learning should be goal oriented.
- Adults desire explanations of the relevance concerning the subject matter.
- Adults typically respond best to learning that focuses on performing common tasks.
- Training should be experiential. Materials should be considered and be aligned with prior participant experience.
- Adults prefer a self-directed approach that allows for discovery on their own.
- Yesterday's individual tutelage is being replaced with facilitation and coaching.
- New technology is a growing enabler.
- Adult learning should include reflection.

And, as my recent dissertation study focusing upon high-potential corporate women as mentees found, it may not hurt to ask people what they want to learn and at what pace; thus, ensuring ownership and accountability.

As a takeaway, managers should ensure that the training experience has strong connectivity and aligned purpose with the individual's current and future responsibilities. This will enhance the learner's readiness, motivation, and appetite to move forward.

Be aware of learning preferences

While gamification as a training methodology is on the rise, lectures still have their place. However, there are drawbacks. According to a McKinsey & Company survey, "adults typically retain just 10% of what they hear in classroom lectures. Cramming all the key learnings into one lengthy training (session) makes logistical sense, but it greatly restricts learning retention."

Ouch! If that statistic is in the ballpark, we are wasting a lot of time and effort.

One way that we can improve upon that subject matter retention rate is to better match individuals with their preferred learning styles. The VAK Learning Styles Model, while it has its detractors and evolved through several variations, still holds face-value relevancy from the 1920s. It suggests that people prefer to learn in one of three ways: visual, auditory, or kinesthetic (or some combination of the three).

As noted on *MindTools:*

- Visual: Absorbs and retains information better when it is in pictures, diagrams, or charts.
- Auditory: Prefers listening to the presented materials. He or she responds best to voices such as in a lecture or group discussion. Hearing their own voice repeating something back to a tutor or trainer is also helpful.
- Kinesthetic: Prefers a physical experience. He or she likes a "hands-on" approach and responds well to being able to touch or feel an object or learning prop. They learn by "doing."

You may know your own style, and there are numerous resources and analytical tools available on the Internet to help begin the journey of self and team awareness The trick is to match the respective learning preferences of your individual team members and align them with the delivery methodology (in person, synchronous, and asynchronous) of the training for your team. To do so should increase the probability of heightened training effectiveness.

Be aware of learning barriers

As noted in Principle 3 (DEI), teams in the corporate world are becoming less and less homogeneous. People are different. We have unique origins and identities. We are the sum of our own life experiences. Our views have been shaped by, among other factors, the influences of genetics, environment, socioeconomics, education, and life events.

For learning to be effective, the environment must be psychologically safe and inviting. This comfort level will encourage participants to feel accepted and to be authentic, enhancing their connectivity with the subject matter. Further, for optimal learning, barriers must be removed. Thus, to the extent possible, you must stay attuned to each participant's well-being and employ appropriate teaching strategies that recognize and are responsive to cultural awareness.

Coach's teaching methodology

Coach viewed teachers as "enablers ... in terms of unlocking (their students') potential." He believed that teaching had eight basic components: demonstration, imitation, correction, repetition, repetition, repetition, repetition, and repetition.

Did I mention repetition?

He felt these eight steps were the keys to teaching anyone with the required learning capacity, anything, at any time—whether in a classroom, on the basketball court, or in life. Personal mastery was a matter of self-awareness, enhanced focus, control, and the constant hunger for improvement.

How do you know that your training programs have had an impact?

Measuring the impact and return of training programs can be an analytical minefield full of confusing metrics, variables, and formulas. Yet, the evidence suggests the benefit is well worth the cost. To this end, a study by Accenture showed "that for every dollar invested in training that companies received $4.53 in return. That is a 353% ROI."

While HR professionals and accountants can debate and evaluate the merit of any program's efficiency, cost-effectiveness, design, delivery, payback, or business alignment, there are some administrative parameters that you should keep in mind to maximize the probability that your team's training and education programs gain traction.

Incorporate training objectives into your performance management system

Training goals should be a part of each employee's performance plan. Focus on two or three targeted outcomes and hold people accountable for advancing their skills to support your team and themselves!

Be clear of the desired outcome

Training without an intentional, pragmatic objective tends to be serpentine and wander, causing participants' interest and engagement to fall.

Before sending your team members off to training ask: What are we trying to accomplish? Beyond sharing subject matter materials, is the training, whole or in part, about broadening horizons, shaping behaviors, or challenging current ways of thinking or doing? Can the training subject matter also incorporate sought-after skills such as problem-solving, innovation, critical thinking, or transformation? Can it be experiential in nature? Be specific with your thinking. Be quantifiable if possible. It is imperative that the program's targeted outcome is aligned with your business objectives and participants realize its value-added relevance.

Of note, training should ideally be linked to individual career development and potential advancement. Without such a connection, you may simply be grooming talent for their next employer.

Participants must apply what they have learned

The worst-case scenario is when a training participant returns to the workplace and puts the course materials on the shelf behind their desk ... only to collect dust.

- As a form of reinforcement, encourage participants to share their new learning with their colleagues. This helps build a community founded upon continuous learning, critical thinking, and the sowing of innovative seeds.
- Even if it takes an uncomfortable push, participants must demonstrate their learning by stretching their new cognitive muscles in your work environment. This is done by applying the newly attained skills. This is how growth occurs.
- As a coaching opportunity, enable participants to reflect upon what they have learned and provide appropriate encouragement and counsel for refinement.
- The newly acquired skills must be translated into habits. Accordingly, regular demonstrations will improve practice efficiency and effectiveness, prompting and inculcating the desired change.

What can we do better next time?

It is always important to survey what worked and what did not, as well as to get suggestions for improvements from program participants. This feedback is used to help make the next training program that much more effective.

Walk the talk

There are several action items that you can undertake to advance the learning of your team members.

Plan ahead

Organizations experience chaos, ambiguity, heightened politics, and needless waste as a direct result of an unexpected or unplanned absence at the helm. They should always have that next generation of leadership and key roles ready at notice to maintain relative continuity. One of your critical responsibilities should be to identify and groom one or more candidates to be your successor.

Be brave!

Today, you can send a fax quietly and efficiently from your cell phone.

I was introduced to the fax machine in the mid-1980s. It sat in the "copy room" at our offices. One of our administrative assistants was showing a small group of colleagues how to use the machine. I was in the group. I remember thinking … Let me get this straight. You put a document on this tray and a copy of it comes out on a similar machine someplace else? This concept was simply … mind-boggling! This invention had to be the result of recreational drug use. I could not wrap my brain around this.

When I saw the demonstration, I wanted nothing to do with it. The machine was huge. It was loud when dialing and made an ear-piercing screech during transmission. I would never remember which side was "up" for the paper. What would I do if it jams? Feeling quite intimidated, I felt it best to rightfully leave its operation to those who knew what they were doing.

Needless to say, I eventually got past my initial trauma. Now, I look back and wonder, what was I thinking?

Have curiosity

"What has become clear to you since we last met?" is a quote attributed to Ralph Waldo Emerson. These few words outline the philosophical underpinning for life-long personal growth and professional development through curiosity and engagement.

How would you answer this question?

Successful leaders have a natural curiosity about their organization and its people. This causes them to ask questions aimed at improving operational effectiveness and efficiency. If you do not have such curiosity, it would be wise to list this as an area for development, as it will serve you well in the long term.

Instill a growth mindset

Dr. Carol Dweck and her colleagues have studied children's attitudes about learning over the past 30 years. Salient among their findings: attitude is everything! Some children thrive when challenged; others seem predetermined to lesser accomplishments.

Conclusively, Dweck found that children have either "fixed" mindsets or "growth" mindsets.

Fixed mindsets are characterized to avoid challenges, give up easily, see one's work as meaningless, ignore negative feedback, and feel threatened by the success of others. As a result, the studied children plateaued early, fell behind, and never achieved their potential.

Growth mindsets believe that they can get smarter. They understand effort makes them stronger. They put in the extra effort, and they realize it will bear fruit. Specifically, they embrace challenges, stay persistent when bowing out might look attractive, see effort as the path to results, learn from feedback, and find inspiration in the success of others.

Dweck and her team found that students with growth mindsets significantly out-performed their peers. Most important, encouraging the development and outcomes of a growth mindset can be done with intervention. In the teaching world, this was done with the feedback that was given to students. For example, simply praising children by telling them that they are smart encourages a fixed mindset. On the contrary, praising a student for their hard work and effort encourages a growth mindset, pushing them to self-develop toward more learning and achievement.

As mentioned earlier, Microsoft has transformed its culture using some of Dr. Dweck's research. They were and are intent on building a company that no longer has all the an-swers, but instead has a thirst for learning. They push themselves and each other to learn, share, and grow.

Microsoft is coming at this topic at the macro-level, but there are some things you can do, specifically with feedback, to encourage your team to have a growth mindset. As noted, begin with self-awareness about the words you use for team member feedback. Telling people that they are "poised," "articulate," "clever," "accomplished," etc. is fine, but not encouraging. These adjectives have finite shelf life and, therefore, limited efficacy. Rightful pride may result, but it may also bring on smugness or arrogant distance from colleagues. This type of feedback may also cause someone to feel like their learning is complete, and/or they have reached the mountaintop.

To bring on the growth mindset, use verbs, not adjectives, for feedback. Recognize someone for their contribution—not as an end, but as part of a forward-looking learning continuum. Phrases indicative of praising new learning, applying an innovative approach, encouraging further work or exploration, or sharing new ideas and suggestions can bring about continued productivity gains.

It's only a slight pivot point with your words, but the message can be truly motivational.

Give of yourself

Thomas J. Watson, Sr., the Founder of IBM (1914–1956), experienced success due to his innovation, business savvy, positive employee relations skills, and leadership capabilities. *None* of what he ultimately accomplished may have come to fruition without his inspirational mentor, John Patterson. It was Patterson (at NCR in Watson's early business days) who personally showed a then-discouraged Watson how to successfully call upon customers and sell. He carried this philosophy and practice forward.

If Patterson could make the investment in Watson, you can do the same.

Yes, you are a role model

One of coach's favorite maxims: "No written word, no spoken plea, can teach our youth what they should be. Nor all the books on the shelves: It's what the teachers are themselves."

Remember, you are a role model. 24/7/365. You live in a goldfish bowl. All of your words and actions are public, both at and outside work.

Attend to your own renewal

Socrates noted, "The unexamined life is not worth living." If you were to take an inventory of your personal and professional assets and limitations, what might be on that list?

Know thyself

Several books and online resources can help with self-analysis related to personality and psychological testing—with something as simple and readily accessible as Myers-Briggs Type Indicator or DISC. *For self-awareness, I especially like the Test for Attentional and Interpersonal Style (TAIS) as a discovery tool. It helps individuals understand the impact of "pressure" (and who isn't under pressure?) and its effects upon our unique information processing and decision-making, and subsequent performance. This tool may also be used by managers to help supplement staff placement and professional development decisions.*

If these more formal assessment options are not appealing, perhaps taking a periodic and regular personal inventory might provide insight, reflecting upon:

- *Write a capsule summary of your background and upbringing, citing the key individuals and events of influence.*
- *What are your professional goals? Personal goals? Is there harmony?*
- *What are your current skills and areas of knowledge?*
- *What skills and areas of knowledge will you need for the future?*
- *What attributes/characteristics/skills are required for you to attain your professional goals?*
- *How do you perceive yourself? Why? What are your overall strengths and development areas? How do you influence others?*

- *What are your professional accomplishments? What did you do to make those happen? (Note: Put your accomplishments in the STAR format—Situation, Task, Action, and Results. This will help you organize your thoughts, as well as prepare you for any future presentations or interviews.)*
- *What do you want in a job? In what type of work environment are you most comfortable and effective? What type of boss do you prefer and thrive under?*
- *If asked, how would you describe yourself to a potential employer in less than one minute? (Note: This is also known as the "elevator pitch.")*

When you are done with this exercise, you may want to consider writing your priorities on your own 3" × 5" card and posting it in an area that you see every day. If you are not working on something on that card, why are you doing it? The bottom line is that the more information and awareness we have about ourselves, the more effectively we will be able to move along on our desired path, as well as deal with and help others.

What's your EQ?

We have all worked with or seen people who are book-smart. These are the folks possessing intellectual horsepower (i.e., logic, reasoning, memory, attention, etc.). However, as author Daniel Goleman points out, one's intelligence quotient ("IQ") is not the only barometer for one's potential fate in this competitive world. Rather, emotional competencies for "self-awareness and impulse control, persistence, zeal and self-motivation, empathy and social deftness" (i.e., one's "EQ" or emotional intelligence) are just as salient in one's personal development and socialization processes (1995, inside jacket cover). *In fact, it is my experience that if your career derails, it will likely be attributable to shortcomings with your EQ.*

EQ is critical for leadership. It is predicated upon self-awareness, being in the moment, self-discipline, and relating to the other party. Social skills, motivation, and empathy are among its key characteristics.

EQ has two primary components: recognizing, knowing, understanding, and managing your own emotions; and recognizing and understanding the emotions of others. People with a high EQ are patient, stable, good listeners, curious, forward-thinking, and consistent with their behavior. They are strong-willed and sound decision-makers. They are focused, warm, and welcoming.

Much like the previously mentioned tests for personality, there are EQ tests available online. If you suspect that your EQ is lacking, it might be time to check under the hood and tune up as needed.

Be a lifelong learner

As the plaque over the Coach's desk implies, the best teachers (and students) never stop learning.

Russell Sarder is an award-winning entrepreneur, best-selling author, and CEO. Under his stewardship, NetCom Learning, a global leader in managed learning services, training, and talent development, has become a multi-million dollar business. As part of his outreach efforts, Russell sponsors "Sarder TV," a forum where business leaders are interviewed on a variety of topics, including organizational and people development. To prompt the on-camera dialog, before each of these interviews, guests are invited to complete a placard with the phrase, "Learning is _____." Inevitably, interview participants often respond with words such as "required," "critical," "necessary," and "vital."

Learning is the essential fuel for the leader. It is the source of high-octane energy that keeps up the momentum by continually sparking new understanding, new ideas, and new challenges. It never ends. It is indispensable under today's conditions of rapid change and complexity when knowledge may have a short shelf life. Learning should be sought and chased with vigor.

Why lifelong learning matters

Lifelong learning = lifelong employability. And your lifetime may be a while.

In their thought-provoking book, *The 100-Year Life*, Lynda Gratton and Andrew Scott make a powerful case that our need or desire to work may soon be spread over a 50 (or dare we say, 60-plus!) year career. Through improved health practices by all, and a better gene pool for some, our upcoming lifespans may hit the century mark as a common happening. This will dramatically impact, if not end, our present traditional three-stage life cycle paradigm—education, work, and retirement, potentially replacing it with multiple stages and careers with different timing, emphasis, needs, and priorities.

Assuming we are on this longevity path, what, when, and how we build and apply our portfolio of learning will transcend all aspects of our lives. As part of our employee experience, organizations will place more emphasis upon individual and team learning. There will be no tolerance for those who are stagnant. Linear career paths will disappear; career and job changes will be required. Learning will be flexible, multi-sourced, and derived through and from others. Resiliency will be part of every job description. To stave off knowledge obsolescence, organizations will insist that their team members prepare for, participate in, help others, and keep momentum toward learning objectives and experiences.

Succinctly, to prevent becoming a dusty relic, we must find ways to upscale and re-scale our learning and skills base, creating value for our organizations and ourselves.

(*Food for thought: Today's talent market is more and more connected and inclusive. It is increasingly likely that you will be competing against talent from all over the world for your next job, especially as you progress on the corporate ladder.*)

Get it done

Education opens doors. It transforms you. It defines you. It shapes your character. It broadens your perspectives. It opens your eyes to previously unseen horizons. It causes you to challenge your previously held beliefs. It promotes critical thinking. It allows you to understand both sides of a debate. It promotes empathy and understanding. It encourages us to be creative and to adapt. It sparks psychological, emotional, and cognitive growth. It is the evolutionary and revolutionary foundation for all of our tomorrows.

Experience is a great part of education; however, if you have the opportunity, get online or in the classroom. Learn about other cultures and languages. Explore facets of business beyond your day-to-day. Get out of your comfort zone. Complete high school. Get an associate's or bachelor's degree. These latter degrees have almost become "must-have" entry tickets into today's professional workplace. Certifications are also useful and necessary, and an advanced degree is becoming more of a requirement. In addition to broadening your horizons, multiple degrees and certifications are a great way to rightfully differentiate yourself and stay fresh in your field.

Note: Your education, while a terrific individual accomplishment, is the product of many people supporting you along the way. It is a treasured gift. Share your experience, knowledge (what you know), and your wisdom (knowledge plus perspective and judgment) with others.

This is personal

Pay attention. The world is changing ... quickly, and STEM (science, technology, engineering, and mathematics) is leading the way!

At the macro-level, technology advances are making an impact ona wide scope of industries. Cars are already driving themselves and may soon fly. Machines are dispensing prescriptions and stocking store shelves. Alexa is running all of the gadgets in your house. For competitive intelligence, eyes in the sky can monitor retail parking lot capacities, crop yields, the number of sheep in a pasture, and oil tanker inventories. Hedge funds now run on far more efficient AI algorithms. Many societies, whole or in part, are already cashless. An upcoming chicken dinner may taste farm-fresh, but it may have test-tube origins. In addition, you certainly want your next mammogram (or that of a loved one) interpreted with artificial intelligent software, which is much faster and almost flawless. And let's not forget that AI can write research papers that pass academic rigor, write music, draft lawsuits, craft advertisements, advance medical exploration, generate personalized messaging around your health and well-being, and build websites almost from scratch. Its potential—to exponentially increase productivity and disrupt—seems boundless. And it's just gettimg started ...

At the individual level, jobs and related tasks are being newly defined. Human and machine collaborations are improving and replacing aspects of jobs that were manual and repetitive in nature. Robots are doing housekeeping and making breakfast. Assembly line workers, data entry clerks, fruit-pickers, stenographers, cashiers, paralegals, record-keepers, and landscaping positions are gradually disappearing and/or becoming redefined. In the office, accounting, administrative, recruiting, and procurement practices are at the tip of the transformative iceberg. And Microsoft Teams, Zoom, and the like are here to stay, changing how we interact.

Related to all the above shifts, what is the future of "employment?" What will this mean for you? What does the future of work look like? Where and what will be the new jobs? Will you be employed by one organization or be a "free agent," whose talent is procured by corporations on a real-time basis for projects? Will there be anything such as job security? Perhaps there will be a rise of professional unions or none at all.

You MUST stay up-to-date in your current and possibly next field as many positions are and will be impacted, enhanced, or transformed. These technological and societal changes are getting closer to your doorstep.

I recently attended a "Think Tank" session held at the New York campus of IESE, one of the world's leading business schools. Here, chief human resources officers from some of the world's largest companies gathered to debate the question, "Is learning the answer to disruption?" As you might imagine, this topic brought out a wide range of opinions concerning the relationship between these two critical constructs. What was most striking, however, was the direction the discussion later took that focused upon the workforce implications of new technologies. Specifically, it was posited that CEOs may need as little as half of their current workforce in five to ten years (i.e., half the number of people, but all with new or enhanced skills).

You do not want to be on the wrong side of these evolving marketplace trends. Stay current and explore.

Be a most valuable player

As a then-recent college graduate, I went to work for a large chemical company. I took an entry-level role in inventory control, wearing steel-tip boots and a hard helmet at one of their manufacturing sites.

Like many 21-year-olds, I did not know what I did not know. My near-term mindset was simply to do a good job, live at home and save a few bucks, play in some basketball and softball leagues, and see where life would take me.

That mindset did not last. I realized that I wanted to make a difference. To this end, I worked hard and started to make a name for myself at my company. I was curious and hungry, even competitive. I wanted to know anything and everything about how our products were made and distributed, and I pushed boundaries and raised my hand in this quest. The company invested in me and my contributions expanded. Job rotations followed, giving me broad business exposure. I went back to school. I was recognized as a key contributor and a future leader. I was becoming a "go to" guy.

After five years in several different functions and roles, I was ultimately placed in the labor relations supervisor position. I loved it. I knew this was home. With an internal customer perspective, it allowed me to leverage all that I knew about the site, its people, processes, policies, etc. It also allowed me to have a holistic impact on the way forward for the site. I was going to be a better HR professional because I knew the business.

To this day, I am grateful for that opportunity. It gave me clarity. It gave me a foundation for a rewarding career. And I gave to them, and continue to give my employers, all of my best in return.

Take responsibility for your own career

This point cannot be overstated. Your future depends on you.

Most employees believe that it is the duty of their employer to steer their respective careers and to provide needed training. On the other hand, the majority of managers overwhelmingly believe that it is the employee's responsibility to take command of and control their own career navigation.

Do not get caught in the former thinking. Your employer may not know best or even care.

Be self-reliant. Seize control of your own career. Think competitively, You need goals, timelines, and assessment points to ensure that your career is headed in your desired direction and at the pace you deem appropriate.

You, and no one else, are responsible for your own financial, moral, social, and personal accountability. No one knows better of your future possibilities and contributions than you.

Should you fear the future?

No. But pay attention and be prepared!

A good example is the role of bank teller. Back in the day, you went to your bank on payday to make your deposit and to get some cash. These transactions were conducted routinely by a bank teller. Today, the ATM (Automatic Teller Machine) has assumed many of the bank teller's basic transactional duties, but that does not mean that the role was eliminated. It has now morphed to take on different and more complex duties, and the qualifications for this role have changed.

Does passion matter?

Yes, passion matters. It is a powerful emotional driver. It is right there with energy, excitement, desire, and enthusiasm. It can be a key element of learning and motivation. It is referenced several times in this book.

Yet, the phrase "chase your passion" is one fraught with problems.

Early in our work lives, we often don't know what we don't know. Therefore, it is hard to find our passion until we have broader exposure to career possibilities. Accordingly, we unintentionally blur the lines between passion as an isolated construct and its possible fruits—such as money, respect, or status. Are we really chasing our passion or its by-products?

Be aware of this distinction. Your real aim is to find something that you are good at (and hopefully, enjoy), and to get better at it every day. Passion may lead, but more likely will follow.

How does this compare to Conventional Wisdom?

If I spend my time teaching, how will anything else get done?

On the contrary, if you do not teach others, you will end up doing all the work yourself and dramatically underserve your organization and the team around you.

Endnotes for Principle 18: A good leader is first, and foremost, a teacher

Introduction

Hill, A. (2000). Interview notes, 1, p. 3.

Why invest in your team?

Eudy, R. (2016, October 19). 5 steps for proving the role of your training investment. Retrieved on July 2, 2018, from: https://www.cornerstoneondemand.com/rework/5-steps-proving-roi-your-training-investment

Know the playing field

Auricchio, G. (2018, October 11). "Envisioning 'the what,'" Global HR Think Tank, "Is Learning the Answer to Disruption?" IESE Business School, New York.

NJ Department of Personnel, Certified Public Manager Program. (1998, June). Development Institute, Learner Guide, Module 1—"Introduction to Public Management, page 10 of 23, citing A. Palmer, "Learning Cycles: Models of Behavioral Change," 1981.

Determine what training is needed

HR-Survey. (2018: copyright). Training needs assessment survey. Retrieved on July 2, 2018, from: https://www.hr-survey.com/TrainingNeeds.htm

U.S. Office of Personnel Management. (Date unknown). Training and development/planning & evaluating/training needs assessment. Retrieved on July 2, 2018, from: https://www.opm.gov/policy-data-oversight/training-and-development/planning-evaluating/

Types of individual or group training and education programs

Sumitomo Corporation of Americas. (2018). Draft of work product for cross-regional training & education. Committee: Teng, S., Leung, E., Hasegawa, R., Lim-Brand, A., Nagai. K., Rueda, F., Neale, L., Franklin, D., Karasawa, K., Zaima, W., Fang, Y., Kakihara, D., Kumseng, L. Margree, J., & Kane, W., New York.

Tailor your approach

Drucker, P.F. (1967). *The effective executive*. New York: HarperCollins Publishers, Inc., p. 170.

Appeal to the adult learner

Rutgers University on-line. (Date unknown). The principles of adult learning theory. Retrieved on July 2, 2018, from: https://on-line.rutgers.edu/blog/principles-of-adult-learning-theory/

Palis, A.G. & Quiros, P.A. (2014, April-June). Adult learning principles and presentation pearls. *Middle East African Journal of Ophthalmology*, pp. 114–122. Retrieved on July 2, 2018, from: https://www.ncbi.nlm.nih.gov/pmc/articles/PMC4005174/

Be aware of learning preferences

Levy, A. (2018, February 23). Why leadership training doesn't work. *Forbes.com*. Retrieved on July 17, 2018, from: https://www.forbes.com/sites/forbescoachescouncil/2018/02/23/why-leadership-training-doesnt-work/#7403e11077a4

MindTools. (Date unknown). VAK learning styles—understanding how team members learn. Retrieved on July 19, 2018, from: https://www.mindtools.com/pages/article/vak-learning-styles.htm

Be aware of learning barriers

Plotts, C. (2022). *Cultural intentions as evidence-based framework and applications of cultural responsiveness in education*. Colonial Beach and Gloucester, Virginia: DBC Publishing, pp. 13, 22.

Coach's teaching methodology

Hill, A. (2002). Interview notes, #JW1-2, pp. 12–14.

Have curiosity

Bennis, W.G. & Nanus, B. (1997). *Leaders: Strategies for taking charge* (Second ed.). New York: HarperCollins Publishers, Inc., p. xv.

Instill a growth mindset

Decades of scientific research that started a growth mindset revolution: Dr. Dweck's research into growth mindset changed education forever. (2017). *Mindset Works*. Retrieved on September 12, 2017, from: https://www.mindsetworks.com/science/

Give of yourself

Bennis, W., Brown, T., Champy, J., Crainer, S., Davis, S., Edwards, H., Goleman, D., Gottlieb, A., Heller, R., Larreche, J.C., Leyden, P., Meyer, C., Norton, B., & Rayport, J. (Advisory Board), (2002). *Business: the ultimate resource*. Cambridge, Massachusetts: Perseus Publishing, pp. 1054–1055.

You are a role model

Hill, A. & Wooden, J.R. (2001). *Be quick but don't hurry*. New York: Simon & Schuster, p. 96.

How do you know that your training programs have had an impact?

Eudy, R. (2016, October 19). 5 steps for proving the role of your training investment. Retrieved on July 2, 2018, from: https://www.cornerstoneondemand.com/rework/5-steps-proving-roi-your-training-investment

Shephard, C. (Date unknown). Assessing the ROI of training. *Fastrack Consulting, Ltd.* Retrieved on July 2, 2018, from: http://www.fastrak-consulting.co.uk/tactix/Features/tngroi/tngroi.htm

What can we do better next time?

Schroeder, P. (2017, December 4). 6 training best practices according to seasoned trainers. *E-Learning Industry*. Retrieved on July 2, 2018, from: https://elearningindustry.com/training-best-practices-according-seasoned-trainers-6

Levy, A. (2018, February 23). Why leadership training doesn't work. *Forbes.com*. Retrieved on July 17, 2018, from: https://www.forbes.com/sites/forbescoachescouncil/2018/02/23/why-leadership-training-doesnt-work/#7403e11077a4

What's your EQ?

Goleman, D. (1995). *Emotional intelligence*. New York: Bantam Books.

Cornerstone University. (2017, June 5). Are you emotionally intelligent? Here's how to tell. https://www.cornerstone.edu/blog-post/are-you-emotionally-intelligent-heres-how-to-tell/

Be a lifelong learner

Schroeder, P. (2017, December 4). 6 training best practices according to seasoned trainers. *E-Learning Industry*. Retrieved on July 2, 2018, from: https://elearningindustry.com/training-best-practices-according-seasoned-trainers-6

Sarder, R., 2018). LinkedIn Biography. Retrieved on July 17, 2018, from: https://www.linkedin.com/in/russellsarder/

Bennis, W.G. & Nanus, B. (1997). *Leaders: Strategies for taking charge* (Second ed.). New York: HarperCollins Publishers, Inc., p. 176.

Why lifelong learning matters

Gratton, L. & Scott, A. (2016). *The 100-year life*. New York: Bloomsbury Business.

This is personal

Frank, M., Roehrig, P., & Pring, B. (2017). *What to do when machines do everything*. Hoboken, New Jersey: John Wiley & Sons, Inc., pp. 1–11.

Take responsibility for your own career

Quast, L. (2014, September 29). Who's in charge of career planning? you. *Forbes*. Retrieved on July 17, 2018, from: https://www.forbes.com/sites/lisaquast/2014/09/29/whos-in-charge-of-career-planning-you/#6ea3346c39c2

A great leader cannot worry about being liked

As Coach often stated, "You control your character; others hold your reputation." Coach understood that leadership was not a popularity contest. Inherent to his system, decisions about who played (and who did not) were seldom made without someone becoming upset. This was especially true as Coach gave the majority of court time to a rotation of seven or eight players, while the balance of players waited for slimmer pickings.

Your coaching imperative: Do the right thing

Know the difference between what you have the "right to do" as leader and what the right thing is to do. After all, you have control over what you do, but not what others say.

You want to be liked, but ...

Most of us want to be liked. It seems natural. Yet, in the workplace, this aspiration generally goes unfulfilled for leaders—as it must.

When one is in a position of authority, they are making daily decisions about allocating fixed resources. The key word here is "fixed." You have a limited budget and time. Thus, if, or should we say when, everyone who works for you wants more money, promotions, plum work assignments, flexible work schedules, enhanced work/life balance, and face time, you can only disappoint. Feelings will be hurt and chasing this idealistic pursuit may prove self-destructive. Here are some traps to avoid:

- "Yes" is too often your response—Your inclination to say "yes" to every request and invitation, expanded responsibilities, committee participation, socialization, conference attendance, association memberships, special assignments, etc. takes away from time you might spend elsewhere. Be careful. This is not a healthy habit. Better to take your time with these decisions in order to weigh the trade-offs.
- Not being decisive—Delaying decisions because you are weighing how they will be received or stalling in an effort to avoid conflict is disingenuous. Be true to yourself and to those around you when it comes to determining the best way forward.
- Patronizing people—Telling people what they want to hear, or otherwise distorting or delaying the truth may cause alienation. You do not need everyone's approval.
- Stop trying to do it all yourself—In your attempt to please everyone, you may be hurting your own credibility. Delegate, work as a team, and mutually support each other.

DOI: 10.4324/9781003456902-28

- Stop trying to be everyone's solution—You need boundaries between people and activities. Set them, control them, and respect them.
- Stop trying to solve everyone else's problems. Place accountability and control where it belongs.
- Stop trying to be everyone's friend—You are their boss!
- Letting the image of who you want to be interfere with the person you are—In doing so, you are being dishonest or a phony. This only drains energy and puts you on a path of mistrust.
- Losing your values—Make sure that the important things in your life are receiving the right time and attention. Stay authentic to yourself!

Coach had close bonds with his players *after* they had hung up their sneakers. In fact, in his later years, he was generally beloved and revered. The hindsight of appreciation is like that. On the other hand, when he was actively coaching, his players generally did not like him. He let his assistants have the closer relationships and be his buffer. Being "liked" was never a concern for Coach. Being authentic was!

Leave your ego behind

Everyone has an ego. Do not let it get in the way.

With each rung of the corporate ladder you climb, you attain more power, authority, and status. Industry recognition might even be a by-product. This success tempts and teases your ego. If you have not placed the right people around you, they may tell you what you want to hear versus what you need to hear. They will want to please you more. They will laugh at your jokes and listen more attentively. They will be more agreeable and may defer their own judgments to yours. They psychologically bow to your positional (or cultural) standing in the organizational hierarchy. Heady stuff!

Be careful when you are feeling best about your mirror's image. (*For me, a person's arrogance is the fastest and greatest turnoff.*) An unchecked and increasingly hungry ego can start to distort your reality and breed questionable motives. Your behavior can become corrupted, your vision can become clouded, and you can lose touch with the people you are responsible for leading.

When humility and gratitude, two cornerstones of leadership, begin to slip, watch for some of the common ego traps.

- Your ego colors your thinking—Those with the "Midas touch" believe that they can do no wrong. They have all the answers and their intuition is the rudder of choice. Help is not required.
- Opportunities are missed—An ego, coupled with a know-it-all attitude, can miss opportunities and be resistant to change. Egos with all the answers can also grossly underestimate challenges, thinking that the wave of a wand should cure most ills.
- You overestimate your abilities—People may come to be masters at some things, but likely not all. They learn the hard way that there are no shortcuts or that necessary details have been missed.
- Egos like command and control—This can lead to autocratic decision-making and micromanagement, likely in an over-bearing and critical manner. In addition, top-down communication will miss much.

- Egos do not need mentors—People with inflated self-opinions prevent themselves from seeking appropriate guidance and advice.
- Egos view every decision in the context of what the decision means for them personally—When the world revolves around you, seeing beyond that horizon is a challenge.
- Egos like credit, but steer away from blame—Large egos tend to be vulnerable and insecure. Pride is their protection. Any news that dents or contradicts that self-image is not going to be warmly greeted. (This was discussed in Principle 17.)

Coach Wooden, with all of his accomplishments and accolades, was the antithesis of this—the absolute antithesis.

Deal with your team's narcissists

Narcissists make themselves look better at the expense of others, which puts your reputation and team dynamics at risk. They are generally not team players. Their inflated view of themselves, tendency to envy others, lack of desire to follow the norms, ability to run roughshod over everyone, obsessive and potentially crippling perception of their own narrow opinions and spin-mastery, and reluctance to accept blame or share the spotlight can make them lone sheep.

That does not mean that they cannot be productive and even play a leadership role. Their "bullet-proof" exterior allows them to see the big picture, as well as to take risks and make decisions without emotional attachments. Some of this generation's most successful entrepreneurs fall into this category.

Be wary when the narcissist is in the room. Try to keep him or her as an asset, not a liability. If possible, it is best to pair him or her with someone who will listen and engage, attend to detail, look at things from a strategic and tactical view, and know how to work the organizational bureaucracy.

Your tolerance for this type of selfish personality (and they can be real jerks!) should be causally related to their level of contribution. Cautiously monitor their contributions, and tolerate them as long as the benefit outweighs any burden.

Deal with your team's "unique" personalities

All companies have their gurus. You know who they are: the rain-makers, the founders, and the innovators. These are the organizations "can't live without" folks. They are responsible for getting the enterprise launched or making the enterprise successful. They come in all shapes and sizes.

The challenge is what, if anything, do you do when the behavior of these critical contributors is so outside the norm?

Case in point. A software developer where I once worked had some quirky habits. He was the creator of software used by the United States government. Its use was classified. This developer's efforts and creations were what drove the company. In fact, it is likely that this $500 million company would not have existed without him.

This gentleman had a few eccentricities. When he arrived at work, he would keep his diesel Mercedes running all day in the parking lot. He would leave his dog in the car, window cracked. He would come into the office, saying hello to no one. He would promptly go to his office and shut the door. The door would remain shut for the balance of the day with exceptions for bathroom breaks. He seldom attended meetings. He interacted with coworkers and his boss only on rare occasions, and if you had to knock on his door, it had best be for an exceptional reason. His office was his play space and no one was welcome.

How do you handle that one? The answer is "very carefully."

After some prolonged interventions of soft cajoling (which I am sure was interpreted as nagging), I was able to appeal to his sense of mission and knowledge transfer. We got him to the point where he would keep his door cracked and attend "as needed" meetings. We took it as a baby-steps victory.

Know how you are perceived

The late Ed Koch, New York City's outspoken mayor, was known for asking his constituents, "How'm I doing?" He proclaimed this in his distinct New York accent, at a pace that was slippery fast. While a bit rough around the edges, his probe was specific and intentional. He wanted feedback. Knowing how you are perceived—liked or not—is important, too.

Your team members make judgments about you every day, and the bad ones can be hard to corral. Once viewed in this manner, things can be exaggerated, negatively construed, or otherwise questioned. These perceptions take on a life of their own and spread.

Feedback is an effective tool to help minimize your blind spots. American psychologists Joseph Luft and Harry Ingham conceived the Johari Window Model in 1955. This model considers an individual's feelings, attitudes, skills, values, behaviors, and motivations by dividing them into four quadrants that are split between what is known and unknown to oneself versus what is known and unknown by others.

As noted in Principle 12 under "self-discovery," to the extent you are comfortable, ask others for their opinions. You want to know how you are perceived and what you can do differently that will have the greatest impact on your success. Best if they can be as detailed as possible and you should manage your reaction if you hear some tough messaging.

Admit mistakes

Stuff happens! It has to. You are learning new things, challenging yourself and your team, and being innovative. Accordingly, mistakes occur, and things fall off the tracks.

When mistakes occur, it is best to admit to them, learn from them, and try to move on. In all likelihood, you will be held in higher regard if you handle the misstep properly. In this vein, in borrowing from the "crisis management" handbook, there are some steps that you can take to amend, especially if your mistake has damaged your credibility, integrity, or key relationships.

- Fear, embarrassment, or ego may cause you to run and hide. This may only exacerbate the situation.
- Admit the mistake. Say you are sorry. Be straightforward and clear. Do not wait. Hold your head high.

  Admitting the mistake has some personal advantages. It gets you out of a defensive mode, starts the restoration process of your credibility, increases transparency to your audience, reduces your stress levels, and provides a "reset" opportunity.

Organizationally, admitting the mistake provides a learning opportunity, builds trust and loyalty, allows for correction, builds collaboration and inclusion, sets a new tone for risk-taking and invention, opens communication channels, and reinforces the desirable aspects of your culture.

- Take ownership of the mistake. While it may be tempting to deflect responsibility or to blame someone or something else, accept accountability.
- Someone is likely frustrated, hurt, or disadvantaged because of your mistake. Pragmatically and emotionally connect with them. Make amends if possible and show empathy.
- Walk through what happened, cause and effect, with the appropriate amount of detail. Take your time. Answer questions. Stick with the facts.
- Provide assurances that this mistake will not be repeated. This includes the why's and how's. Highlight key learnings. Share remedial steps with aligned accountabilities and timelines. Start the healing.

Have a sounding board

Leadership can be a lonely endeavor. A very lonely endeavor. Its pace is a sprint, but you must also be marathon-ready. Occasionally, the path in front of you has forks and surprises.

Just as Coach had his trusted assistants, make it a point to have a trusted confidante you can occasionally bounce off ideas and suggestions, as well from whom you may receive candid feedback. This person can be objective, provide contrarian views and complementary competence, share insight, and ask pointed questions. In this regard, a former coworker, a trusted colleague, a mentor, or an executive coach can be a valuable asset for today and the days to come. In addition, make your human resources function as your business partner, as often they can be helpful with organizational perspective and practical advice.

Be grateful

Leadership is a privilege, not a right. You have been or will be appointed to this leadership role because someone(s) recognized potential in you. This is an amazing opportunity, as well as a major responsibility. Do not take it lightly and strive not to disappoint. Be grateful to everyone who helps pave your way and stay on the narrow course.

How does this compare to Conventional Wisdom?

I want everyone to like me.

If this is the case, maybe a leadership role is not your calling.

Endnotes for Principle 19: A great leader cannot worry about being liked

You want to be liked, but ...

Grover, S. (2017, February 10). How wanting to be liked gets you rejected. *Psychology Today.com*. Retrieved on February 7, 2019 from: https://www.psychologytoday.com/us/blog/when-kids-call-the-shots/201702/how-wanting-be-liked-gets-you-rejected

Morin, A. (2015, December 22). 5 signs you're trying too hard to be liked. *Forbes.com*. Retrieved on February 7, 2019 from: https://www.forbes.com/sites/amymorin/2015/12/22/5-signs-youre-trying-too-hard-to-be-liked/#25b40986deea

Leave your ego behind

Hougaard, R., & Carter, J. (2018, November 6). Ego is the enemy of good leadership. *hbr.org*. Retrieved on February 7, 2019 from: https://hbr.org/2018/11/ego-is-the-enemy-of-good-leadership

Petch, N. (2016, July 26). Why a big ego reduces your chance at business success. *entrepreneur.com*. Retrieved on February 7, 2019 from: https://www.entrepreneur.com/article/279633

Rampton, J. (2016, July 12). 8 ways my ego killed my business. *entrepreneur.com*. Retrieved on February 7, 2019 from: https://www.entrepreneur.com/article/278901

Deal with the narcissists

Flora, C. (2016, June 9). Big egos in business. *Psychologytoday.com*. Retrieved on February 7, 2019 from: https://www.psychologytoday.com/us/articles/200401/big-egos-in-business

Know how you are perceived

Communication Theory. (2013 estimate). "The Johari window," Communication Models, Group Communication. Retrieved on March 22, 2019 from: https://www.communicationtheory.org/the-johari-window-model/

Gallagher, B. (Date unknown). How are you being perceived in the workplace? *TeamWorks*. Retrieved on March 22, 2019 from: www.teamworks-works.com/_literature_156099/Perceptions

Garfinkle, J. (Copyright: 2005–2019). Perception is reality: 8 steps for changing how others see you. *Garfinkle Executive Coaching*. Retrieved on March 22, 2019 from: https://garfinkleexecutivecoaching.com/articles/power-of-perception/perception-is-reality-8-steps-for-changing-how-others-see-you

People Matters Editorial team. (2018, January 17). A 4-step guide to find how you are perceived at work. *People Matters*. Retrieved on March 22, 2019 from: https://www.peoplematters.in/article/employer-branding/a-4-step-guide-to-find-how-you-are-perceived-at-work-17268?media_type=article&subcat=life-at-work&title=a-4-step-guide-to-find-how-you-are-perceived-at-work&id=17268

Admit mistakes

Fisher, S. (2018, December 5). How to admit to your customers that you messed up. *Mojomedialabs.com*. Posted on December 5, 2018. Retrieved on February 7, 2019 from: https://www.mojomedialabs.com/blog/

Leadership Directions. (2015, August 5). Sorry, I was wrong. Good leadership involves admitting your mistakes. *Leadership Directions, an SGS Company*. Retrieved on February 7, 2019 from: https://www.leadershipdirections.com.au/2015/08/05/admit-your-mistakes/

Prichard, S. (2016, June 13). The power of admitting a mistake. *skipprichard.com*. Retrieved on February 7, 2019 from: https://www.skipprichard.com/the-power-of-admitting-a-mistake/

Whitehurst, J. (2015, June 9). Be a leader who can admit mistakes. *hbr.org*. Retrieved on February 7, 2019 from: https://hbr.org/2015/06/be-a-leader-who-can-admit-mistakes

Have a sounding board

Jordyn, B. (2014). Why every executive needs a sounding board. *Accelera Consulting Group*. Retrieved on February 7, 2019 from: https://consultants.betsyjordyn.com/blog/why-every-executive-needs-a-sounding-board

Rightway. (2017, August 24). How a trusted sounding board can set you up for success. *Rightway.co.nz, New Zealand*. Retrieved on February 7, 2019 from: https://www.rightway.co.nz/blog/how-a-trusted-sounding-board-can-set-you-up-for-success

Be honest, direct, and willing to risk it all for your beliefs

Among others, there are two poignant examples that point to Coach staying true to his values and convictions. In 1947, Indiana State won its conference title; however, Coach rejected an invitation for his team to play in the post season NAIA tournament because African Americans were not allowed to play. (Note: The NAIA changed this rule the next year, and Indiana State participated in the tournament with one of Coach's players, Clarence Walker, becoming the first to break the color barrier.)

Another example occurred on the first day of practice in 1973 when All-American center and returning national champion Bill Walton was begiining his senior season. Bill took exception to Coach's requirements regarding facial hair and hair length, and arrived in the gym looking less than tidy. Calling Bill aside, Coach reminded Bill about the need for grooming. Bill protested. Coach replied that while he respected Bill's political and social views of the day, he reserved the sole right to determine who would see playing time. Ultimately, Bill grabbed a bicycle and raced to a nearby barbershop.

Your coaching imperative: If you don't stand for anything, you will fall for anything

This principle is about courage, having convictions, and sticking to them.

When we think about courage, it is often in the context of someone responding to danger: a soldier, a police officer, a nurse, a fire fighter, or other first responder, risking their own life to save another's. We may also see courage when someone takes a strong, unpopular, or unprecedented political or social stand. People like Nelson Mandela, Rosa Parks, Martin Luther King, Eleanor Roosevelt, John Lewis, and John McCain come to mind. They saw the world through a different lens, understood the sense of timing and gravity about their causes, and took their challenging journeys of burden, accepting personal responsibility to the end.

Courage in an organizational setting is generally not predicated upon a life or death situation; it is about intentional bold action. Its examples include having difficult performance and personal discussions, standing up to bullies, taking on the naysayers, confronting questionable management choices, breaking disappointing news, sailing unchartered waters, and fighting for time-tested values and principles.

Courage as a skill

Coach had a saying, "Don't be afraid to act. Don't be afraid to fail."

DOI: 10.4324/9781003456902-29

Courage is not taught in a classroom. It is not in your gene pool. It is not a behavior for which you can be conditioned. It is also not possible if you have a fear of failure.

Courage is a voluntary willingness to make yourself vulnerable, to open your kimono. It is highly personal. It is only gained through a magnitude of experiences involving risk-taking.

Contemplating courage

Kathleen Reardon argues that courage in a corporate setting is not about impulsive action-taking. It is about calculated risk, where, in most cases, time is not yet an enemy. When matters are of high importance and involve the potential use of significant political capital, Reardon suggests that your situational analysis should include confronting questions such as:

- Why am I pursuing this now?
- Am I contemplating a considered action or an impulsive one?
- How long would it take to become better prepared? Is that too long?
- What are the pros and cons of waiting a day, two days, a week or more?
- What are the political obstacles? Can these be removed or reduced in the near future?
- Can I take steps now that will create a foundation for a courageous move later?
- Am I emotionally and mentally prepared to take this risk?
- Do I have the expertise, communication skills, track record, and credibility to make this work?

The tipping point of courage

As James M. Murray, former director of the United States Secret Service mentioned in his 2023 commencement address at the University of Scranton, the essence of courage, in any environment, is captured in these two questions:

1 If not you, then who?
2 If not now, then when?

Courage exemplified

Courage comes in several different flavors. In both public and private environments, it is often accompanied by ambiguity, doubts, chaos, and threats.

The courage to create

It takes bold decisions, unconventional initiative, and risk tolerance to start any company. In Silicon Valley, Singapore, Zhongguancun (the technology hub in the Haidian district of Beijing), and in garages beyond, would-be entrepreneurs are working today on the next generation of technological products and services that may holistically and dramatically impact our lives and livelihoods. As time evolves, not all of these entrepreneurs, or their potential or early investors, will have the stomach for the chase; however, in looking back, we can find several notable and inspirational examples of individuals who have helped shape both the United States and global business landscape by rolling the dice. Among them:

- In creating the virtual bookstore on Amazon.com in 1995, Jeff Bezos left a blossoming Wall Street career to become an Internet pioneer. In less than four years, the company became profitable. Bezos showed early critics that the Internet was more than information dissemination and exchange as he built a business that is today's dominant force in e-commerce.
- When Ingvar Kamprad was 17, he started his own company. He began by marketing a hodgepodge of products, mostly affordable furniture, via mail order. After a slow start, he changed course, shifting from the competitive mail order industry to allowing customers to see and "touch" the furniture before deciding to buy. It was a gamble. His first exhibition opened in 1953, when he greeted 1,000 customers with coffee and buns. Ultimately, his company manufactured its own furniture and he later introduced flat packaging in 1956. By the turn of the century, IKEA had 150 stores in 30 countries, employing over 44,000 people.
- In 1954, at the age of 52, Ray Kroc changed the way America ate. After spending the previous 17 years of his life selling mixers, he was introduced to the McDonald's restaurant in San Bernardino, California. Here, he witnessed the "recipe" for operational efficiency and customer service. By 1961, after experiencing severe financial problems that almost caused bankruptcy, he bought out the owners for $2.7 million. He built new restaurants with the "pillars" of "quality, service, cleanliness, and value."

The courage to stay the course

Coach Wooden would not let outside parties dictate his decision-making. Fans, parents, media critics, alumni, skeptics, competitive pressures, or others would not influence him with their parochial interests. He had a system. He believed in that system. He believed in himself and his players, even if the banners at Pauley Pavilion would take a few years to come. With university support, he could be patient in his early years with the progress shown.

The courage to transform

If you stand still, you might be left behind.

In 1989, the five largest companies in the world by market capital valuations were NIT, Industrial Bank of Japan, Sumitomo Bank, Fuji Bank, and DKB. ExxonMobil was eighth. Fourteen of the twenty companies were Japanese. Three (NIT, IBM, and AT&T) were technology-driven.

Almost 20 years later, the top of the list features Apple, Amazon, Google/Alphabet, Microsoft, and Facebook/Meta—all companies that either were not in existence in 1989 or in their infancy. ExxonMobil, the only company to still be on the list, was now tenth. There are NO Japanese companies. There are eight technology-driven companies and China has a growing presence.

WOW! The pace of change is stunning. Blink, and your company could sadly share the fate of Sears, Blockbuster, Borders, J.C. Penny, Lord & Taylor, or Toys "R" Us.

To keep pace, much less get ahead, may take some foresight, courage, and prayer to transform your organization. Bill George, a Harvard faculty member and former CEO of Medtronic, captured some prolific examples.

- When Alan Mulally arrived at Ford, it was losing $18 billion a year. (Yes, that is a "B"!) In response, he convinced the Ford family to pledge their support, stock, and name in order to borrow the money to retool the entire product line. It worked. Unlike their competitors, Ford never declared bankruptcy, regained market share, and returned to profitability, saving thousands of jobs in the process.
- How would you like to take the helm of a company whose products once had 50% of the market share, which had dipped to 18%? Welcome to General Motors. It was Mary Barra in 2014 who set the course of a different direction by killing off duplicative and inwardly competitive brands, while transforming the product line. They had to go the route of a government bailout, but they re-established the company, killed off many of their former "cultural problems," and streamlined and redesigned their vehicle line-up.
- Embracing a sustainable living platform, Paul Polman set stretch goals at Unilever in 2009 to double revenues and to generate 70% of that from emerging markets. In his first eight years at the helm, aligning 175,000 employees around defined metrics, he returned 214% to company shareholders.
- When Indra Nooyi was named CEO of Pepsi in 2006, she foresaw the marketplace shift from carbonated sugar-flavored sodas and salty snacks to healthy alternatives. Under the mantra "Performance with Purpose," she pushed the company to expand in that direction, returning a sizable increase in Pepsi stock, as compared with competitors.

Beyond the above, George also mentions the leaders of Delta, Starbucks, Xerox, Nestle, Merck, and Alibaba as examples of leaders who had the courage to transform their companies.

The courage to stand your ground

Sometimes, courage is about holding firm to your convictions.

On November 15, 2018, British Prime Minister Theresa May faced some brutal clashes at the House of Commons as she attempted to make the case for her negotiated Brexit terms. In what *The Times* called the worst day of her premiership, standing alone, she was weakened by an attempted coup, stirrings of a no-confidence vote, and a wave of same-day resignations.

At a news conference later that day on Downing Street, she stood at the podium. Some expected her to wilt or change her mind. More drastic forecasts claimed she might leave office. Yet, despite her relatively unpopular stance, she defiantly told those in attendance and others watching, she was not modifying her stance. In fact, she proclaimed, "I believe with every fiber in my being that the course I have set out is the right one for our country and all our people." She further added, "Leadership is about taking the right decisions, not the easy ones."

In a political environment fraught with overwhelming negativity, cynicism, and unrelenting criticism, her line in the sand was drawn. And while her stance ultimately did not turn out to be the basis for the way forward, she remained steadfast and firm until her resignation. Interpersonal courage and fortitude personified.

The courage to speak up

Would you confront a colleague who just accepted an excessive gift from a supplier? How might you handle the situation if you came to know that your company's inventory reports have been altered to make the short-term balance sheet look better? Would you have the moral fortitude to expose an injustice, even if its repercussions could possibly jeopardize your company's viability and subject you to coworker isolation?

Hold that last thought …

In 2001, Sherron Watkins, the former vice president of Corporate Development for Enron, wrote an internal memo to Ken Lay, the company founder, detailing her concerns about the company's creative accounting methods. She cautioned their improper practices were too risky and that they might not withstand scrutiny. Her fear was that scandals were on the horizon absent immediate change. She urged the company's leaders to come clean about its misleading accounting statements.

The leaders ostensibly did not listen or choose to ignore Ms. Watkins' warnings. Her memos later went public during a congressional committee hearing, exposing and labeling Ms. Watkins as some type of corporate "whistleblower." The company did ultimately implode and its executives went to jail.

Watkins did all she could to right the wrongs. And we cannot imagine her lost sleep and sweaty pillows. She must have been consumed with "ratting out" others, loyalty divisions, conflicts about personal ethics, and her own internal struggles with integrity and reputation. This is a woman with true gumption!

The courage to do the right thing

Andrew S. Grove was born in 1936 in Hungary. He survived scarlet fever at age four, grew-up in poverty, was sheltered from Nazis, and ultimately escaped communist Russia into Austria in 1956. He arrived in the United States in 1957 and enrolled in and subsequently graduated from the City University of New York. His degree was in chemical engineering. He later received his Ph.D. at UC Berkeley.

His first job was at Fairchild Semiconductor. He later joined a start-up, Intel, in 1968, where he rose through the ranks to COO, and then CEO. In 1987, a minute technical flaw was detected in the company's flagship Pentium processor. It may have gone unnoticed by unsuspecting or unknowing retailers or consumers. Instead, Grove made the $475 million decision to recall and replace the product.

While Intel suffered a significant financial hit, the recall left the company's reputation intact, if not enamored. Any potential public relations issues were avoided, and profits eventually rose.

The courage of transparency

This type of courage was shown by Jerry Senion in the mid-90s. Jerry was the general manager of an appliance manufacturing facility in central New Jersey, where I headed-up the HR team. At the time, we were being threatened by off-shore competition that had shuttered similar manufacturers. Jerry knew that in order to sustain, some difficult decisions needed to be taken, many of which involved rebuilding the site's relationship with organized labor. To this end, he opened the company's books (within context) to the local unions and sought their partnership in a turnaround.

The unions were at first skeptical about this approach. Perhaps they were even suspicious. However, the partnerships unfolded—locally and with the international union heads. As a result, the site moved forward with training and incentive programs for flexible, multi-craft practices. Much needed cost savings were attained in other areas. Ultimately, these efforts, along with other re-engineering initiatives, led to a 25% increase in productivity and a 30% increase in return-on-assets.

Production from this site was eventually moved to China, but Jerry's leadership kept that facility and its 2,000-plus jobs viable well beyond its expected shelf life.

The courage to endure

Can you push yourself when you have little left to give?

In October 1803, Meriwether Lewis and William Clark set off on what was to be the most famous adventure of their lives. Given the mandate by President Jefferson to explore the lands of the vast Louisiana Purchase that he had bargained from Spain, their mission was to record the geography, geology, and commercial possibilities of the newly acquired region. Two and a half years and over 8,000 miles later, their "Corps of Discovery" reported back, after undergoing extreme hardships under extraordinary conditions.

The expedition was fraught from the start with mistakes and misgivings, yet somehow it attained its goal. Maps were poor or non-existent, guides were unavailable or untrustworthy, and communication with the Natives was difficult at best. Along the way, this group encountered dangerous wildlife, roaring rivers, leaking boats, harsh weather, and threatening situations … conditions that would have caused others to turn back. One can only imagine the homesickness and depravity they must have experienced as they trekked across the unknown.

Lewis and Clark knew the risks, weighed the odds, and accepted Jefferson's mandate—a task many others would have shunned. They never lost track of their goal nor wavered in their faith as they charted the American West. Although many mistakes were made along the way, the results of their efforts helped map out an entire new region, and it stands as one of the greatest accomplishments in American history.

In the corporate world, you may not be asked to make these types of physical sacrifices, but your energy, patience, and dedication may be tested.

The courage to go forward

The passing of a well-liked co-worker who was close to many is a steep personal and professional challenge. Hopefully, you never have to experience this.

In 2018, my company lost a long-service employee. She was a friend and colleague. She reported to me in HR. We had worked side-by-side for almost ten years. She was scheduled to retire shortly. Unfortunately, she was taken far too soon.

Jan's absence left our company's workplace with a terrible void. She was an integral part of our team, with involvement in many projects and initiatives. She was also a role model and mentor to many, deeply entrenched in our organizational fabric. It was suddenly strange to walk by an empty desk; stranger still to refer to her in the past tense.

There is no textbook on how to handle these types of tragedies. I can only say that I did my best. I spoke with her husband and helped coordinate related benefits and activities; I gave time and space to all team members; we held private meetings to talk and/or listen to stories;

I crafted related messages and announcements; and with my voice cracking, I delivered words of remembrance at her memorial service.

As a team, we grieved. As a team we (slowly) picked up the pieces. As a team, we each showed courage to go forward.

Why courage is hard

Hypothetically (or not) …

Let's say that you have worked hard and smart your whole career. You sacrificed. You strategically changed jobs a couple of times, keeping yourself on a fast track. You took night classes and earned the advanced degree. You belonged to the "right" professional associations and got the "right" accreditations. You worked for some terrific mentors who sponsored your next steps. You put in the long hours at work, traded off family time, traveled extensively as needed, and established your reputation as an "up and comer." No assignment was too challenging. People inside the industry came to respect your opinions and you attained a heightened professional stature. Well-deserved rewards finally came your way. Your dream job was finally realized and your future seemed even brighter!

And then, conflict is at your doorstep …

You come to work on Monday. There is a rumor that your closest coworker and someone you consider to be a friend, may have been involved in a serious compliance violation. Innocent or not, the company's gossip grapevine is in overdrive. You have no direct knowledge of the potential indiscretion, but, with the benefit of hindsight and reflection, you can connect quite a few suspicious dots. What to do?

At least two choices await you. In option one, you report nothing. You mind your own business and ignore the possible indiscretion. You ask nothing, volunteer nothing, and hope that you will not to be tarnished by any worst case association. You might even be able to rationalize your inaction by convincing yourself that nothing good is going to come out of this anyway. Maybe it will blow over or go away.

Your other choice involves doing something. Saying something. Options here can take you down many rabbit holes, some of which point to why courage is fleeting in today's corporate environment.

- *You could be humiliated. Why didn't you originally report your suspicions? Might you be faulted for not recognizing the concern and saying something sooner? Would your reputation be put at risk? And everyone knows that you both worked closely together …*
- *You could damage relationships. If you report your suspicions, will your friend hold it against you? Assuming he survives, would you be able to continue working together?*
- *Your credibility could become damaged. Would you be considered a snitch? Who is going to trust you going forward?*
- *You could lose your job.*

Goodness knows where this investigation may go. It may mean spending endless time with HR. There may even be lawyers involved if it gets serious. Might your friend try to save himself by implicating others? Could your job be on the line if you have to decide between devotions?

No easy choices, but if you are reading this book, I think you will do something.

Everyday courage

While you may have early doubts or hesitation, exhibiting courage is good for your self-confidence and esteem. It can be empowering. Notably, it does not have to be a life-changing event or a strategic shift to do so. Here are small some ways you can demonstrate courage in a corporate setting:

- Fight your inner-introvert and express your opinion.
- Stand-up for yourself. If you don't, who will?
- Hire people who have diverse opinions, contrasting your point of view.
- Challenge the status quo.
- Say "no" if you need to keep your work/life balance or manage other priorities.
- Assuming it is feasible, ask to occasionally work remotely and demonstrate correlating productivity.
- Push yourself to give a presentation, knowing that you are anxious about public speaking.
- Listen openly to what your critics have to say.
- Continuously learn.

Periodic reflection

In the early days of the Vietnam War, Coach Wooden, a veteran of World War II, believed that individuals had an obligation to serve their country. While not outspoken in his views, he made it clear to his players that he frowned upon their protest efforts.

His view about sending our troops to war later changed when, by chance, he read and reflected upon an article about the cruelties of armed battle and how, in many cases, our young men and women were sacrificed for the causes and means of a few.

While your personal core values and beliefs, by definition, have deep roots, one should periodically assess them, especially as they compare with your organization's values for alignment. Such introspection develops deep thinking, identifies a stronger sense of self, and encourages independence of thought.

How does this compare to Conventional Wisdom?

Play it safe. Stay low. This, too, will pass.

To the contrary, you do not want to be sitting home second-guessing yourself about courses of action that you wish you would have otherwise taken. Your choice is to act or to be potentially acted upon.

Endnotes for Principle 20: Be honest, direct, and willing to risk it all for your beliefs

Introduction

"Wooden, John," Wikipedia. (Date unknown). Retrieved on November 16, 2018 from: en.mwikipedia.org

Your coaching imperative

Furnham, A. (Date unknown). The four types of corporate courage. *Insights*. Retrieved on October 19, 2018 from: https://www.managers.org.uk/insights/news/2015/october/the-4-types-of-corporate-courage

George, B. (2017, April 24). Courage: The defining characteristic of great leaders. *Forbes.com*. Retrieved on October 19, 2018 from: https://www.forbes.com/sites/hbsworkingknowledge/2017/04/24/courage-the-defining-characteristic-of-great-leaders/#2f517c7711ca

Hyland, P. (2006, July 4). Private conversation.

Kane, W. (2008). *The truth about thriving in change*. Upper Saddle River, New Jersey: Pearson Education, p. 29.

Coaching as a skill

Hickem, C. (Date unknown). Corporate courage: where has it gone? *Arden Coaching*. Retrieved on October 19, 2018 from: https://ardencoaching.com/corporate-courage-where-has-it-gone

Contemplating courage

Reardon, K.K. (2007 January). Courage as a skill. *Harvard Business Review*. Retrieved on October 19, 2018 from: https://hbr.org/2007/01/courage-as-a-skill

The tipping point of courage

Murray, J.M. (2023, May 21). *The university of Scranton, undergraduate commencement ceremony, address to the graduates*. Mohegan Sun Arena at Casey Plaza, Wilkes-Barre, PA.

The courage to create

Bennis, W., Brown, T., Champy, J., Crainer, S., Davis, S., Edwards, H., Goleman, D., Gottlieb, A., Heller, R., Larreche, J.C., Leyden, P., Meyer, C., Norton, B., & Rayport, J. (Advisory Board). (2002). *Business: The ultimate resource*. Cambridge, Massachusetts: Perseus Publishing, pp. 1064–1065, 1102–1103, 106–107.

Jeff Bezos: The king of e-commerce. (2008, October 10). *Entreprenuer.com*. Retrieved on November 26, 2018 from: https://www.entrepreneur.com/article/197608

The courage to transform

George, B. (2017, April 24). Courage: The defining characteristic of great leaders. *Forbes.com*. Retrieved on October 19, 2018 from: https://www.forbes.com/sites/hbsworkingknowledge/2017/04/24/courage-the-defining-characteristic-of-great-leaders/#2f517c7711ca

The courage to stand your ground

Elliott, F., & Coates, S. (2018, November 16). Lonely may staggers on. *The Times*, p. 1.

The courage to speak up

Associated Press. (2006, March 15). Enron whistleblower tells of 'crooked company.' *NBCnews.com*. Retrieved on November 26, 2018 from: http://www.nbcnews.com/id/11839694/ns/business-corporate_scandals/t/enron-whistleblower-tells-crooked-company/

Capozzi, C. (Date unknown). Moral courage in the workplace. *Chron.com*. Retrieved on November 26, 2018 from: https://smallbusiness.chron.com/moral-courage-workplace-20589.html

The courage to do the right thing

Bennis, W., Brown, T., Champy, J., Crainer, S., Davis, S., Edwards, H., Goleman, D., Gottlieb, A., Heller, R., Larreche, J.C., Leyden, P., Meyer, C., Norton, B., & Rayport, J. (Advisory Board). (2002). *Business: The ultimate resource*. Cambridge, Massachusetts: Perseus Publishing, pp. 1088–1089.

The courage to endure

Furnham, A. (2018, October 19). The four types of corporate courage. *Insights*. Retrieved on October 19, 2018 from: https://www.managers.org.uk/insights/news/2015/october/the-4-types-of-corporate-courage

Kane, D.E. (2003, January 20). Private conversation.

Why courage is hard

Weinstein, B. (2015). *The good ones: Ten crucial qualities of high-character employees*. Novato, California: New World Library, pp. 100–107.

Everyday courage

Marcus, B. (2017, July 17). 10 ways you show courage every day. *Forbes.com*. Retrieved on October 19, 2018 from: https://www.forbes.com/sites/bonniemarcus/2017/07/17/10-ways-you-show-courage-every-day/#3ef9890062b4

Tobak, S. (2013, February 15). 8 ways to be a courageous leader. *Inc.com*. Retrieved on November 26, 2018 from: https://www.inc.com/steve-tobak/the-most-important-leadership-attribute.html

Game time is when the coach's job is almost over

Prior to the start of each game, with his "OK" signal to Nellie, a grasp of the small crucifix in his palm (given to him by his minister when he enlisted in the Navy), and his rolled-up program, Coach would settle on the bench. He knew his team was individually and collectively prepared for most any eventuality. He wanted them to run the show and ideally, he would have minimal intervention during the game. Game tapes will show that the players rarely looked to the bench for guidance once the ball was in the air. They knew the plays, had run the drills, and knew their roles and expectations. In essence, he had complete control by letting go.

Given a choice, his preference would have been to sit in the stands and eat popcorn.

Your coaching imperative: Liberation!

The late Jack Welch, CEO of General Electric, once pronounced, "The idea of liberation for our workforce is not enlightenment. It's a competitive necessity."

Give 'em an inch, a foot, a yard

Frank Winfield Woolworth, founder of The Great Five Cent Store (1879), became the most successful retailer of his time with his basic bargain-basement offerings. He attributed his decades of business success to entrusting others to attend to the details of running the business by giving them "power and responsibility." He knew that employees need responsibility for self-management and continuous improvement. They need freedom to act and to control their jobs. To the extent possible, they should design their jobs, create the processes around them, fix their own problems, and do whatever it takes to keep a customer satisfied.

Woolworth was an early practitioner of employee empowerment.

Empowerment leads to several positive outcomes. Benefits include boosting team performance and capacity, increased confidence, provision of new learning opportunities, and the building of future leaders. Empowered employees feel a sense of ownership of their work and will give more of their discretionary effort, thus enhancing productivity. Further, empirical evidence supports the highly desirable correlation between empowerment and employee engagement. More of the former gets you the latter.

Here are some of the key ingredients and leadership practices for an empowered team. You will note that many of these have received expanded discussion earlier in this book. It is no coincidence that we started our writing focusing upon staffing and we close by outlining how you optimally engage with your team.

DOI: 10.4324/9781003456902-30

- Lead—Give people purpose.
- Be clear with your strategy—Strategy gives your team context and a framework for their actions and decision-making. Let your team know your destination, as well as the path to get there.
- Surround yourself with those you trust—Your team will represent you and your values in their business interactions. Trust them. Encourage them to trust each other.
- Be open to new ideas—Listen. Be respectful. Show that you value the opinion of others. Push them to be innovative and to challenge the routine.
- Be an effective communicator—Up, down, and all around. Be accessible.
- Fight the urge to micromanage—This will stifle creativity and erode morale. Encourage autonomy.
- Pay attention to culture—Transparency counts. Manage conflict. Make timely decisions. Treat everyone fairly. Focus on team building.
- Let your team grow and develop—Enhance individual and team skills by investing in your people. Share experiences and expertise. Give them the tools they need. The dividends are priceless.
- Accountability counts—People need to feel safe to use their authority, but they should not step over the line.
- Recognize extra effort, as well as results—Rewarded behavior gets repeated. Show your appreciation.
- Stand up for your team—"Have their back" if or when needed.
- Brag about them—Be an ambassador. Assuming it is warranted (or even if some modest liberties are taken), let your leadership team know the strides your team is taking. It will help build their confidence.
- Be a role model—Demonstrate your values. Never sacrifice your integrity.

Bring empowerment to life

How much control, direction, and supervision is required in order for someone to feel "empowered?" The answer is, "It depends." In many respects, empowering an employee is like guiding a toddler to take his or her first steps and knowing when to let go.

At the organizational level, some companies seem to have figured out how empowerment is a critical strategic benefit, and they go the extra step to inculcate it into their culture and business policies. They hire smart people, get out of their way, and ensure that nothing gets in their way. They embrace the management practices previously noted. They want team members doing their jobs, feeling trusted, being comfortable about sharing their ideas, and acting with appropriate freedom and latitude.

Nordstrom's, while battered by the pandemic, is one of the best-known examples of employee empowerment. Their "above and beyond" customer service reputation is legendary, and it has become their differentiator in the marketplace. Embracing a corporate culture committed "100 percent" to the customer, empowered employees have wide latitude in helping customers with all aspects of their shopping experience, even at the sacrifice of profit. Nordstrom employees are expected and encouraged to put customers first, knowing that criticism will never come from taking care of a customer, but it will if they do not.

Here are some other examples of how companies empower and partner with their employees:

- Disney—"Cast members" are renowned for making the experiences of their guest magical! Part of Disney's formula to encourage employees to give the extra efforts lies in the way the company shows its care. To this end, the company listens to, thanks, rewards good work, and shares positive customer stories with their employees.
- Google—As an innovative market leader, the company has several vehicles, most notably "Google Cafes" to encourage employees to interact with each other, promoting shared ideas. They also allow their engineers a fixed percentage of time to work on projects of personal interest.
- Timpson—The British multinational retailer allows employees a certain financial allocation to solve any customer issues before the need for management involvement.
- American Express—Employees are evaluated equally upon what they accomplish, as well as how they get things done. The highest performers understand that their behavior and the way they treat others counts.
- John Lewis—Employees are referred to as "partners" at this U.K. retailer. By doing this and by using a participative management style for decision-making, the company is expressing a sense of shared responsibility for business outcomes.
- Hyatt—In an industry prone to high staff turnover, the company focuses upon continuous development of their "associates," as well as promoting from within.
- Virgin—The company is known for listening to employee suggestions and acting upon them to become more innovative. Listening makes employees feel valued, want to reciprocate, and to do their best.
- Ritz Carlton—Another "gold standard" company for customer service, they allow employees to spend up to $2,000 per incident to solve a customer problem.
- Costco—Their no-risk return policy empowers employees to take back items, make exchanges and ensure issues are resolved hassle free. This approach is best for the customer and allows employees control of the solution, as well as avoidance of potential conflict.
- Trader Joe's—Employees are encouraged to serve customers quickly without sacrificing quality. They will open packages, take returns, and help you to your car. They want to connect with the customer individually.
- Adobe—Creativity in the digital world requires flexibility and freedom. The company defines responsibilities and expected outcomes, and then employees chose their own path toward solutions.

Whether it is enhanced customer service, eager expansion of one's job description, creation of new processes, or collaborative teams, the companies above see and realize the benefits of empowering their team members. Their untethered employees are more engaged and enthusiastic about their employment experience, which is good for them and the bottom line of their business.

Take your work seriously, but not yourself

Coach was as comfortable with himself as anyone was. He could laugh at himself. He knew not to take himself too seriously.

Easier said than done, try not to get caught up in worrying about the opinions and expectations of others. When this happens, we let others' opinions define us. We become driven by the need for their approval or not to disappoint, as if we must uncharacteristically modify our actions in a manner subject to their scrutiny and judgment. Stage fright and fear of ridicule set in, insecurity abounds, confidence splinters, and we leave our best selves behind.

To be like Coach, the only expectations you need to meet are your own. The only pressure there is to perform is that which you place upon yourself. If you are prepared and performed at your peak, there are no regrets.

In order to take yourself less seriously and have greater psychological security, consider:

- Confront the source of your fear.
- Rebound quickly from mistakes.
- Change the conversation. Not everything is black or white.
- Think—What is the worst thing that could happen?
- Success, recognition, and the approval of others are not your values. .
- Add humor to your life.
- Your image is not you.

Have fun!

Those who had the privilege to play for Coach and to enjoy his company through his later years would say that he often spoke with a quick quip, had a boyish grin and a contagious smile, and he made conversation and trips down memory lane fun, if not funny. However, no one would have used the word "fun" to describe a typical UCLA practice session. As noted, Coach's practices were physically challenging and grueling.

The fun and lasting memories made for the Bruins' players were to be found elsewhere in their academic and playing experience. They reveled in the electric build-up to a game's tip-off, the camaraderie from the road trips, the rock star treatment at home versus the less-than-hospitable treatment elsewhere, the friendships formed, the shared late night meals, and the post-graduation fraternal gatherings. There was also the fun associated with being on the court, every day, with each other as the best amateur basketball players in the world.

Work may not be fun per se, but that does not mean that you cannot find or make opportunities when some pleasure and laughter can make things more enjoyable, and perhaps even more productive. After all, in most cases, you are spending the majority of your awake time with your work associates.

Intuitively, when people are having fun they work harder, are more committed, and hold organizational needs as paramount. In fact, research has proven that when leaders ease off the gas pedal, there is an increase in employee trust, creativity, camaraderie, and communication—resulting in decreased turnover and enhanced morale. Engagement is also amplified.

Succinctly, "fun" is a direct characteristic or by-product of a productive work environment. It is a clear indicator of a strong, positive workplace culture.

Fun comes in many forms. Playing games, competitions, using humor, milestone recognition, and celebrations are the headlines. Former Southwest Airlines CEO Herb Kelleher had a mantra that work could be fun, exemplified through management practices around casual dress, practical jokes, birthday celebrations, employee holiday garb for greeting customers, delivering safety instructions on the plane with stand-up comedy, and having attendants pop out of overhead compartments. Crazy? Perhaps, but the zaniness was an overlay to a highly effective and profitable business that produced low staff turnover rates and no disruptive labor disputes. Sales grew from $270 million to over $5 billion on Kelleher's watch.

Here are some "fun" examples cited by Marelisa Fabrega to consider, many of which are at little or no cost. (Note: The pandemic may be shifting some of these approaches.)

- Designate a day per month or per quarter for "happy hour" after work. Celebrate personal accomplishments and milestones here.
- Have sports tournaments. Foosball, pool, darts, ping-pong, table-top hockey, and like games can be fun and create a team-bonding experience.
- Decorate the workplace.
- Bring in a yoga instructor. It breaks the routine and may provide some participants physiological and psychological benefits.
- Post a "Wall of Fame." Publicize customer testimonials, noteworthy news, or success stories.
- Have a success "bell." Not only will an angel get his or her wings, but co-workers can cheer knowing a colleague just experienced success.
- Toys such as blocks, Legos, hula hoops, and Etch-a-Sketch may have a place and serve as stress release avenues.
- Create art, memes, and videos together. Go at it by creating a mural on a nearby wall.
- Pizza and ice cream socials serve as fun rewards for achievement.
- Post employee pictures on a wall. This is a fun way to build community.
- Bring in the music (appropriately!). At Microsoft, music is pumped in and up at 3:00, just when the day's energy is waning.
- Compare vacation notes. At staff meetings, devote a segment to hearing about your team member's outside interests.

I recall one April Fool's Day—an occasion of practical jokes and hoaxes—I discreetly brought several cans of aerosol confetti string into the office. My first "attack" was on our recruiter when he was in the middle of an interview. It made for some harmless fun and great laughs. By unintended extension, it also sent a message to the interview candidate (who witnessed the "stringing"), that lighter moments were part of our culture.

Glance back, but focus ahead

After speaking of "fun," I now change gears in a more cerebral direction. In doing so, fittingly, I believe that the following three topics—and their reflections—are apt ways to wrap-up this writing ...

When Life Gives You Lemons

I have switched jobs several times in my career. In most cases, I left voluntarily. Three times, I did not:

- *I was asked to leave one position by a newly hired CEO. He was bringing in someone to head up the HR function with whom he had long-standing relationship. It happens. He had done it in other places. Of course, it is still unfortunate when it happens to you—even if you know it is coming.*

- *In a second instance, the company had high-hopes to bring a Parkinson's drug to the market. Unfortunately, after a sizable investment of time and money (think hundreds of millions of dollars), we did not get needed regulatory approvals in our first pass. The company was ostensibly dismantled. After coordinating the downsizing, my position was also eliminated.*
- *The third time, there was fault in many directions. There were yellow flags during the recruiting process. There were orange flags at the job offer stage. There were many red flags at on-boarding and beyond. I thought I could "fix" everything, but my invincible (ignorant? arrogant?) attitude was wrong. I misread the tealeaves, misjudged motives, misplaced trust, and never got traction. It was never a good "fit."*

There is a lot of psychological baggage to sort when you go through a sudden (or even fore-seeable) job divorce. Feelings are hurt. Self-esteem and confidence evaporate. Depression becomes your shadow. Your mind tosses in turbulence between "what if?" and "what am I going to do next?" It feels like a grieving period and it may take weeks or months to process.

There is some good news here. Despite the onset of dark clouds, I have always found a way, in time, to land on greener grasses. You can, too. I have found that the key is to turn rejection into redirection and opportunity as soon as possible. After all, our job is only what we do; it is not who we are.

Paul Schnabel's "Destination: Inspiration! Charting Your Career During Turbulent Times," (2020) is a great reference if you are at or approaching a career crossroads.

Your search for meaning

Viktor Frankl is the author of *Man's Search for Meaning*, a personal and moving memoir based upon his experiences in the Nazi concentration camps of World War II. During this period, he was broken physically, psychologically challenged and battered, and was subject to the atrocities of humankind's cruelest and harshest treatment.

Frankl persevered long enough to enjoy his freedom. His parents, brother, and pregnant wife did not.

In returning to his professional practice, Frankl, a psychologist, theorized, based upon his own experiences and those shared by others, that those prisoners who had purpose and meaning in their lives had a greater probability of surviving. They had heightened coping capabilities. He went further to state that the functional objective of psychotherapy should be to help individuals find their respective ends to be attained. He went forward to make this his vocational calling.

Answering, "What is the meaning of life?" is a complex and challenging issue. It comes at us at different times and in different stages of life. The question rarely arises when the sun is shining; rather, it is more likely when storm clouds are upon us. On the one hand, answering this question seemingly has universal consequences, with almost a mystic or ethereal quality. On the other hand, such answers may be deeply personal and individualized, attitudinal in nature, and highly motivational.

Coach Wooden was a man of inner peace. He found the intersection of his professional love for sports and teaching in coaching. He did it with grace and decorum. He did it with uncompromised values and endless enthusiasm. His life's meaning was in helping others to become their best.

As you contemplate where you have been and where you are going, you may contemplate "What is the meaning of life?" However, your time may be equally well-spent confronting the question of "What is the meaning of YOUR life?" This one word makes a dramatic difference!

Define your legacy

A person's legacy is about what they achieved. It also concerns how they treated those around them, Words like love, empathy, integrity, compassion, and making a positive difference come to mind,

Jim Collins, author of *Good to Great*, would have surely recognized Coach as a "level five" leader for his demonstration of compelling humility, calm determination, reliance upon principles or values, and his ability to apportion success to others. Likewise, in his book, *The Servant: A Simple Story about the True Essence of Leadership,* Jim Hunter stated "... the true foundation of leadership is not power, but authority, which is built upon relationships, love, service, and sacrifice." Certainly, this description fits Coach like a glove.

Legacies evolve over time, in moments and in phases, with decisions, shared experiences and learning, setbacks, adversity, and accomplishments. It is never too late to start a legacy, but sooner is better than later. To do so, keep these attributes in mind:

- To thyself be true—Be true to who you are and to your core values.
- Translate your values into guiding principles—Your core values should be consistent in your behavior and attitude. People should set expectations accordingly.
- Be courageous—Calculated risks are part of leadership. Challenge the status quo and bring innovative solutions to the table.
- Care for others— You will never regret an act of kindness. Genuinely care for and support those around you. This is particularly critical in advancing others' careers, and encouraging growth and development. Be a mentor and a sponsor. Their success is yours.
- Create a productive and engaging culture—It is all about team success, not yours.
- Hold yourself accountable—Ask no one to do what you would not. Be self-disciplined, abide by the highest ethical standards, and be a role model for contribution.
- Pass it on—Uphold the important traditions of your organization and secure them for the next generation.
- Seek respect over recognition—Praise and gratitude can be fickle.

How will you be remembered? An interesting (and sobering) exercise might be to write your obituary and reflect upon any qualitative gap between who you currently are and who you want to be.

How does this compare to Conventional Wisdom?

How many of us enjoy being the hub of the wheel? The "Big Cheese?" The "Big Kahuna?" "Da Man?"

The top spot on any organizational chart does have its intangible enticements, and no one said removing your hands from the steering wheel would be easy. However, when decision-making and authority are distributed appropriately—with skills training, systemic resources, process control, and supervisory support—the empowered organization is well on its way to attaining new levels of productivity and success.

Endnotes for Principle 21: Game time is when the coach's job is almost over

Introduction

Hill, A. (2000). Interview notes, #2-1, p. 8.
Wooden, J.R. (2002, August 22). Private conversation.

Liberation

Harris, J. (1996). *Getting employees to fall in love with your company*. New York: AMACOM, a division of the American Management Association. p. 97.

Give 'em an inch, a foot, a yard

Bennis, W.G., Brown, T., Champy, J., Crainer, S., Davis, S., Edwards, H., Goleman, D., Gottlieb, A., Heller, R., Larreche, J.C., Leyden, P., Meyer, C., Norton, B., & Rayport, J. (Advisory Board). (2002). *Business: The ultimate resource*. Cambridge, Massachusetts: Perseus Publishing, pp. 1162–1162.
Daisyme, P. (2017, February 22). Trust the process: 10 tips to empower and encourage staff. *Business.com*. Retrieved on February 15, 2019 from: https://www.business.com/articles/trust-the-process-10-tips-to-empower-and-encourage-your-staff/
Drucker, P.F. (1980). *Managing in turbulent times*. New York: HarperCollins Publishers, Inc., p. 192.
Folkman, J. (2017, March 2). The 6 key secrets to increasing empowerment in your team. *Forbes.com*. Retrieved on February 15, 2019 from: https://www.forbes.com/sites/joefolkman/2017/03/02/the-6-key-secrets-to-increasing-empowerment-in-your-team/#23b21ff377a6
Hamel, G., & Prahalad, C.K. (1994). *Competing for the future: Breakthrough strategies for seizing control of your industry and creating the markets for tomorrow*. Boston, Massachusetts: Harvard Business School Press, p. 290.
Hassen, A., & Shea, G.F. (1997). *A better place to work*. New York: AMA Membership Publications Division, p. ix.
How to lead and empower your team. (2018, September 27). *Experteer Magazine*. Retrieved on February 15, 2019 from: https://us.experteer.com/magazine/how-to-empower-your-teams-as-team-leaders/
Lambert, N. (2017, December 11). How empowering your employees helps improve business. *Huffingtonpost.com*. Retrieved on February 15, 2019 from: https://www.huffingtonpost.com/entry/how-empowering-your-employees-helps-improve-business_us_5a2eec0ee4b0bad787126f08
Ramsey, D. (Date unknown). 4 ways to empower your team. *Ramsey Solutions*. Lampo Licensing 2019. Retrieved on February 15, 2019 from: https://www.daveramsey.com/blog/4-ways-to-empower-your-team
3 things you need to empower your team. (2015, December 29). SEI. Retrieved on February 15, 2019 from: https://seic.com/knowledge-center/3-things-you-need-empower-your-team

Bring empowerment to life

Abdi, N. (2017, July 19). 4 examples of how companies effectively engage their employees. *Talaera Thoughts blog*. Retrieved on March 7, 2019 from: https://blog.talaera.com/2017/07/19/companies-empower-engage-employees
Cooper, L. (2015, September 22). 3 excellent examples of employee empowerment. *Print-Print.co.uk*. Retrieved on February 15, 2019 from: https://www.blog.print-print.co.uk/3-excellent-examples-of-employee-empowerment/
Flint, M., & Vinberg Hearn, E. (2015, December 11). 6 companies that get employee engagement – and what they do right. *Managers.org.uk*. Retrieved on March 7, 2019 from: https://www.managers.org.uk/insights/news/2015/december/six-companies-that-get-employee-engagement-and-what-they-do-right

Morgan, B. (2018, March 14). 10 companies that arm employees with tools to fix customer problems. *Forbes.com*. Retrieved on March 7, 2019 from: https://www.forbes.com/sites/blakemorgan/2018/03/14/10-companies-that-arm-employees-with-tools-to-fix-customer-problems/#6cc6e8bd4a30

Page, F. (1997). A framework for looking at well-run organizations. *OD Practitioner*, 29, p. 9.

Sallym. (2016, November 9). Nordstrom's customer service is the definition of above & beyond. *Sharpen blog*. Retrieved on March 7, 2019 from: https://sharpencx.com/blog/nordstrom-customer-service/

Take your work seriously

Razzetti, G. (2018, November 7). How to stop taking yourself too seriously. *Psychologytoday.com*. Retrieved on February 26, 2019 from: https://www.psychologytoday.com/us/blog/the-adaptive-mind/201811/how-stop-taking-yourself-too-seriously

Have fun!

Bennis, W.G., Brown, T., Champy, J., Crainer, S., Davis, S., Edwards, H., Goleman, D., Gottlieb, A., Heller, R., Larreche, J.C., Leyden, P., Meyer, C., Norton, B., & Rayport, J. (Advisory Board). (2002). *Business: The ultimate resource*. Cambridge, Massachusetts: Perseus Publishing, p. 1105.

Fabrega, M. (Date unknown). 25 ways to have fun at work. *Daring to Live Fully*. Retrieved on February 25, 2019 from: https://daringtolivefully.com/have-fun-at-work

Gostick, A., & Christopher, S. (Date unknown). Why fun at work matters. Excerpted from *The Levity Effect: Why It Pays to Lighten Up. Monster.com*. Retrieved on February 25, 2019 from: https://www.monster.com/career-advice/article/fun-at-work-matters-levity-effect

Smith, J. (2014, October 31). 8 easy ways to have fun at work. *Businessinsider.com*. Retrieved on February 25, 2019 from: https://www.businessinsider.com/easy-ways-to-have-more-fun-at-work-2014-10

Your search for meaning

Exploring Your Mind. (2018, June 29). The meaning of life according to Viktor Frankl. Retrieved on March 6, 2019 from: https://exploringyourmind.com/the-meaning-of-life-according-to-viktor-frankl/

Sparks, K. (Date unknown). "Viktor Frankl: Austrian Psychologist" Encyclopedia Britannica. Retrieved on March 6, 2019 from: https://www.britannica.com/biography/Viktor-Emil-Frankl

Define your legacy

Collins, J.C. (2001). *Good to great: Why some companies make the leap and others don't*. New York: HarperCollins Publishers, Inc., p. 36.

Hunter, J. (1998). *The servant: A simple story about the true essence of leadership*. New York: Crown.

Publishing group, inside jacket

Llopis, G. (2014, February 20). 5 ways a legacy-driven mindset will define your leadership. *Forbes.com*. Retrieved on February 25, 2019 from: https://www.forbes.com/sites/glennllopis/2014/02/20/5-ways-a-legacy-driven-mindset-will-define-your-leadership/#23e6076d16b1

Proctor, P. (2015, October 20). Want to leave a lasting legacy? read this. *Entrepreneur.com*. Retrieved on February 25, 2019 from: https://www.entrepreneur.com/article/249968

How does this compare

Kotter, J. P. (1996). *Leading change*. Boston, Massachusetts: Harvard Business School, p. 102.

Summation

Closing thoughts

In recapping, this book has shared and brought to organizational life the philosophy and principles, honed and recorded over time, refined on-the-job, day-by-day, over a span of 40 years of Coach Wooden's unique and unparalleled approach toward achieving optimal organizational performance. My hope and intent are that you will consider these principles in a manner that will allow for personal reflection and professional application. In doing so, I believe that you will enhance your team building and leadership skills, and that your team will achieve optimal productivity and results.

You will also become an exemplary leader!

- **Staffing:** Attracting and Selecting Talent
- **Cultivating Culture:** Defining How People Should Interact
- **Organizing and Planning:** The Need for Direction and Focus
- **Reinforcing Desirable Behavior:** Managing Performance
- **Engaging the Organization:** A Leader's Role and Responsibility

Thank you for reading!

Closing thoughts

Some additional perspective of the man simply referred to as "Coach."

- I asked Coach to describe his coaching "style."
  He was hesitant to respond and did so in the third person. He said that he had heard others say he emphasized preparation, maintaining self-control, discipline, talent development, and conditioning.
- I asked Coach about a common view that success is about passion.
  He said passion is fleeting; love is enduring. Find something to do that you love.
- I asked Coach if he could have selected another vocation, what would it have been?
  He said teaching (as if there was anything else).
- I asked Coach from where he derived the most satisfaction.
  He said from watching his players grow.
- I asked Coach what he might have done differently.
  After a significant pause, he cited the one or two occasions where he felt his disciplinary decisions may have hurt the young men beyond the court.
- I asked Coach if he had any regrets.
  His eyes grew sullen as he expressed not dancing more with Nellie.
- I asked Coach how he wanted to be remembered.
  He humbly stated, "as a considerate man."

As I reflect upon the man, his career, and his contributions, I recall his definition of success …

Success is the peace of mind, which is a direct result of self-satisfaction in knowing you made the effort to do your best to become the best that you are capable of becoming.

Personal reflections

Figure 24.1 Coach and Bill, 2003.

With all his unprecedented and unique career achievements, Coach's warmth and openness led me down a personal path of enlightenment and transformation. For as I came to realize, he was always true to his first vocation—teaching—as he welcomed inquiries from students like myself in his desire to share his experience and observations.

When we first met in Los Angeles in 2002 at Andy's introduction, Coach beat me to the punch with his initial salutation—telling me what an "honor" and a "privilege" it was to meet me, based upon some generous words he had heard from Andy and another mutual acquaintance, Steve Ford. In response, I froze and sputtered, incoherently mumbling something that was intended to sound like "Hello, Coach."

Shortly thereafter, my initial nervousness was cast aside. The conversation was free flowing. Our relationship grew into a meaningful friendship with occasional visits (VIP's Café in Tarzana is the best!) and phone calls that grew more frequent over time. On one noteworthy visit, we read poetry to each other in the privacy of his den for a few hours. Surreal!

In my quest to learn about team performance and leadership, I asked Coach every reasonable question about his style, his playing days, his upbringing, and the salient influences in his personal life. Although he had been asked many of these same inquiries hundreds of times, he continued to answer as if I were the first to broach any topic. His thoughts were measured, deep, and fraught with the wisdom of the years—often citing his own experience or drawing upon quoted words from Abraham Lincoln or Mother Teresa. For me, his scholarly replies were but a temporary satisfaction of a humanistic and academic appetite, as I always wanted to hear more. We laughed, discussed philosophy, and exchanged perspectives and emotions. He opened his heart through sharing reflections, always speaking of "love" and "balance." He always had a joke or two.

I found Coach to be inspirational, as well as kind and sincere. He was indeed a national treasure. I always left his condo or put down the phone feeling special, important, loved, and eager to share my newfound and richer perspective with my own family. He was indeed the wise and nurturing grandfather that Norman Rockwell would have depicted, always putting others first.

I once shared with him that I thought "serenity" was an appropriate and holistic one-word descriptor of him. His responsive smile told me that he was pleased with that reference.

By investigating Coach's principles, I came to know and validate what Andy and other former UCLA players already knew—that his values-based principles do have far-reaching and universal application for individuals and organizations interested in enhancing their leadership and performance standards. As part of my investigative journey, I also learned about the gift of giving from this most compassionate man.

To Coach, I am forever grateful. I miss your friendship and love.

To Andy, I cannot thank you enough for the introduction, your selfless and generous support, and endearing enthusiasm. I am truly blessed.

Acknowledgments

This book was made possible with the help of many.

Andy Hill deserves the lion's share of credit. In addition to bringing the Coach into my world, he shared personal and professional memories, and relatable anecdotes for this writing. Andy opened his mind, heart, and home to me. Simply, not one word of this 20-year labor of love would have been possible without him or the inspirational bedrock of *BQBDH*. I am forever in his debt.

Needless to say, with a similar sentiment, Coach Wooden's shared insights and evolving friendship with me was and remains one of my life's most notable impressions. His words, wit, and wisdom left an indelible mark and made me a better person. He gave to this writing without limits.

To Meredith Norwich, Bethany Nelson, Yogesh Malhotra, and the rest of the Routledge team. Your trust and support brought these pages to life. Your help was invaluable!

I would like to thank various people for their help and encouragement—Robert Chell, the late Charlie Seashore, Bruce Weinstein, Bob Kulhan, Russell Sarder, Bill Milani, Jon Margree, the late Debbie Franklin, Joe McCune, Laura Kriska, the late Gary Kehler, Jan Seele, Joe Schaffer, Nick Molinaro, Sayed Sadjady, Winter Nie, Larry Krampf, Dale Winston, Steve Ford, and the late Richard White.

Special thanks to some of my former bosses and business colleagues for providing leadership modeling behaviors. These include the late Jerry Senion, Kaz Nambu, Shigeru Kobayashi, John Warren, Sam Parker, Phil Chaikin, Bill Cassidy, Jim Moore, and the late Dick Furlough.

Key advice, support, and enthusiasm were also provided by Tom Cox, Keith Melville, Bruce Wexler, Dan O'Leary, Mark Kays, Brendan Cox, Nancy Hancock, Bill Cannon, Bob Cahill, Rick Elliott, Chris Loder, Rob Gilbert, and Jim Spanarkel.

Special thanks to this book's early readers for their candor and suggested course adjustments—Linda Shor, Gail Howell, Bob Lackaye, and Bob Kane. And a deserved "shout out" to my early editors—David Kane and Franci Ferguson.

To Tom Moran for many things; in particular, for giving me my first job and later talking me out of what would have been a career-limiting decision.

To the guys with whom I shared those formative years on the hoops courts at Holy Trinity, Gumbert Park, and Tamaques Park. Countless hours of games with relentless competition—winners stay on. While the sweat and sharp elbows are behind us, the camaraderie, memories, and influence of the game continue. In this vein, thanks to Steve Reddy, Bruce Moran, Bruce Johnson, Dave Miller, Tom Decker, Jay Boyle, Boo Bowers, Spud Monroe, and Chucky Murray for reminding me of those special days.

To my Westfield High School '77 basketball coach, Neil Horne. Coach Horne shares many of John Wooden's traits and philosophies. Each minute of our two-plus hour practices had detailed forethought and defined purpose—conditioning, continuous improvement, team over selfish play, and, of course, repetition. (To this day, I can still run our "one game" offense.) He demanded the best and got the most from his players, and his multiple state championships are evidence of his proven recipe. While hardly appreciated at the time of all those endless sprints and demanding "box-out" drills, there were later-realized lessons about self-reliance, self-discipline, and perseverance. Many belated thanks.

To my Mom and Dad. Your love was felt from above. And Dad, some of your early suggestions were carried forward! I was listening.

Last, and of most importance, my heartfelt thanks to Coleen (for her many questions, suggestions, and contributions), Billy, David, and Michael … laughter and ever-lasting love personified. (And Max, too!)

Bill, Coach, and Andy, 2002.

About the authors

Figure 0.2 Bill Kane.

Bill joined the faculty of the Rutgers University School of Management and Labor Relations in the fall of 2022. When not in the classroom, Bill coaches corporate executives and consults with business leaders. His subject matter expertise is in the fields of leadership, organizational change, team-building, and talent development.

Prior to joining RU, Bill was a highly accomplished chief human resources officer, administrative head, and board advisor in the *Fortune* 500, with over 25 years in senior roles. Most notably, as the long-standing senior vice president of the Human Resources Group at Sumitomo Corporation, one of the world's leading corporate investors and business partners, he was responsible for the human resources function and human capital management strategy for the regional corporate entity, as well as its broad portfolio of group operating companies ($14 billion in annual revenue with over 40,000 employees across multiple industries). Prior to Sumitomo, Bill worked with sector leaders in the fields of chemicals, consumer products, technology, and life sciences.

He is the author of *The Truth about Thriving in Change*, published by Prentice Hall/Pearson Education in 2008, which has been translated into Chinese, Russian, and Arabic.

Bill has served on numerous advisory boards, including as an elected member of the Smithsonian Science Education Center in Washington, DC, promoting STEM in the classroom. He has also been a member of the Conference Board, CHRO Council.

Bill has been active with and had leadership roles with several HR associations. He speaks at human resources and business conferences, and his views have been featured and quoted in multiple media outlets.

A lifelong learner, Bill earned his PhD at the Fielding Graduate University in Santa Barbara, California. He holds three master's degrees: an MA from Fielding in human & organizational systems, an MBA in management, and an MA in organizational psychology from Fairleigh Dickinson University. He has taken executive education programs at the International Institute for Management Development (IMD) in Lausanne, Switzerland, and he received his executive/organizational coaching certification from the Institute of Executive Coaching and Leadership (IECL) in Sydney, Australia. His undergraduate degree is from Rutgers College.

Longtime residents of Westfield, New Jersey, Bill and his wife, Coleen, now reside in Long Beach Township, New Jersey. He may be contacted at wmskane@gmail.com or through www.LeadingBusinessTeams.net.

Figure 0.3 Andy Hill.

Andrew Hill is a successful author and motivational speaker who has appeared before audiences throughout the United States and Canada. His book, *Be Quick But Don't Hurry: Finding Success in the Teachings of a Lifetime*, is now in its 15th printing.

From January 1991 to April 1996, Andrew Hill served as president of CBS Productions in charge of development and production for all CBS-owned entertainment programming. During Mr. Hill's presidency, CBS Productions became the network's leading supplier of primetime programs. In addition to increasing network advertising profits, these series returned more than $1.5 billion in foreign and domestic syndication income.

During his tenure at CBS Productions, Hill was responsible for some of the decade's most successful primetime programming, including TOUCHED BY AN ANGEL; DR. QUINN, MEDICINE WOMAN; WALKER, TEXAS RANGER; CAROLINE IN THE CITY; DAVE'S WORLD; and RESCUE 911. In fact, when the CBS lineup featured DR. QUINN, TOUCHED BY AN ANGEL, and WALKER on Saturday night, it was the first and only time in broadcasting history that one studio supplied an entire successful night of programming to any network.

In 1997, Hill was named president of Programming for the Channel One Network, the largest source of news and information for America's teens. Hill left Channel One in July of 2000 to write *Be Quick But Don't Hurry: Finding Success in the Teachings of a Lifetime*. The book was published by Simon and Schuster and was co-authored by John Wooden, the man voted by ESPN as "the greatest coach of the 20th century," and named by *The Sporting News* as the greatest coach of all time.

Hill's educational credentials include a master's degree in education and an undergraduate degree in psychology, both from UCLA. While at UCLA, he was a member of three consecutive N.C.A.A. championship basketball teams under the guidance of Coach Wooden. This makes Andy a member of an exclusive club since only 12 other men have been on three championship teams. Not surprisingly, these players have one thing in common—they all played for John Wooden at UCLA. In 2017, Andy was inducted into the Southern California Jewish Sports Hall of Fame.

In addition to speaking and consulting to corporations and professional organizations, Andy has had the honor of introducing Coach Wooden at an awards presentation at the 2002 Final Four in Atlanta, has addressed the UCLA Men's Basketball team and the University of Michigan Football team, and gave the commencement address at the University of Michigan School of Music and at the UCLA Anderson School Executive Training Program. Andy also has been featured on such television programs as REAL SPORTS with Bryant Gumbel on HBO; NIGHTLINE with Ted Koppel; THE NEWS-HOUR with Jim Lehrer; CNBC's POWER LUNCH with Bill Griffeth, FOX SPORTS NET ROUNDTABLE with Bill MacDonald; Bill Walton's LONG STRANGE TRIP on ESPN; the TEN GREATEST COACHES OF ALL TIME that aired on CBS; and was the subject of a segment on FOX SPORTS NET narrated by Todd Donoho. Hill spent 15 years giving value added presentations on behalf of T. Rowe Price to their clients across the country.

Andy lives with his wife of 48 years, Janice, in Los Angeles, California. Janice is a psychotherapist in private practice and a certified yoga instructor. They have a daughter, Alexandra, who is a graduate of the University of Pennsylvania, happily married to Mickey Berman and mother of Zach, Izzy, and Grant. Their son Aaron, a graduate of Michigan and Yale, is an oboe professor at the University of Nevada Reno. Aaron and his wife Dr. Laura Smith have a son, Ronan.

Index

Printed in the United States
by Baker & Taylor Publisher Services